GW01081533

NON-APPEARANCE BEFORE
THE INTERNATIONAL COURT OF JUSTICE

LEGAL ASPECTS OF
INTERNATIONAL ORGANIZATION

S. Rosenne, *Procedure in the International Court*. A commentary on the 19⁰¹
rules of the International Court of Justice. 1983.
ISBN 90 247 3045 7

Taslim O. Elias, *The International Court of Justice and some Contempora*
Problems. Essays on international law. 1983.
ISBN 90 247 2791 X

Ijaz Hussain, *Dissenting and Separate Opinions at the World Court*. 1984.
ISBN 90 247 2920 3

J. Elkind, *Non-Appearance before the International Court of Justice*. 1984.
ISBN 90 247 2921 1

E. Osieke, *Constitutional Law and Practice in the International Labour Orga*
zation. In press.
ISBN 90 247 2985 8

JEROME B. ELKIND

Senior Lecturer in Law
University of Auckland
New Zealand

Non-Appearance before the International Court of Justice

Functional and Comparative Analysis

1984 **MARTINUS NIJHOFF PUBLISHERS**
a member of the KLUWER ACADEMIC PUBLISHERS GROUP
DORDRECHT / BOSTON / LANCASTER

Distributors

for the United States and Canada: Kluwer Academic Publishers, 190 Old Derby
Street, Hingham, MA 02043, USA
for the UK and Ireland: Kluwer Academic Publishers, MTP Press Limited
Falcon House, Queen Square, Lancaster LA1 1RN, England
for all other countries: Kluwer Academic Publishers Group, Distribution Center
P.O. Box 322, 3300 AH Dordrecht, The Netherlands

Library of Congress Cataloging in Publication Data

```
Elkind, Jerome B.
   Non-appearance before the International Court of
Justice.

   (Legal aspects of international organization ; v. 4)
   Bibliography: p.
   1. International Court of Justice.  2. Jurisdiction
(International law)  3. Provisional remedies.
I. Title.  II. Series: LAIO ; v. 4.
JX1971.6.E59  1984      341.5'52          83-27165
```


ISBN 90-247-2921-1 (this volume)
ISBN 90-247-3044-9 (series)

Copyright

© 1984 by Martinus Nijhoff Publishers, Dordrecht.

PRINTED IN THE NETHERLANDS

To Judge Philip C. Jessup
for his encouragement

In the world community, as in the individual State, there is no more powerful incentive to good order than the expectation and example of good order

C. Wilfred Jenks, *The prospects of international adjudication*

We have always been for peace, but some things are more important

World Leader speaking as her armies were invading the territory of another country.

TABLE OF CONTENTS

FOREWORD

The Institute of International Law was pleased to be able in 1983, at its Cambridge session, to award Dr. Jerome B. Elkind, Senior Lecturer in Law at the Department of Law of the University of Auckland, the Francis Lieber prize for his dissertation on *"Non-Appearance before the International Court of Justice – a Functional and Comparative Analysis"*. For the first time the prize founded by James Brown Scott "in a spirit of gratitude towards the Institute and with the thought of paying a tender tribute to the memory of his mother, Jeanette Scott, who had a lasting influence on his life", goes to honour an American lawyer. One cannot but note the happy coincidence that makes Dr. Elkind beneficiary of the prize which bears the name of Francis Lieber, praised so highly by James Brown Scott in his capacity of President of the Institute of International Law at the session held in the United States, at Briarcliff, in 1929.

Admitted to the Institute some twenty years earlier, James Brown Scott decided in 1931 to pay personally the amount for a prize the laureate of which would be designated by the Institute. Through a clause in his will he ensured later that the payment would be continued after his death, which occurred in 1943, by a legacy in favour of the Institute. It was at the 1947 Lausanne session, the first to be held after the second world war, that this demonstration of James Brown's loyalty came to the knowledge of his fellow-members. Already as Director of the Legal Division of the Carnegie Endowment for International Peace he had had the Institute approved as counsellor by the Foundation's trustees. In this "exceptional position as major patron" he managed to direct his initiatives towards achievements that played a decisive part in the training of specialists in international law throughout the world. It has been written of him that he was *"avec une magnifique compréhension dans le sens de l'universalité du droit et de la justice un merveilleux animateur"*.[1]

The award of the Francis Lieber prize and the publication of the dissertation upon which it was bestowed by the Institute should make a most useful contribution to the study of a problem in which the international judicial institution is particularly concerned to-day. The situation which arises when a State cited before the International Court of Justice fails to appear has held in particular the attention of the Institute of International Law, principally on the initiative of Sir Gerald Fitzmaurice, who, made aware of the significance of this problem in the performance of his duties at the Court, published an important article on the subject in the British Yearbook of International Law for 1980 (pp. 89-122). The Bureau selected this subject for the competition in January 1980, and the Fourth Commission, with Mr Arangio Ruiz as Rapporteur, was entrusted with the examination in 1981. Undoubtedly the Institute will have occasion to refer to Dr. Jerome B. Elkind's dissertation in its future work. The author concerned himself in the main with clarifying the legal situations accounting for the decision of a State which, after having accepted compulsory jurisdiction, declines to appear before the Court when the beneficiary of such acceptance decides to rely upon it. Particular attention is devoted to the debates that resulted in the adoption of the famous Connally reservation and to the discussions to which it gave rise in practice. The author also examined with great care the background of Article 53 of the Statute of the Court, which because of the concept of failure to appear contained in it led to a search for similarities with domestic judicial systems. On the latter, Dr. Elkind provides information which shows the great variety of existing rules and practices, but which also highlights the specific problem arising at international level.

The author has discerned very well that the attitude of States failing to appear may be explained by some more or less justifiable misgivings about international justice. In this regard his comments deserve to be considered both by those who play a role in the choice of people called upon to exercise such functions and by

---

1. A. de la Pradelle, *Maîtres et doctrines du droit des gens*, 2nd edn., 1950, p. 420.

those who accept compulsory jurisdiction for their States without weighing properly the consequences thereof. They should also induce members of the Court, whether individually or as a body, to give special thought to the matter in the performance of their duties.

Finally, the subject calls for reconsideration of the role incumbent on the judge in contemporary international society. The contribution made by Dr. Elkind's book on this topic is of undeniable interest.

Suzanne Bastid

Member of the Institute of International Law

Honorary Professor at the Paris University of Law, Economics and Social Sciences

AUTHOR'S PREFACE

All too frequently in recent years, a State which has been the subject of a unilateral application to the International Court of Justice, has refused to appear in the action, claiming that the Court lacked jurisdiction to hear the case.

Increasing resort to this behaviour is serious because it calls into question the effectiveness of the unilateral application procedure and the concept of compulsory jurisdiction itself. The phenomenon of non-appearance needs to be studied. It needs to be studied from a comparative point of view to see if the treatment of non-appearance in municipal jurisdictions can contribute to our understanding of non-appearance in international law. It needs to be studied from a functional point of view in order to understand what motivates it and what can be done about it. Why do States which are willing to agree, in the abstract, to submit at least certain classes of disputes to the compulsory jurisdiction of the International Court of Justice decide, when they are faced with an actual attempt to use these procedures against them, that they are no longer willing to abide by the promises which they made?

The first Chapter is a historical and comparative study of non-appearance in municipal law. The second Chapter will look at the actual cases in which States have either refused to appear or failed to appear before the International Court of Justice and its predecessor, the Permanent Court of International Justice. The insights gained from the first Chapter will be applied to international law in the Third Chapter.

Since many of the cases of non-appearance have involved requests by the applicant for provisional relief, the fourth Chapter will study interim protection, in order to see what there is about the provisional remedy that motivates respondent, or more accurately, non-responding defendant States to stay away from the Court when a request for interim protection has been made.

States which refuse to appear very often purport to decide for themselves that the Court has no jurisdiction to hear the merits of the case. Thus the fifth Chapter will study the validity of the various forms of self-judgment. The last Chapter will aim at drawing the study together and examining why States do not yet seem to have reached a stage where they are prepared to submit their disputes to international adjudication.

This book follows naturally and logically from the present author's earlier work, *Interim Protection: A Functional Approach*, which was also published by Martinus Nijhoff in 1981. But the rules of the James Brown Scott competition, for which this work was submitted, require that the manuscript be submitted to the *Institut de droit international* under conditions of strict anonymity. Therefore the reader will find that references to the present author's previous work are made in what must appear to be an oddly circumspect manner.

The rules also require that the manuscript be published only subject to such changes as are specified by the *Institut*. But the author would like to acknowledge an interesting suggestion made by his colleague, Dr. P.J. Evans, after the manuscript had been submitted to the *Institut*. The suggestion concerned the Court's duties under Article 53(2) of the Statute to satisfy itself, in the case of non-appearance, that the Court has jurisdiction in accordance with Articles 36 and 37 and that the claim is well-founded in fact and law.[1]

The suggestion is that, if the Respondent does not give notice of its intention to appear by a certain specified time limit, the Court should appoint an *amicus curiae* to argue the Respondent's case for it.

This proposal would require amendment of the Statute and it is open to the objection that the Court should never abandon the hope that the respondent will appear, nor should it withdraw from it the opportunity to do so. None the less, it is a proposal worth considering.

1. See Ch. 3.

ACKNOWLEDGMENTS

The author would like to thank first of all the *Institut de droit international* for its most generous award.

Secondly the author would like to thank the New Zealand Institute of International Affairs and the New Zealand Legal Research Foundation. Both of these organizations provided grants which assisted in the production of the manuscript.

On his own faculty the author wishes to thank the late Dean, Professor J.F. Northey, Dr. P.J. Evans, and Mrs. Nadja Tollemache.

Thanks are also due to Dr. Judith Grant of the Romance Languages Department for her assistance with translation.

Last but not least the author would like to thank the three students who assisted him, Ms. Christina Muller, Mr. David Stanley Niven and Ms. Jane Parcell.

CHAPTER 1

DEFAULT IN MUNICIPAL LAW

INTRODUCTION

Engelmann, in his book *A History of Continental Civil Law* remarks that the development of the law of procedure usually comes
about for many people through the subjection of self-help to the
supervision of the Community.[1] In this process, the activity of the
individual becomes dictated by fixed forms. The forms then comes
to be vested with coercive power.

Early proceedings seldom began with an appeal to a court. They
usually involved the question of whether self-help remedies had
been executed according to the proper form. Was the exercise of
private coercion in accordance with the law? At this stage, non-
appearance was scarcely a problem.

At a much later stage it was considered that the decision as to
the legality of private coercion ought to precede the exercise of
such coercion and that execution should not take place until a
tribunal had decided that such coercion would be lawful. At a still
later stage, the exercise of coercion came to be regarded as the
prerogative of the community or State.

Once the community takes shape and the individual is sub-
ordinated to the rule of the community, individuals come under
an obligation to submit their disputes to the judgment of some
third person or institution (third-party settlement). Those who
resist this tendency may come to be regarded as unworthy to
belong to the community and thus excluded from its protection.
This "putting from within the peace" or outlawry was the only

1. Engelmann, *A History of Continental Civil Procedure* (1928), p. 241.

means which society possessed at that stage of "terrorising and overpowering the individual".[2] Power to apply this measure rests only in the community or in the organ which exercises its authority.

ROMAN LAW

The above observation particularly characterises Roman Law. The development of Roman procedure had its inception at a time when people were just starting to emerge from a primitive state. It arose from the custom of submitting a difference of opinion to an impartial third person to decide the difference. By doing so and by undertaking to comply with the consequences of an adverse decision they were able to effect peaceful settlement of controversies which, at an earlier time, would have been decided by force.[3] Outlawry was practised in Roman Law as late as the 4th Century B.C.[4]

The fundamental character of classical Roman civil procedure was the division of judicial proceedings into two sections, proceedings *"in jure"* and proceedings *"in judicio"*.

The object of the former was, first to determine whether plaintiff's claim was admissible (was there any form of civil procedure to enforce it) and then to fix the nature of the claim and the condition under which it could be asserted.[5]

Proceedings *in jure* were held before a magistrate exercising the power of the State. If one party admitted his opponent's title, that was a *confessio in jure* and terminated proceedings.[6] At this stage the Magistrate or *"Praetor"* decided whether and to what extent the case involved a legal controversy calling for a judicial decision.[7] If he decided that plaintiff's case was admissible, he issued a *litis contestio* formulating the legal issue for the *judicium*.[8]

At the jucidium stage, the judge or *judex*, who represented the

---

2. Id. at p. 248.
3. Id. at pp. 247-248.
4. Id. at p. 248.
5. Sohm, *The Institutes: A Textbook of the History and System of Roman Private Law* (Transl. Ledlie 3rd ed. 1907), p. 226.
6. Id. at p. 56.
7. Supra note 1 at p. 242.
8. Supra note 5 at p. 226.

people, was usually a private person or several private persons acting under oath. The legal issues were decided by means of a judgment (*sententia*). The judge first received evidence in order to ascertain the facts and then pronounced judgment.[9]

The earliest form of procedure was called the *"legis actio"*, or *"legis actio sacramentum"* a proceeding according to statute in which both parties solemnly affirmed their legal claim.[10] The plaintiff appeared before the *praetor* with a fully formulated legal conclusion with the judgment outlined in the conclusions.[11] The *legis actio* carried all the formalism of the *jus civile*. The procedure was based on oral *formulae* which were immutable because the wording of the statutes was immutable. It was restricted to a definite number of statutory claims.[12]

From about the middle of the third century B.C., as the inroads of the *jus gentium* became stronger, the *Praetor Peregrinus*, who was responsible for claims between foreigners, was faced with a large number of fresh claims which were not based on recognised Roman statute.[13]

When a *praetor*, faced with such issues, granted a *lis contestio* he had to formulate the issues himself. He also appointed the judges. So in drawing up the decree of appointment he indicated the duty of the judges. In his decree he stated the issues and ordered the judges, "by virtue of his *imperium*," to decide the case according to certain specified conditions.[14]

This formulation of the issues was done by the *preator* himself in his decree. This decree was called the *formula*. It was framed on the basis of certain forms or *formulae* in the *preator's album*.[15] The proceeding was known as "the formulary procedure". Eventually it passed into civil procedure.[16]

At about the time of the beginning of the Empire a new form of procedure (*extraordinarium cognitio*) came to be permitted in certain cases. Toward the end of the third century A.D., the

9. Id. at p. 229.
10. Id. at p. 230.
11. Supra note 1 at p. 392.
12. Supra note 5 at p. 241.
13. Id. at 243.
14. Ibid.
15. Id. at p. 244.
16. Id. at p. 246.

4

formulary procedure began to give way to it. In this procedure the separation of proceedings *in jure* and proceedings *in judicium* was abolished.[17]

There were three basic differences between the *legis actio* and formulary procedure:

> a. In the formulary procedure the magistrate's formulation influenced the trial, in the *actio juris*, it did not.

> b. In the *actio juris* judicial decisions were permitted. In the formulary procedure they were commanded.

> c. In the *actio juris* both the magistrate and the judge were governed by statute. In the formulary procedure, the judge was governed by the magistrate's edict.[18]

Default in Roman law could occur at either the *in jure* proceedings or *in judicium.*

In jure proceedings

The aim of *in jure* proceedings was to bring about a *litiscontestation*. This involved an agreement of the parties to submit to a *judicium*. But failure to defend was treated quite differently in the *actio* and formulary proceedings. In the *legis actio*, the plaintiff appeared before the *praetor* with a fully formulated pleading or conclusion with the requested judgment outlined in the pleading. If the defendant failed to offer any contradiction, it was treated as a *confessio* and defendant was considered *pro damnato*. Thus, silence was treated as a confession.[19]

In the formulary proceeding this was not the case. As we have seen, it was not plaintiff, who presented the legal conclusion. It was the *preator*'s formula. Thus, failure to plead in contradiction was not, in itself, a *confessio*. There had to be either a clear confession by plaintiff or defendant would have to prove his issues at a *judicium.*[20]

17. Supra note 1 at p. 243.
18. Id. at p. 242.
19. Karlowa, *Der römische Civilprozess zur Zeit der Legisactionen* (1872), p. 112; Buckland, *A Textbook of Roman Law* (2d ed. 1932), p. 613.
20. Buckland, ibid.

But there was another problem. Submission to a *judicium* was regarded as contractual. If denfant failed to appear or appeared but refused to enter into a contract, it was impossible to have a *judicium*. He had to be coerced into participating. To do this *preator* granted the plaintiff a *"missio in bona"* in which he empowered the plaintiff to seize the defendant's property and sell it. Then plaintiff could proceed against the purchasor as the defendant's successor.[21]

It has been suggested that, if plaintiff failed to appear, he forfeited his claim.[22]

In judicium proceedings

In these proceedings, it was not necessary to coerce the defendant. In *legis actio* proceedings, if either party failed to appear, the court waited until noon and then rendered judgment in favour of the appearing party without considering the merits of the case.

In the formulary proceedings, if plaintiff failed to appear judgment went to the defendant. But judgment for plaintiff was not automatic in the event of a default of appearance by defendant.

The judge was acting under orders from the *preator* to investigate the claim and decide according to the proofs. Thus, plaintiff had to state his claim and prove the facts supporting it in order to obtain a judgment in his favour. A non-appearing party was however under certain procedural disadvantages:[23]

> Although it might thus happen that a judgment of absolution was rendered, in spite of the defendant's failure to appear, the disadvantage under which his default placed him was in most cases sufficiently serious. For the judge heard the case without having had brought to his attention any of the facts and arguments which, adduced by the defendant, might have brought about a judgment in his favour.[24]

If plaintiff failed to appear, the facts on which he based his case could not be proved and the defendant was absolved.[25]

21. Supra note 1 at p. 393.
22. Livy, *Ab Urbe Condita*, The History of Rome, Vol. 4 (transl. W.A.M. Devitt 1815).
23. Supra note 1 at pp. 394-395.
24. Id. at p. 395.
25. Ibid.

6

Imperial procedure

When *jus* and *justicium* ceased to be separate stages, a *litiscontesation* was unnecessary although its use persisted for a long while. But defendant's co-operation was no longer needed in order to try the issue. A non-appearing defendant could be fined or even brought in by force in certain circumstances.[26]

The defendant had to be summoned three times or he had to be served with a peremptory summons acquanting him with the consequences of failure to appear. Once that had occurred and the default continued, the plaintiff could either ask for a *"missio in bona"* or procede to an *ex parte* hearing. It has been suggested that plaintiff had to prove the facts alleged in an *ex parte* hearing.[27] But Engelmann says that this view is not borne out by the examples cited in support of it.[28] If the judge was not satisfied with the plaintiff's claim, he could, at his discretion, insist upon proof. If the plaintiff failed to appear, the defendant was absolved *ab instantia.*

MEDIAEVAL GERMAN PROCEDURE

Mediaeval German procedure was characterised by formality. In earliest times defendant's counter-allegation had to correspond word for word to the allegations of the plaintiff. If they failed to do so, the counter-allegations were either deemed a nullity or they were deemed contradictory only in so far as the words actually contradicted the opposing allegations.[29]

In the German view the allegations of each party were given the same weight. Engelmann says that the absence of contradiction brought about "not exactly the fiction of an admission (for fiction was alien to the German law) but a continuance of the belief which had previously been accorded to the words of the alleging party".[30]

In this sense, no distinction was made between non-appearance

6. D.2.5.21; 2.8.25.
27. Puchta, *Geschichte des römischen Civilprozess* (10th ed. 1893), p. 185.
28. Supra note 1 at p. 396.
29. Id. at p. 181.
30. Id. at p. 180.

and failure to answer. In either case, the defendant's default led to defeat. But default by virtue of non-appearance had other consequences for the defendant.

Where the claim was one of debt and defendant failed to appear, plaintiff's claim was taken as established and plaintiff could distrain defendant's goods. If the action was one for the recovery of property and the complaint had been alleged in three successive terms of court, plaintiff was put in possession of both movables and immovables.[31]

Otherwise the Court did not have the power to execute its judgments. So implementation of plaintiff's rights could only be secured if the defendant gave a promise to perform the judgment. This was known as a duty of court service and failure in such a duty was regarded as contumacy toward the King's court and entailed a public punishment.[32]

Someone who refused to give such a promise set himself apart from the law. Initial contumacy could involve a provisional form of outlawry entailing a fine. If the defendant was summoned three times in three successive terms of court and persisted in his failure to appear, plaintiff could apply to the King to have him declared a definitive outlaw or "peaceless".[33] A peaceless man forfeited all protection of the law for his person or property until he consented to give the required promise.[34] Peacelessness might even result in excommunication.[35]

In order to incur these penalties, the default had to be genuine. Defendant had to be duly summoned and he had to be absent without lawful excuse. Initially distinct excuses were recognised under Frankish Law. But later they were all subsumed under the head of genuine necessity such as where a person was imprisoned or absent in the service of the King, his Lord or of God.[36]

In an action for debt, default could be set aside by the defendant. Where plaintiff had been put in the possession of real property by virtue of the default of the defendant, the defendant had a

---

31. Hübner, *History of Germanic Private Law* (transl. Philbrich) (Reprinted 1968), pp. 185, 404 ff.
32. Supra note 1 at p. 181.
33. Id. at p. 182.
34. Id. at pp. 163-164.
35. Id. at p. 182.
36. Ibid, citing Brunner, *Deutsche Rechtsgeschichte* (1892), Vol. II, p. 336, note 21.

8

year and a day to annul the transfer of possession and defend his title.[37]

In the case of non-appearance of the plaintiff, the defendant could declare his readiness to defend the action in three successive terms of the court. If plaintiff still failed to appear, the defendant was absolved from the complaint. If the claim involved property, defendant could demand a judicial confirmation of his title.[38]

ROMANO-CANONICAL PROCEDURE

In the late middle ages, a revived Roman law spread from the confines of Italy and in some cases incorporated Germanic procedures. Italian statutory law incorporated and developed the Germanic institution of peacelessness and seizure of property in the case of breach of a court duty.[39]

Other penalties which might be imposed on a non-appearing defendant were fines, imprisonment and excommunication. But these were not often applied.

To be guilty of contumacy, defendant must have been summoned three times in the regular and proper manner and the time set by the court for his appearance must have expired. If he simply failed to appear, he was guilty of constructive contumacy. But if he expressly refused to appear he was guilty of true contumacy and lost his right to appeal an adverse judgment.

Yet Romano-Canonical procedure was quite lenient in the procedural disadvantages that were imposed on a non-appearing defendant.

Default of appearance was not deemed an admission of the facts alleged by the plaintiff nor an acquiescence in his demand. In the event of non-appearance by the defendant, an *ex parte* hearing took place in which plaintiff had to show that he, and not the defendant, should prevail. Thus "Canon law has the utmost tenderness for the '*contumax*'".[40]

In cases of real action, plaintiff, after a summary investigation,

37. Id. at p. 183.
38. Planck, *Das Deutsche Gerichtsverfahren im Mittelalter nach dem Sachsenspiegel und dem verwandten Rechtsgueblem* (1874), pp. 319 et seq.
39. Supra note 1 at pp. 463-464.
40. Id. at p. 464.

was put in possession of the property demanded where defendant failed to appear before the *litiscontestation*. But this was subject to the right of the defendant to regain possession within a year's time by paying costs. After a year, defendant could proceed anew against the former plaintiff for recovery of the property. In a personal action, the plaintiff was put in possession of defendant's property as security for his claim.

Contumacy of the defendant in a real property action after the *litiscontestation* resulted in an *ex parte* hearing. It was possible for a judgment to be rendered in favour of the *contumax* but not unless the cause was clearly in his favour. Otherwise the *res* was awarded to the plaintiff.

In personal actions, there was a *missio* which transferred *custodia* to plaintiff for a period of one year. After further attempts to summon defendant, the plaintiff's possession was made permanent.

Where plaintiff failed to appear before the *litiscontestation*, a hearing was held in which only the allegations in his pleading could be considered while all of defendant's allegations and proofs were heard. If plaintiff failed to appear after the *litiscontestation* then all of the allegations and proofs of both parties were considered. But defendant could adduce new allegations and proofs at the hearing. Defendant was absolved only if the evidence did not show a clear right to relief on the part of the plaintiff.[41]

GERMAN AND AUSTRIAN PROCEDURE

A manual of Canonical procedure appeared in Germany as early as 1227.[42] In the 14th Century there were instances of a written procedure based upon Canon Law principles. The final stages of reception took place in the 15th and 16th Centuries.[43] In 1497 Emperor Maximillian I accepted the Roman *Corpus Juris* as the law of the Holy Roman Empire. With Roman Law came the Romano-Canonical procedure. It became the procedure of the Imperial Chamber of Justice (*Reichskammergericht*) as well as of numerous territorial courts.[44]

41. Ibid.
42. Id. at p. 513.
43. Id. at p. 518-519.
44. Id. at p. 507.

The *Reichskammergericht* was strict in dealing with contumacy however. It made a distinction between failure to appear and failure to plead.[45] Instead of merely putting the plaintiff into possession subject to the right of the defendant to decide to defend, it revived the coercive measures of outlawry and excommunication. Plaintiff was entitled to specify his proof in his complaint.[46] Failure to plead by the defendant resulted in *poena confessi*.[47]

A reaction to Roman Law in the 16th Century led to the development of a German Common Law Procedure in which elements of Germanic and Roman Law were combined. The common law of procedure contained a considerably heavier admixture of German law than did the substantive law.[48]

Under this procedure, plaintiff had two courses open to him in the event of a non-appearing defendant:

(a) He could apply for *immission* (provisional possession of defendant's property) together with outlawry and excommunication; or

(b) he could apply for an *ex parte* hearing.[49]

Immission and outlawry were later abolished.

The *ex parte* hearing proceeded on the theory that the defendant had denied plaintiff's claims. So the plaintiff had to prove his allegations. By contrast, where a defendant appeared but failed to plead, then the *Reichskammergericht* considered that he had admitted plaintiff's allegations.

A non-appearing defendant did lose certain procedural advantages. If, in the face of an order to appear or face the consequences of contumacy and a motion by plaintiff to set the proceedings on foot, he continued to stay away, then he lost the benefit of any dilatory (delaying) and peremptory (barring) exceptions.[50]

The Prussian legislation of 1876 envisaged two stages in the proceedings, a pleading stage and a proof stage. At the pleading stage, plaintiff could either lodge a written complaint with the court or

45. Id. at p. 528.
46. Id. at p. 535.
47. Id. at p. 528.
48. Id. at p. 542.
49. Id. at p. 549.
50. Ibid.

state it orally to a judge who drew up a "protocol". The complaint or protocol was served on the defendant with a time limit for an answer. If defendant failed to appear or lodge a written answer at or before the designated time, affirmative *litiscontestation* was deemed to exist. If the judge found the plaintiff's complaint legally sufficient, he rendered judgment in accordance with plaintiff's prayer.

The present German system has been described as being governed by the principles of orality and immediacy.[51] Under the principle of orality, nothing can be considered except what is presented orally at the hearing. The principle of immediacy means that the proceedings, including oral presentation and the taking of proof, takes place before the court itself and not before a delegated official. In the case of default, the present system is modelled on the Prussian system in its strictness. Each party is entitled to be heard. The defendant is usually summoned by means of a writ at which time he is informed of the consequences of default. If he wants to defend the case, he must notify the court in writing within two weeks of receiving the writ unless the writ must be served in a foreign country. He is then granted a further two weeks to answer the charge.[52] The consequence of non-appearance at a court hearing is that the non-appearing party is excluded from the hearing.[53]

An alleged fact need not be proved in four circumstances:
(a) judicial admission;
(b) failure to deny the allegation;
(c) judicial notice, and
(d) legal presumptions.[54]

If the defendant does not appear at the hearing, the plaintiff may apply *ex parte* for a default judgment on the basis of the pleadings. If the pleadings support the application then default judgment is granted. If not, the petition is dismissed. If the defendant's declaration arrives, before the judgment with the judge's signature has been received by the court office, the default judgment does not take effect.[55] All default judgments are provisionally enforceable.[56]

51. Id. at p. 606.
52. *ZPO* § 276.
53. *ZPO* § 230.
54. Supra note 1 at p. 607.
55. *ZPO* § 331.
56. *ZPO* §§ 708-714.

The development of French Civil procedure involved elements of primitive German law, elements of Romano-Canonical Law and elements of customary law.

Between the 14th and 16th Centuries defendants were given three chances to heed a summons in an action concerning title to land. The first and second failures had no other consequences than a judgment for costs.[57] Plaintiff had to sue out repeated summonses. On the third default, defendant was debarred from all defences and judgment was rendered against him in accordance with plaintiff's proofs.

If the subject matter concerned a personal right, defendant forfeited additional procedural advantages with each default.

The practice regarding burden of proof varied from court to court. In some courts plaintiff had immediate judgment. In others, he had to present his proofs although the defaulting defendant was barred from all defences, contradictions and from the right to contradict witnesses. None of these defaults were self-executing. They required a motion by the opposite party and a pronouncement of judgment by the Court.

By 1500, the law of contumacy had been simplified.[58] A distinction was made between default (*défaut*) and dismissal (*congé*). Dismissal resulted from plaintiff's failure to prosecute. Default resulted from a failure to defend. The law recognised four kinds of omission:

1. Failure to appear (*faut de se présenter*), a failure attributable to either party.
2. Failure by plaintiff to give the defendant documents to support his claim (*faut de donner copie des pièces*).
3. Failure to defend (*faute de défendre*) by failing to deliver the answer and documentary evidence.
4. Failure by either party to plead (*faute de plaider*).

The opposite party had to present a motion to obtain a default or dismissal. If it was found "just and duly verified", the motion was granted although a production of proof might be required.

If the failure to act was a failure to lodge papers or to introduce

57. Supra note 1 at p. 684.
58. Id. at p. 724.

proof, the party at fault was barred (*forclos*) from later rectifying the defect.

All earlier rules regarding default were abolished by Ordinance in 1667.

In modern French Civil Procedure, a distinction is recognised between failure to plead (*défaut faute de conclure*) and failure to appear (*défaut faute de comparaître*).[59] *Défaut faute de conclure* occurs when the defendant appears, but one side or the other fails to submit its pleadings (*conclusions*) to the court.

At one time *défaut faute de conclure* resulted in a default judgment. Under *article 154 bis* of the *Code de Procédure Civile* [*Ancien*], if defendant failed to serve his *conclusions*, a new *avenir*[60] was served on defendant's *avoué*. If defendant failed to serve his *conclusions* after that, then plaintiff could obtain judgment in his favour that was not subject to reopening. A similar procedure was available if the plaintiff failed to submit his *conclusions*.[61]

With a *défaut faute de comparaître*, under the old code, the plaintiff could request a default judgment as soon as the time limit for appearance ran out, but defendant could appear up until the time the hearing was terminated.

The procedure for obtaining a default judgment was the same as that for obtaining a judgment in a contested case except that the case did not have to wait its turn on the calendar.

The judgment was not automatic. The Court examined, in a summary fashion, whether plaintiff's claim was well-founded. This could be done on the basis of documentary evidence. Proof in the form of examination of witnesses was rarely ordered unless public policy was strongly involved.[62]

Default judgment was usually served on the defendant by a *Huissier* appointed by the presiding judge.[63] The judgment would indicate the time available to defendant for reopening or appeal. It had to be served within 6 months or it became void.

---

59. Cuche et Vincent, *Précis de procédure civile et commerciale* (12th ed. 1960), pp. 411-412.

60. An *avenir* was a notice served on defendant's *avoué* by plaintiff's *avoué* requesting him to serve his defensive pleading and to be present in court on a specified date not less than 15 days from the date of service.

61. [*Ancien*] *art.* 154.

62. Supra note 59 at pp. 414-417.

63. [*Ancien*] *art.* 156.

14

The remedy for a default judgment was (and still is) reopening by way of *opposition*. Previously every defaulting defendant could reopen his or her case in this way. But reform in 1958 curtailed the *opposition* and provided that it could not be obtained if the defendant was personally served or if the judgment was not subject to appeal.[64] In the case where the plaintiff has not been personally served, a second attempt to serve him could be made.[65] *Opposition* has the effect of staying the execution of the judgment.[66]

In the New Code of Civil Procedure, promulgated in 1975, Ch. I, s.II of Title XIV is headed '*Le défaut de comparution*'. But articles 469 and 470 deal with situations in which parties appear but fail to complete procedural acts within the required time limit. In those cases, the judge can rule as if rendering a contested judgment taking into account those matters which have been raised or he can officially declare the summons void.

After a final warning addressed to the parties or their representative, he can officially dismiss the case by a decision which is not open to appeal. But the more important distinction, when dealing with non-appearance is the distinction between judgments by default (*par défaut*) and contested or trial judgments (*le jugement contradictoire*).

A judgment is contested as soon as the parties appear either in person or by a representative according to the terms appropriate to the jurisdiction before which the claim is brought.[67]

If the plaintiff fails to appear without lawful excuse, the defendant may request a contested judgment on the merits, although the judge has a discretion to defer the case for a further hearing.[68]

If the summons has not been delivered to a defendant in person, a defendant who does not appear can be reinvited to appear either on the initiative of the plaintiff or pursuant to an official decision of the judge. The new summons must usually follow the form of the first one except that it must mention the appropriate provisions of the Code relating to default. The judge may also inform

64. Giverdon, "La réforme par la procédure par défaut" [1959], *Recueil Dalloz, section Chronique* 201.
65. [*Ancien*] *art.* 150.
66. Supra note 59 at p. 439.
67. *Nouveau Code de Procédure Civile, art.* 467.
68. Id. *art.* 468.

the interested party of the consequences of his or her failure to appear by a simple letter.[69]

If the defendant fails to appear, the judge may give a decision on the merits. But he can only uphold the demand if he is satisfied that it is regular, admissible and well-founded (*régulière, recevable et bien fondée*).[70]

Following the Old Code and the 1958 reforms, a judgment in the event of the non-appearance of the defendant is a judgment by default in two circumstances, where the decision is one from which no appeal is allowed and where the defendant has not been personally cited. On the other hand, where the decision is appealable and where the summons has been delivered in person to the defendant, the judgment is deemed to be a contested judgment.[71]

A default judgment can usually be attacked by *opposition*.[72] But a judgment which is deemed to be a contested judgment cannot be attacked by *opposition*. Defendant must pursue the means of recourse which are open to contested judgments.[73]

Opposition is a procedure by which a defaulting party obtains a retraction of the judgment.[74] It results in having the matters which have been adjudged by default remanded to the same judge who must rule again on questions of both fact and law.[75]

ENGLISH LAW

Holdsworth places the beginning of the history of English Law at the time of the coming of the Saxons to England.[76] He dates the Saxon period from 449 to the time of the Norman Conquest in 1066. He cites a large body of eminent opinion to support the assertions that the rules of Saxon Law were almost entirely Germanic without any appreciable admixture of Celtic or Roman elements. There were a few Roman elements as a survival of Roman occupation but he did not think that these were significant.

69. Id. *art.* 471.
70. Id. *art.* 472.
71. Id. *art.* 473.
72. Id. *art.* 476.
73. Id. *art.* 477.
74. Id. *art.* 571.
75. Id. *art.* 572.
76. Holdsworth, *A History of English Law* (3d ed. 1944), Vol. 2, pp. 2-3.

The plaintiff began by summoning his opponent to the court. This summons was a private and extra-judicial act and plaintiff had to prove it by producing witnesses who had been present at service. Service had to take place before sunset at the defendant's permanent residence and had to be made personally on the defendant or on his wife, seneschal or steward if he were not at home. Either the summons had to set a definite time to answer or the time was set by special agreement.

With the passage of time, the custom developed of sending the summons by an officer furnished with the King's writ.[77]

> Whether the summons to a particular plea was required to be be made in a set formalism of words is unknown; probably it was not, but all that can be certainly affirmed is that it must have sufficiently described the cause of action as to identify it, and have required the party on refusal of the demand to appear before such a court on such a day, there to hear judgment.[78]

On the day fixed by the summons, defendant had to either appear or give some recognised essoin (excuse for non-appearance).[79] Essoins could include absence beyond the seas, absence in the service of the King or of his Lord, sickness or tempest.[80] If he did not appear, plaintiff summoned him again for another term and if he had sent no essoin, plaintiff would require him both to answer and to pay a fine of thirty pence. If he failed to appear without excuse, in the second term, another thirty pence fine could be levied. If after the third summons, he still failed to appear without excuse he could be proceeded against by distraint. Plaintiff however surrendered the distress back to him upon his giving security for further appearance and submission to the court. Later, in the thirteenth century, the King's Court required four summonses.[81]

The system of frankpledge was a pledge of corporate responsibility by the inhabitants of a tithing for the general good behaviour and willingness to answer legal summonses of each free-born citizen in the tithing above the age of twelve.[82]

77. Bigelow, *History of Procedure in England* (1880), p. 217.
78. Id. at p. 224.
79. Id. at p. 219.
80. Supra note 76, vol. 2 at p. 92.
81. Supra note 77 at p. 219.
82. Id. at p. 143.

In the King's Courts, the essoins came to an end with the third excuse. If the party failed to appear or send an attorney on the expiration of the third term, the court ordered him to come or send an attorney. If he appeared at the fourth term he had to prove the truth of his essoins on oath and with one witness. If he did not appear, the land (if it were a suit for land) was taken by the King and the defendant could take it back after fifteen days by exculpation of default and replevin.[83] If he still did not appear within that time seisin was granted to the plaintiff. But the defendant could still sue out a Writ of Right and try title to the land.

If the defendant did not appear within fifteen days, he was commanded to appear at a fourth term "and have justice there". If he duly appeared and found pledges to guarantee that he would abide by the judgment, the seisin would be returned to him.[84] Under Saxon Law and indeed until as late as 1832, English Courts had no power to try a cause in the absence of the other party. Holdsworth draws a parallel with the Roman *Legis Actio* procedure, the law courts being considered as tribunals of arbitration.[85]

Where the plaintiff failed to appear, the defendants who had been summoned were bound to wait until the fourth day after appearance day. If they did not wait, the plaintiff might appear and put the defendant in default. If the plaintiff did not appear within three days, the defendant was entitled to go *sine die*. If the plaintiff failed to send an essoin, he was punished by a fine.[86]

Outlawry was used only at last resort and in extreme cases of contumacy or unyielding disobedience to the requirements of the law or the commands of the King. When the defaulting party was the plaintiff, no damage was done. When he was the defendant, there were usually adequate means, in the form of distraint or of pledges, of satisfying the demands of the plaintiff. When this was not so, then refusal to abide by a judgment requiring him to give security probably subjected the defendant to outlawry.[87]

These procedures extended well into the mediaeval period (1066-1485) and beyond. In Holdsworth's view, the main outstanding feature of the law of civil procedure had been fixed by

83. Id. at p. 238.
84. Id. at p. 239.
85. Supra note 76, Vol. 2, p. 93.
86. Supra note 77, at p. 237.
87. Id. at p. 548.

the end of the thirteenth and the beginning of the fourteenth centuries. However, as rules of pleading became more technical, so did the means of compelling the defendant to come to court. Even Holdsworth was unwilling to canvass these detailed and technical rules in their entirety.[88] There were as many methods of bringing the defendant to Court as there were forms of action. He did discuss the procedure in real actions. It did not greatly differ from procedure in the Saxon period.[89]

When we consider procedure in the period between 1487 and 1700, we have to look separately at proceedings at common law and proceedings in the Courts of Chancery. In this period, there were numerous ways to bring an action.[90] In legal theory, an action was brought by the service of an Original Writ of Summons and both plaintiff and defendant were required to appear in court either personally or by their attorneys.[91] In fact, the most common method of starting an action in this period was by suing out a Writ of *Capias Ad Respondendum* directing the sheriff to arrest the defendant. This Writ was available in all of the most common actions and by the nineteenth century it came to be used in the first instance, the Original Writ being either suspended or ignored.[92]

Likewise personal appearance became a fiction. A defendant who was not arrested made certain formal entries in the court record expressing his appearance. If he was arrested, he expressed his appearance by "giving bail to the action".[93]

As far as the plaintiff was concerned, there were no formalities observed. Once the defendant entered an appearance, both parties were considered "as in court".[94]

The principle still prevailed that there could be no proceedings against an absent defendant. In 1725, it was enacted that if the plaintiff provided an affidavit that the defendant had been personally served with a copy of process, he might enter an appearance for the defendant.[95] Otherwise plaintiff had to choose between

88. Supra note 76, vol. 3 at p. 624.
89. Compare Holdsworth, ibid with material cited supra notes 85-87 and accompanying text.
90. Id. vol. 9 at pp. 249-250.
91. Id. at p. 252.
92. Id. at p. 250.
93. Id. at p. 252.
94. Ibid.
95. 12 Geo. 1, c. 29, extended by 45 Geo. 3, c. 124, §§ 3 and 7; 8 Geo. 4, c. 71, § 5.

distraint, *capias* or attachment and commission of rebellion. This would depend on the nature of the action. *Capias* was the most common. "Attachment and Commission of Rebellion" involved the appointment of four commissioners who were ordered to attach the defendant wherever he could be found in the United Kingdom "as a rebel and contemnor of the King's laws and government by refusing to attend his sovereign when required".[96]

There were two types of bail, bail below and bail above. Bail below was taken by the sheriff as security for the defendant's appearance at the return of the Writ. Bail above was taken by the court as security for satisfaction of the judgment. Once bail above was given, bail below would be vacated.

If defendant were not within the jurisdiction and had no fixed abode and no property which could be distrained, the plaintiff would have to proceed to outlawry. The next writs were a Writ of *Alias* and a Writ of *Pluries* and finally a Writ of *Ultigatum Capias* by which he was declared an outlaw.[97]

By this time, the institution of outlawry had, according to Holdsworth, been perverted and overlaid with a mass of conventional rules.[98] Originally it had given the defendant "ample and reiterated" notice of the suit and only the contumacious and fraudulent were outlawed. By the 18th century the defendant was never summoned during the whole course of the proceedings. None of the above writs were even delivered to the sheriff to be executed. They were returned as a manner of form.

The defendant had no previous notice of the suit and his property could be seized and sold and the proceeds paid over to the plaintiff before he was aware that there was any action pending against him.[99] But there were steps which an outlawed defendant could take to get his outlawry reversed. He could apply to set aside the outlawry in which case he had to pay costs and enter an appearance. But if he took proceedings to get the outlawry reversed by writ of error, he did not have to pay costs or enter an appearance.[100]

Proceedings in Chancery were almost as lengthy and complex as proceedings at common law. A rule of the court in the sixteenth

96. Supra note 76, vol. 9 at p. 349.
97. See chart, id., at pp. 436-437.
98. Id. at p. 254.
99. Id. at p. 255.
100. Ibid.

century that no process could enforce an appearance until a bill signed by counsel had been filed came to be disregarded in the seventeenth century. It was therefore specifically enacted in 1705.[101]

The stages were:

(1) attachment — "a writ in the nature of a *capias* directed to the sheriff directing him to take up the defendant and bring him into court".

(2) If the sheriff returned *"non est inventus"*, attachment with proclamation.

(3) If this be returned *"non est inventus"*, a commission of rebellion...".

(4) If this was unavailing, a sergeant-at-arms was sent to find him.

(5) If the sergeant-at-arms could do nothing, "a sequestration issues to seize all his personal estate and the profits of his real estate".[102]

In 1732 it was enacted that where a defendant was suspected of leaving the realm or otherwise absconding to evade service, the plaintiff could apply to have his bill taken *pro confesso*.[103] But if this procedure was not available, the old law had to be applied in all its unsatisfactory complexity.[104]

The complication of the process to compel an answer was "equal to if not greater", than the process to compel an appearance. The chief difference was that once a defendant avoided all process, an application might be made to take his bill *pro confesso* even before the Statute of 1732. But, whether he was in custody or not, repeated Writs of *Habeas Corpus* to bring his body before the court were required before this could be done.[105]

It would seem to be outside the scope of this work to detail the processes of reform commenced in 1832 with the Uniformity of Process Act.[106] Suffice it to say that civil procedure was unified and simplified, uniform writs of summons for real and personal actions were instituted and the powers of the plaintiff to enter an appearance for a non-appearing defendant were expanded.[107]

101. 4 Anne, c. 16, § 22.
102. Supra note 76, at p. 349.
103. 5 Geo. 2, c. 25, § 1.
104. Supra note 76, vol. 9 at p. 350.
105. Id. at pp. 351, 437.
106. 2 & 3 Wm., c. 39.
107. See e.g. id., § 3.

In 1920, when the Statute of the Permanent Court of International Justice was drafted, the *British Annual Practice* (also called the *British Whitebook*) had a number of provisions dealing with default. Order 13 dealt with "Default of Appearance" (and continued to do so until 1979). Order 27 related to "Default of Pleading".

Where any defendant failed to appear, and plaintiff wanted to proceed upon default of appearance he was required to file either an affidavit of service or notice in lieu of service.[108] Where the writ was endorsed for a liquidated demand, the plaintiff could enter final judgment for a sum not exceeding the sum indicated on the writ together with interest and costs.[109]

Where the claim was for pecuniary damages or detention of goods with or without a claim for pecuniary damages and defendant failed to appear, the plaintiff could enter interlocutory judgment and a writ of inquiry issued to assess the value of the goods and/or the damages.[110] If the claim was for a liquidated sum, then final judgment was for the liquidated sum plus interest and costs.[111]

In an action for land the plaintiff was entitled in the event of non-appearance to enter a judgment that the person whose title was asserted in the writ should recover possession.[112]

In most of the actions under Order 13 when the party served with the writ failed to appear within the time limited for appearance, plaintiff filed an affidavit of service and the action proceeded as if the defendant had appeared.[113]

A judgment entered pursuant to Order 13 could be set aside or varied by the judge upon such terms or conditions as might be just.[114]

Order 27, Rule 11, provided that, in most actions, if the defendant made a default in delivering a defence, the plaintiff could set down the action on motion for judgment. Judgment was to be given upon the statement of claim alone.[115] It was not necessary on the hearing of the motion to prove the case in evidence.[116]

---

108. Order 13, Rule 2 *Annual Practice* (1920), p. 134.
109. Rule 3, id. at p. 135.
110. Rule 5, id. at p. 139.
111. Rule 7, id. at p. 143.
112. Ibid.
113. Rule 12, id. at p. 146. See also Rule 15, id. at p. 149.
114. Rule 10, id. at p. 145.
115. Id. at p. 441.
116. Id. at p. 444 & 445.

Order 36, Rule 31, dealt with "proceedings at trial". It provided:

> If, when a trial is called on, the plaintiff does not appear, then the plaintiff may prove his claim, so far as the burden of proof lies on him.[117]

In the 1982 *Whitebook*, now entitled *The Supreme Court Practice*, Order 13 is no longer called "Default of Appearance". The title has been changed to "Failure to Give Notice of Intention to Defend".

The change is based on the idea that an acknowledgement of service of process is equivalent to an appearance. Hence the new form asks the defendant three questions:

1. Whether he has received the writ,
2. Whether he wishes to contest the proceedings; and
3. Whether he wishes to apply for a stay of execution of any judgment for the debt or liquidated demand against him.[118]

"Default of Pleadings" is now dealt with in Order 19.

There are close similarities between the Rules listed under Order 13 and Order 19. Rule 1 of Order 13 and Rule 2 of Order 19 provide that, if the claim is for a liquidated demand and the defendant fails either to give notice of an intention to defend or to plead, then, after the appropriate time limited for these steps, plaintiff may enter a final judgment against the defendant for a sum not exceeding that claimed in the writ plust costs. There is also a final judgment where the action is for the recovery of land.[119] But, in a case involving unliquidated damages or the detention of goods, plaintiff may have interlocutory judgment.[120] Such a judgment is interlocutory only as to amount. It is final as to the right of plaintiff to recover damages. Plaintiff may proceed to trial with or without jury as to assessment of damages.[121]

The following requirements must be fulfilled to entitle plaintiff to enter judgment in default of notice of intention to defend being given. He must show:

117. Supra note 108 at p. 608.
118. 13/8/1.
119. 13/4 & 19/5.
120. 13/2 & 3; 19/3 & 4.
121. 12/1/1.

(1) that the writ has been duly served;
(2) that the time for acknowledgement of service has expired with no such acknowledgement having been returned;
(3) that the acknowledgement of service has been returned but it contains a statement that the defendant does not intend to contest the proceedings;
(4) that there is due proof of service of the writ, either by filing an affidavit of service or producing the defendant's solicitor's endorsement of acceptance of service...;
(5) that in a claim for recovery of land, no relief [of a certain sort] is claimed... .[122]

A judgment in default is not a judgment on the merits[123] but rather a very limited estoppel precluding the defendant from setting up defences in subsequent actions which were "necessarily and with precision" dealt with in the judgment.[124]

There is an exception. Under Order 13, Rule 6, in the case of claims not covered by Rules 1 to 5, the plaintiff does not get judgment in the case of default. But he can proceed as if the defendant had given notice of an intention to defend. If a default judgment is given, the defendant may apply to set aside the judgment if he subsequently wishes to defend the action.[125]

Order 19, Rule 1, relates to default of pleading by the plaintiff. Where the plaintiff is required to serve a statement of claim on the defendant and he fails to serve it, the defendant may, after the period fixed for service, apply to the court for an order dismissing the action and the court may dismiss it on such terms as it thinks just. Rules 2-6 substantially replicate the provisions of Order 13, Rules 1-5. But Rule 7 allows the plaintiff to apply for a judgment in cases not covered by Rules 2-6.

When the defendant fails to plead, the plaintiff may apply to the court for a judgment. The court may hear the application, and give such judgment as the plaintiff appears to be entitled to on the basis of his statement of claim.[126]

Where the defendant has given notice of intention to defend but

122. 13/1/2.
123. *Oppenheim v. Mahomed* [1922] 1 AC 482.
124. *New Brunswick Ry. Co. v. British & French Trust Co.* [1939] AC 1; *Kok Hong v. Leong etc.* [1904] AC 993 (PC).
125. 13/9/2.
126. 19/7.

24

has made no defence or his defence is struck out, plaintiff may apply by summons or a motion for judgment.[127] But, a defence served after the time to defend has expired but before judgment, cannot be disregarded. It will generally prevent the plaintiff from securing judgment even though he or she has ordinarily served the summons or notice of motion.[128] If so, plaintiff is entitled to proceed to trial.[129]

On default of pleading, the court cannot receive any evidence. It must give judgment according to the pleading above. It is therefore not necessary on the hearing of the summons or notice for judgment to prove the case by evidence.[130] Judgments under Order 19 may be set aside or varied by the court on such terms as it thinks just.[131]

At the trial, however, a different rule applies. Order 35, Rule 1, says:

(1) If when the trial of an action is called on, neither party appears, the action may be struck out of the list, without prejudice, however, to the restoration thereof on the direction of a judge.

(2) If, when the trial of an action is called on, one party does not appear, the judge may proceed with the trial of the action or any counterclaim in the absence of that party.

The note on the "Effect of Rule 1" says that the rule is taken from the former Order 36, rr. 31 and 32:

If... the plaintiff appears but the defendant does not appear at the trial the plaintiff may prove his claim, so far as the burden of proof lies on him.[132]

So, at the trial, the practice is still much the same as it was in 1920.

UNITED STATES LAW

Suits between States. In drafting Article 53 of the Statute of the Permanent Court of International Justice, the Advisory Com-

127. 19/7/3.
128. 19/7/4.
129. 19/7/6.
130. 19/7/10.
131. 19/9.
132. 35/1/2.

mittee of Jurists was most interested in suits between States in the United States.[133] As a quasi-sovereign entity, a defaulting State cannot be compelled to come to Court. It cannot be punished or outlawed. Nor can execution be levied against it.

In other respects, suits between States are not too different from suits by citizens against States. The case of *Chisholm v. Georgia*[134] served as a precedent for inter-State suits. In that case, the United States Supreme Court held that a state could be sued by a citizen of another State in *assumpsit*. Service on the Governor and Attorney-General of the State was sufficient and if the State did not appear, a judgment by default could be entered.

The case of *The State of New Jersey v. The People of the State of New York*[135] was a suit for the purpose of ascertaining a boundary between the two States. A subpoena had been served upon the Governor and the Attorney-General of New York State sixty days before the return day of service. A second subpoena was served upon the Governor only. There was no appearance by the State of New York. At the hearing the question arose as to whether the subpoena had been validly served and whether the Court had jurisdiction.[136] Counsel for the plaintiff (The State of New Jersey) then said that he would be glad to have a day assigned to argue the point of jurisdiction. Chief Justice John Marshall said that the Court would have no difficulty assigning a day to hear the motion. Notice of the day was served on the Governor and the Attorney-General of the State of New York. But the State did not enter an appearance.[137]

Chief Justice Marshall then said:

> ... as no one appears to argue the motion on the part of the State of New York, and the precedent for granting the process has been established upon very grave and solemn argument in the case of *Chisholm v. The State of Georgia* ... and *Grayson v. The State of Virginia* ... the Court do not think it

---

133. League of Nations, *Procès verbaux of the Committee of Jurists to draft the statute for a Permanent Court of International Justice* [hereinafter *Procès verbaux*] (1920), 11th Mtg. at p. 247.
134. 1 US (2 Dallas) 419 (1773).
135. 28 US (3 Pet.) 461 (1830).
136. Id. at 463.
137. Id. at 465-466.

proper to require *ex parte* argument in favour of their authority to grant a subpoena, but will follow the authority heretofore established.

The Court are the more disposed to adopt this course, as the State of New York will be at liberty to contest the proceeding at a future time in the course of the cause, if it shall choose to insist upon the objection.[138]

At a later stage of the proceedings,[139] the State of New York had still not appeared. Chief Justice Marshall said:

In this case the subpoena has been served as is required by the rule. The complainant according to the practice of the Court, and according to the general order made in the case of *Grayson v. The Commonwealth of Virginia*, has a right to proceed *ex parte*; and the Court will make an order to that effect, that the cause may be prepared for a final hearing. If upon being served with a copy of such order the defendant shall still fail to appear or to show cause to the contrary, this Court will, as soon thereafter as the cause shall be prepared by the complainant, proceed to a final hearing and decision thereof. But inasmuch as no final decree had been pronounced or judgment rendered in any suit heretofore instituted in this Court against a State, the question of proceeding to a final decree will be considered as not conclusively settled until the cause shall come on to be heard in chief.[140]

Thus, the case established the plaintiff's right to proceed *ex parte*. But the plaintiff had to prove his case.

The case of *The State of Massachusetts v. The State of Rhode Island*[141] also involved a boundary dispute. Defendant appeared but then moved to withdraw its appearance. The jurisdictional question was whether existing legislation was sufficient to allow the Court to proceed in boundary cases without special legislation.[142]

138. Id. at 466-467.
139. 30 US (5 Pet.) 284 (1831).
140. Id. at 291.
141. 37 US (12 Pet.) 755 (1838).
142. Id. at 760.

The Court cited *New Jersey v. New York* and considered Acts of Congress in relation to the process and the power of the Court to make and establish all necessary rules. It decided that they were sufficient to authorise process in proceedings between States.

The Court cannot compel the appearance of a State. But it can allow the complainant to proceed *ex parte* if the State does not appear.[143] Unless a State appears on a given day, judgment by default will be entered. In the opinion of Mr. Justice Thompson:

> ... the practice seems to be well-settled, that in suits against a State, if the State shall refuse or neglect to appear, upon due service of process, no coercive measures will be taken to compel appearance; but the complainant, or plaintiff, will be allowed to proceed *ex parte.*[144]

In a commentary on the draft Statute of the Permanent Court of International Justice as it was presented to the League of Nations by the Advisory Committee of Jurists, James Brown Scott said of the U.S. procedure:

> ... the plaintiff shall prepare the case for final hearing. Judgment is not to be entered upon the pleadings of the plaintiff; counsel cannot rest with folded arms and ask that a judgment be entered in accordance with their contentions. The plaintiff must proceed, albeit *ex parte*, and the court enter judgment in accordance with the plaintiff's contentions if, and only if, and to the extent that it finds them to be founded in fact as well as in law.[145]

Suits between individuals. United States law encompasses so many jurisdictions, that we will confine ourselves here to examining the generalised treatment of the subject found in the legal encyclopedia *Corpus Juris Secundum.*

The meaning of appearance in the United States is similar to that in the United Kingdom. Traditionally, a default judgment has been taken against a defendant who, having been dully summoned

143. Ibid.
144. Id. at 761.
145. Scott, *The Project of a Permanent Court of International Justice and Resolutions of the Advisory Committee of Jurists* (1920), p. 124.

28

in an action, failed to enter an appearance in time; but the term is not applied to a default after appearance as well. A default occurs whenever either of the parties omits to pursue the ordinary means of prosecution or defence in the regular manner at any time between the commencement of the suit and the decision.[146] It is taken to apply where the defendant fails to answer and plead within the time allowed or when he fails to appear at a trial. The technical term, where a defendant has entered an appearance but fails to plead or has his defence struck out in judgment is *nil dicit*. Once issues of fact are joined, a judgment on them is not a judgment by default but where there has been a proper default, the taking of *ex parte* proof on which to found a judgment does not make it other than a default.

Where some defendants default, but others appear, an interlocutory judgment can be entered against those who default but no final judgment can be entered until the issues are successfully disposed of as to the other defendants.[147]

In order to sustain a judgment by default, defendant must have violated or disregarded some statute, order or rule. Even then, he or she is not in default if a good excuse can be shown.[148]

A distinction is recognized between default in appearance and default in pleading. Default in appearance relates to the failure to enter an appearance within the proper time. Where a plaintiff's failure to proceed justifies the inference that he has abandoned his suit, then judgment by default cannot be taken against the defendant because of a failure to appear.[149]

Where defendant fails to appear for trial after the issue has been tried, plaintiff may be required to establish (prove) his cause of action before judgment is entered.[150]

Even where a defendant has entered an appearance, he may be in default if he fails to plead unless the undisputed evidence shows that he is not liable to the plaintiff.[151] In general a default has the same effect as a judgment rendered after a trial on the merits.[152]

146. 49 CJS § 187.
147. Id. at § 191.
148. Id. at § 193.
149. Id. at § 196.
150. Id. at § 198.
151. Id. at § 199.
152. Id. at § 200.

In some jurisdictions, a party may even take a judgment by default on the other party's failure to answer interrogatories. If plaintiff is required to reply to the defendant's answer, failure to do so may result in a judgment against him.

A default in pleading operates as an admission of the truth of the allegations set forth in the pleadings. It is not an admission of law that the facts set forth in the pleadings are sufficient to constitute a cause of action. Where the action is in tort for an unliquidated claim, then the amount must be ascertained before plaintiff can recover.[153]

SUMMARY

From this brief, very sketchy view of municipal civil procedure, we can draw a number of generalisations. In early Roman law, in Germanic law and indeed in English law up until the early nineteenth century, a trial was not regarded as possible without the consent and presence of both parties. We cannot say that jurisdiction was based on consent but rather that consent was an essential precondition to the action.

The absence of the plaintiff was not much of a problem. Having initiated the action, he could be taken to have abandoned it if he did not appear. Nonetheless, procedures varied as to the formalities which the defendant would have to go through before he could be absolved of the action.

The absence of the defendant presented more of a problem. If the court could not adjudicate without him plaintiff could not have judgment and non-appearance might thereby frustrate a just claim. Procedure under these conditions was primarily concerned with compelling the defendant to come before the court. This was accomplished by a number of devices such as distraint of property, the arrest of the defendant and, usually as a last resort, punishment of a contumacious defendant either by fine or by outlawry. At this time also appearance was actual physical presence either of oneself or of a representative or counsel.

As time went on appearance came to be manifested by the performance of some act or formality by which the defendant

153. Id. at § 201.

submitted to the authority of the court. At this stage fictional appearances become possible and plaintiff could enter an appearance for the defendant.

Almost all jurisdictions draw a distinction between failure to plead and failure to appear. A defendant who has not appeared or pleaded is usually in default once the time set for appearance or pleading has expired. But the party is usually allowed to cure the defect before judgment and in some cases even a default judgment may be set aside. Failure to appear necessarily involves a failure to plead. The reverse is not necessarily the case although in some jurisdictions appearance may be manifested by the act of pleading. The procedural significance attached to this distinction varies from one jurisdiction to another.

Jurisdictions also vary as to the extent to which a plaintiff needs to prove his case in the event of a default by a defendant. In some jurisdictions he need only prove that a defendant has been duly served. In most jurisdictions, the court will merely deem his allegations uncontradicted. In others, he will have to educe evidence to support his allegations. He need only prove his case, in so far as the burden of proof falls on him. In no jurisdiction is he required to negate all possible affirmative defences as well.

We can illustrate this last point with an example drawn from defamation in English Common Law. Plaintiff must prove a cause of action. That means that where the defendant is present and has pleaded, he or she must prove authorship, publication by the defendant of a statement relating to the plaintiff and the defamatory nature of the statement. In the absence of the defendant these matters may be deemed admitted. In either case, it is not necessary to prove that the statement is false. Truth is an affirmative defence that must be pleaded and proved by the defendant. The same is true of other affirmative defences such as "fair comment" and "qualified privilege". The right to raise these defences is a procedural advantage which a non-appearing or non-pleading defendant will forfeit. In all jurisdictions, a non-appearing and/or non-pleading defendant can expect to forfeit some procedural advantages regardless of plaintiff's burden of proof and regardless of whether or not he can be otherwise punished for failure to appear or to plead.

CHAPTER 2

NON-APPEARANCE AND THE CASES

Sino-Belgian Treaty Case

The phenomenon of non-appearance is not new. The Permanent Court of International Justice was confronted with a case of non-appearance not long after its creation. This was the *Case of the Denunciation of the Treaty of 2 November 1865 Between China and Belgium (Sino-Belgian Treaty Case).*[1] The case arose out of the unilateral denunciation by China of the Treaty of Peace, Commerce and Navigation of November 2, 1865, which involved the treatment of the nationals of each party in the territory of the other.

Article 46 of that Treaty provided that ten years after the date of the exchange of ratifications, the Government of Belgium could open negotiations for the modification of the Treaty by giving notice to the Government of China. In the absence of such notice, the Treaty was to continue for an additional ten years. At the end of each successive ten year term, Belgium would, once again, have the right to modify the Treaty. The Government of China was given no similar right to modify, much less to terminate, the Treaty.

Nevertheless the Chinese Government gave notice to the Belgian Government on April 26, 1926, that it would consider the Treaty terminated. The Government of Belgium denied that the Chinese

---

1. [1927] PCIJ, Ser. A, No. 8, p. 6.

Government possessed the right of unilateral denunciation and offered to negotiate a friendly settlement. The negotiation did not succeed and Belgium proposed bringing the dispute to the Permanent Court of International Justice. This, the Government of China refused to do.

Both parties had filed declarations accepting the compulsory jurisdiction of the Court under Article 36(2) of the Statute. But the Chinese Government, in a Memorandum of November 16, 1926, refused to agree to the matter being submitted to the Permanent Court of International Justice. It maintained that the dispute was political in character and that "no nation can consent to the basic principle of equality between States being made the subject of a judicial inquiry". It was prepared to agree to the dispute being submitted only if the Belgian Government agreed to its being settled *ex aequo et bono*.[2]

China denounced the Treaty by Presidential Decree[3] and enacted measures contrary to the Treaty. On November 25, 1926 Belgium filed an application[4] with the Court asking it to give judgment that China was not entitled to denounce the Treaty unilaterally. The application also contained a request for provisional measures asking the Court, pending judgment, to indicate measures necessary to safeguard the rights of Belgium and her nationals.

The Court was not sitting at the time. So the application was received by the President, Max Huber, who considered whether to inciate interim measures — a power which he had under Article 57 of the 1922 Rules of Court. He initially declined to do so.[5] But later he reversed his position.

The Order of January 8, 1927 laid down certain fairly detailed rules relating to the treatment of Belgian Nationals and their property in China.[6]

Despite the fact that China had accepted the compulsory jurisdiction of the Court, it did not appoint an agent or participate in the proceedings.

On January 3, 1927, Belgium filed a Memorial in the case, but,

2. [1926] PCIJ, Ser. C, No. 16(J), p. 78.
3. Id. at p. 75.
4. [1926] PCIJ, Ser. A, No. 8, p. 4.
5. See Hudson, 2 World Court Reports, p. 3.
6. Supra note 1 at pp. 7-8.

on January 17, the Belgian Government informed the Court that it had arrived at an agreement with China for the reopening of negotiations.

On February 3, the Belgian Government notified the Court, through the President, that it had reached an agreement with the Chinese Government on a provisional regime to be applied to Belgian nationals.[7]

The President, again acting *proprio motu*, issued an order on February 15, 1927 revoking the interim measures because he considered that the new regime would take the place of the regime in the Treaty and hence of measures designed to protect that regime.

The Chinese Government continued to stay away, although the Belgian Government did convey to the Court the Chinese desire for an extension of its deadline for the submission of its countermemorial. On February 13, 1929, just before that deadline expired, the Belgian Government informed the Court that the dispute had been settled by the Treaty of Nanking of November 22, 1928.[8] Accordingly, the Belgian Government withdrew the action.[9]

In the light of the Chinese Government's desire for an extension, it is likely that China would have participated had the case not been settled.

Electricity Company of Sofia and Bulgaria Case

In this case, non-appearance was not voluntary. It involved a Belgian company which had been taken over by the municipality of Sofia in 1916 during World War I. After the war, Article 182 of the Treaty of Neuilly[10] provided for restitution and established a Belgo-Bulgarian Mixed Arbitral Tribunal which, in its award of May 27, 1925, established a formula for fixing the selling price of electric current.[11]

---

7. Id. at pp. 9-11.
8. 87 LNTS 287.
9. [1929] PCIJ, Ser. A, Nos. 18/19, p. 5.
10. 112 British & Foreign State Papers 781, 848 (1919).
11. (1925) 37 *TAM* 308.

In 1934, a dispute arose over the application of this formula. The Tribunal ruled that it was without jurisdiction since the dispute related to the previous award and not to the Treaty of Neuilly. The Bulgarian municipal courts ruled in favour of the Municipality on all points. The Belgian Government also complained of a tax which it claimed only operated against the company in question and no other distributor of electricity in Bulgaria.[12]

The Belgian application was filed on January 25, 1938. It asked the Court to declare that Bulgaria had failed to fulfill its international obligations and to order reparations.[13] Belgium also asked for interim measures of protection[14] in order to forestall measures of execution against the company.

On July 13, a public hearing was held on the request, but the Bulgarian agent was not present. So action on the request was postponed and later withdrawn.

Belgium, as we have seen, had accepted the compulsory jurisdiction of the Court on March 10, 1926. Bulgaria's acceptance was dated August 12, 1921. In addition, Belgium relied on a Treaty of Conciliation, Arbitration and Judicial Settlement concluded between the two countries on June 23, 1931.

Bulgaria appointed an agent and a judge *ad hoc*. It also filed a counter-memorial containing preliminary objections.[15] The Bulgarian Agent appeared and argued at this stage of the Case. On April 4, 1939, the Court dismissed Bulgaria's preliminary objections.

On October 17, 1939, the Belgian Government made a second request for the indication of interim measures. The request was notified to the Bulgarian Government on October 18, 1939, asking that Government for any observations it might wish to make before November 24, 1939. A telegram dated November 18, 1939 by the Bulgarian Agent informed the Court that, because of the war which had broken out, the Bulgarian Agent and judge *ad hoc* had been forbidden to attempt to cross belligerant country to reach The Hague.[16]

12. Application, January 25, 1938, Court Document Distr. 4010 (1938).
13. Ibid.
14. July 2, 1938 [1939] PCIJ, Ser. A/B, No. 79, p. 194.
15. November 25, 1938 [1939] PCIJ, Ser. A/B, No. 77, p. 64.
16. Supra note 14 at p. 197.

The Court, probably taking account of previous dilatory manoeuvres by the Bulgarian Government, refused to delay and granted the measures requested.[17] Proceedings on the merits never took place.

The Eastern Carelia Case

The *Status of Eastern Carelia Case*[18] is not a case of non-appearance of one of the parties. There were no parties. The case involved a request made by the Council of the League of Nations for an Advisory Opinion on the status of the territory of Eastern Carelia. However, an Advisory Opinion may be a way of getting the Court to adjudicate a dispute between two States one of which has not consented to the jurisdiction of the Court[19] − a form of compulsory jurisdiction.

On January 13, 1922, the representative of Finland made a statement pursuant to Articles 11 and 17 of the Covenant concerning a dispute between Finland and Soviet Russia about the status of Eastern Carelia. The dispute involved Russia's obligations under the Treaty of Dorpat 1920, a peace treaty between Finland and Russia. The Council suggested that a Member of the League of Nations might use its good offices to bring the two parties together for negotiations. This, the Esthonian Government attempted to do.[20] Soviet Russia which was not a member of the League of Nations, declined to participate claiming that the matter was a purely a domestic one.[21]

Since Soviet Russia was not a Party to the Statute of the Permanent Court of International Justice, there was no question of the Court having jurisdiction to hear and determine a contentious dispute between Finland and Soviet Russia. So the Finnish representative asked the Council to request the Court to give an Advisory Opinion on the matter. The Council voted to do this on April 21, 1923.[22] The Soviet Government formally declined to

17. Id. at p. 199.
18. [1923] PCIJ, Ser. B, No. 5, p. 7.
19. See Keith, *The Extent of the Advisory Jurisdiction of the International Court of Justice* (1971), p. 89.
20. Supra note 18 at p. 24.
21. Ibid.
22. Ibid.

take part in the proceedings[23] and the Court heard arguments on the question of its competence by the representative of Finland.

The Court replied to the Council's request on July 23, 1923. It rejected the Council's request for an Advisory Opinion on the ground that the subject matter of the opinion requested involved an actual dispute between Finland and Russia.

Saying that the principle is well established in international law that "no State can, without its consent, be compelled to submit its disputes with other States either to mediation or arbitration or any other kind of pacific settlement",[24] the Court noted that such consent had never been given by Russia, that Russia had, in fact, clearly indicated that it would accept no intervention by the League.[25] The Court therefore found it impossible to give its opinion on the dispute.[26]

But then it went on to say that there were other cogent reasons which rendered it inexpedient for the Court to deal with the matter.

The question involved was really one of fact requiring the ascertainment of evidence. Russia's refusal to take part in the case put the Court at a considerable disadvantage in its attempt to obtain such evidence. Consequently, said the Court, it was doubtful that materials would be available to the Court which would enable it to arrive at a judicial conclusion on the questions of fact.[27]

It would seem that, in contentious cases, the Court is under a duty to overcome this disadvantage. Article 53 of the Court's Statute, which will be discussed in greater detail in Chapter 3, requires the Court, in the absence of one of the parties, to assure itself that the claim is well-founded in fact and law.

But the Court's position on the main issue relating to actual disputes pending between two States has been substantially modified in subsequent cases. In the *Interpretation of Peace Treaties Case*,[28] the International Court of Justice accepted jurisdiction over a request by the United Nations General Assembly on the question of whether Hungary, Bulgaria and Romania were complying with

23. Id. at pp. 12-13.
24. Id. at p. 27. See Lalonde, "The Death of the Eastern Carelia Doctrine: Has Compulsory Jurisdiction Arrived in the World Court?", 37 U. Tor. Fac. L. Rev. 80 (1979).
25. Id. at pp. 27-28.
26. Id. at p. 28.
27. Ibid.
28. [1950] ICJ 65.

certain human rights obligations in treaties which those States had concluded with the United States and the United Kingdom. The Court dismissed objections based on the *Eastern Carelia Case* saying that they revealed a confusion between the principles governing contentious procedure and those which were applicable to advisory opinions. It pointed out that the Court's reply, in the latter is only of an advisory character and, as such has no binding force:

> It follows that no State, whether a Member of the United Nations or not, can prevent the giving of an Advisory Opinion which the United Nations considers to be desirable in order to obtain enlightenment as to the course of action it should take.[29]

But it recognised that lack of consent might constitute a ground for declining to give an opinion requested if, in the circumstances of a given case, considerations of judicial propriety obliged the Court to refuse to give an opinion.[30]

In the *Western Sahara Case*, an advisory opinion was requested of the Court on competing claims by Morocco and Mauritania to the territory of Western Sahara which Spain as the governing colonial power was about to relinquish. Spain objected to the advisory opinion on the ground that it had not consented to the submission of those questions to the Court.[31] It cited the *Eastern Carelia Case.*[32] The Court agreed that the case involved a legal controversy. But it was one which arose during the proceedings of the General Assembly and in relation to matters with which the General Assembly was dealing at the time. "It did not arise independently in bilateral relations".[33] But the Court left open the possibility that "in certain circumstances the lack of consent of an interested party may render the giving of an advisory opinion incompatible with the Court's judicial character.[34]

29. Id. at 71.
30. Id. at 71-72.
31. [1975] ICJ 11, 22.
32. Id. at 23.
33. Id. at 25.
34. Ibid. Also on this issue see *Legal Consequences for States of the Continued Presence of South Africa in Namibia (South West Africa) notwithstanding Security Council Resolution 276 (1970)* [1971] ICJ 16.

BEFORE THE INTERNATIONAL COURT OF JUSTICE

The Corfu Channel Case

On October 22, 1946, two British destroyers struck mines and were heavily damaged in the North Corfu Channel on the Albanian side of the Channel, which is a frontier between Albania and Greece.[35] Following the incident, on November 12 and 13, 1946, British minesweepers swept the Channel despite Albanian protest.[36]

The United Kingdom accused Albania of responsibility for material damage and loss of life which occurred as a result of the October 22 incident and complained to the United Nations Security Council. Although not a Member of the United Nations at the time, the Government of the People's Republic of Albania was invited to take part in the proceedings pursuant to Article 32 of the Charter. On April 9, 1947, the Security Council adopted a resolution which read "The Security Council ...recommends that the United Kingdom and Albanian Governments should immediately refer the dispute to the International Court of Justice in accordance with the provisions of the Statute of the Court".[37] Great Britain filed a unilateral application with the Registrar of the Court. The U.K. claimed, as a basis for the Court's jurisdiction, the fact that Albania, in order to participate in the Security Council debate, had accepted, for the particular dispute, all of the obligations incumbent on a United Nations Member including the duty, under Article 25 of the Charter, "to accept and carry out the decisions of the Security Council."[38] In a letter to the Registry dated July 2, 1947, Albania objected on the ground that the recommendation of the Security Council had required that the issue be submitted by agreement. Subject to this reservation, it accepted the jurisdiction of the Court[39] although it cautioned that acceptance was not to be regarded as creating a precedent for the future. It also appointed an agent.[40]

It should be noted that the Security Council Resolution was a

35. *Corfu Channel Case [Merits]* [1949] ICJ 3, 28.
36. Id. at 33.
37. S.C.O.R. No. 34 (9 April 1947) p. 720 cited *Corfu Channel Case [Preliminary Objections]* [1947-48].
38. [1949] ICJ Pleadings, Vol. I, p. 8.
39. Id. at 19.
40. Id. at 28.

"recommendation" rather than a "decision" and consequently it was not binding under the terms of Article 25.

Undoubtedly, the Albanian Government realised this fact after the letter of July 2, 1947, had been received by the Registry of the Court. So it filed a Preliminary Objection on the ground of inadmissibility in which it argued that the Security Council Resolution was not binding in form and was therefore insufficient to found the Court's jurisdiction.[41] It asked the Court to hold the British Application void for irregularity.

The Court held that, even if the original British application had been irregular, the Albanian declaration in its letter of July 2 constituted a voluntary and undisputed acceptance of jurisdiction.[42] Accordingly it rejected Albania's preliminary objection. Thus the Court acquired jurisdiction on the basis of *forum prorogatum*.[43]

Immediately after the decision on Albania's preliminary objection, the two parties concluded a special agreement submitting the dispute to the Court in the form of two questions:

(1) Is Albania responsible under international law for the explosions which occurred on 22nd October 1946 in Albanian waters and for the damage and loss of life which resulted from them and is there a duty to pay compensation?

(2) Has the United Kingdom under international law violated the sovereignty of the Albanian People's Republic by reason of the acts of the Royal Navy in Albanian waters on the 22nd October and on the 12th and 13th November 1946 and is there a duty to give satisfaction?[44]

In its judgment of April 9, 1949, the Court held, on the first question, that the People's Republic of Albania was responsible under international law for the explosion of October 22, 1946 and for the damage and loss of human life that resulted.

It also held that the United Kingdom did not violate Albanian sovereignty by reason of the acts of the British Navy in Albanian waters on October 22 but that the actions of November 12 and 13 did violate Albanian sovereignty. It reserved the assessment of the amount of compensation for further consideration[45] and fixed a

41. Id. at 25-26.
42. Ibid.
43. See Rosenne, *The International Court of Justice* (1957), p. 238.
44. [1949] ICJ 3, 6.
45. Id. at 36.

40

time limit for the Parties' observations regarding the amount of compensation due the United Kingdom.

Up to this point, Albania, though somewhat dubious about the Court's jurisdiction, had participated fully in the proceedings.

In a telegram dated June 23, 1949, the Deputy Minister for Foreign Affairs of Albania asked the Court for an extension of the time limit for the presentation of its observations.[46] This extension was granted by the Court.[47]

But then, on June 29, the Albanian Agent informed the Court that the Albanian Government considered that the special agreement of March 25, 1948, only gave the Court jurisdiction to decide on the principle of compensation but not to assess the amount.[48] He reasserted this opinion in a telegram dated November 15.

The United Kingdom filed its observations within the prescribed time limit and invoked Article 53 of the Statute. The Albanian Government filed no reply or other document,[49] and did not participate in the oral hearings.[50]

Then, in a letter signed by the Albanian *Chargé d'Affaires* dated December 10, after the expiry of the time limit for submission of its written observations, the Albanian Government asked for a change in the procedure for the submission of observations and failing that, for an extension of the time limit.[51]

The Court, in its Judgment of December 15, 1949, pointed out that it had given ample time to the Albanian Government to defend its case and that, instead of availing itself of the opportunity, Albania had twice disputed the Court's jurisdiction, had failed to file submissions and declined to appear at the hearing. It refused the Albanian request.[52]

It then noted that the position adopted by the Albanian Government "brings into operation Article 53 of the Statute which applies to procedure in default of appearance".

Article 53 entitles the United Kingdom to call upon the Court to decide in its favour. At the same time the Court must satisfy it-

46. [1949] ICJ 222.
47. Id. at 223.
48. *Corfu Channel Case [Assessment of Compensation]* [1949] ICJ 243, 246.
49. Ibid.
50. Id. at 247.
51. Id. at 248.
52. Ibid.

self that the claim is well-founded in fact and law. But, it cautioned:

> While Article 53 thus obliges the Court to consider the submission of the Party which appears, it does not compel the Court to examine their accuracy in all their details; for this might in certain unopposed cases prove impossible in practice. It is sufficient for the Court to convince itself by such methods as it considers suitable that the submissions are well founded.[53]

The Court then went on to fix the amount of compensation due from the People's Republic of Albania to the United Kingdom at £ 843,947.[54]

After the Judgment, the United Kingdom and Albania entered into negotiations. Albania offered the sum of £ 40,000 in final settlement of the British claim. The offer was rejected.[55]

Monetary Gold Case

In considering this case, we are departing somewhat from strict chronological order. But the departure is justified because the case stems directly from the Court's judgment in the *Corfu Channel Case*. In fact it involved a rather intricate series of maneuvres by the British Government to get an unwilling and contumacious Albania into a position where it would have to assert its legal rights before the International Court of Justice as either an applicant or an intervenor.

The case involved the Final Act of the Paris Conference on Reparations of January 14, 1946, which provided that looted monetary gold found in Germany would be pooled for the purpose of reparation amongst countries which could prove that the gold had belonged to them.[56] The Governments of France, the United Kingdom and the United States were entrusted with the implementation of the Agreement.

53. Ibid.
54. Id. at 250.
55. See Rosenne, supra note 43 at p. 98.
56. [1954] ICJ 19, 25.

A dispute arose in which Albania and Italy each laid claim, under the Paris Act, to the gold of the National Bank of Albania which had been taken from Rome by the Germans in 1943. The three custodial governments decided by an agreement known as the Washington Agreement of April 25, 1951, to submit the question to arbitration.

The Washington Agreement was accompanied by a statement whereby, if Albania was successful, the gold would be delivered to the United Kingdom in partial satisfaction of the *Corfu Channel* Judgment[57] unless Albania, within 90 days of notice of the Award being communicated to it, submitted to the International Court of Justice the question of whether it was proper for the gold to be delivered to the United Kingdom for that reason.

But the Arbitration, confined as it was to rights under the Paris Act, did not wholly dispose of Italy's claims, some of which arose from an Albanian Law of 1945 which Italy claimed was contrary to international law.

Therefore, Italy too was to have the option, within 90 days, of applying to the International Court of Justice to determine whether the British or Italian claims would have priority should the occasion arise.[58] The three custodial powers agreed to accept the Court's jurisdiction as respondents in either case.

Albania refrained from taking part in the Arbitration. Nevertheless, on February 20, 1953, an award was rendered which favoured Albania. Albania made no application to the Court.

Italy was also reluctant to go to the Court, under the Washington Statement. However it suddenly realised that if it allowed the 90 days to elapse without going to the Court, British title to the gold would be perfected.[59] So it submitted an application. At the same time, since it was not a Member of the United Nations, it accepted the Court's jurisdiction *ratione personae* under Article 35, paragraph 2 of the Court's Statute.[60] Then, even though it was technically the claimant, it raised a preliminary objection claiming that the Washington Statement was not a sufficient basis upon which to found the jurisdiction of the Court.[61] This course of

57. 91 UNTS 21.
58. Ibid. See supra note 56 at 21.
59. Rosenne, supra note 43 at p. 102.
60. [1952-53] ICJYB, p. 37.
61. Supra note 56 at 24.

action stemmed from the difficulty which the Government of Italy had in preparing a memorial due to the fact that the case between Italy and the three custodial powers arose from matters concerning the international responsibility of Albania, a State which was not before the Court.

The United Kingdom attempted to claim that Italy's preliminary objection amounted to a withdrawal of its application which, in turn, perfected the United Kingdom claim to the gold.[62]

The Court noted that it was unusual for an applicant State to subsequently challenge the jurisdiction of the Court.[63] But it was not contrary either to the Statute or to the Rules of Court.[64] It did not amount to a withdrawal or cancellation of the application.[65] The Court also noted that Italy's claim raised questions of Albania's international responsibility.[66]

The crucial question, namely whether the Albanian Law of 1945 was contrary to international law, involved the international responsibility of a third State. Therefore, the Court did not feel able to give a decision on the issue binding upon that State without its consent.[67]

The United Kingdom suggested that Albania could have intervened under Article 62 of the Statute which allows intervention on the part of a State "which considers that it has an interest of a legal nature". The fact that it did not choose to do so, it argued, should not make it impossible for the Court to give judgment on the rights as between the parties[68] especially in the light of Article 59 which holds that the judgment of the Court in any given case is binding "only between the parties and in respect of that particular case".[69]

The Court rejected that argument noting that, in the case before it, Albania's legal interest would not merely be affected by the decision but would form the very subject-matter of the dispute.[70] That being the case, the Court could not, without the consent of Albania, give a decision binding upon any State.[71]

62. Id. at 25.
63. Id. at 28.
64. Id. at 29.
65. Id. at 30.
66. Id. at 32.
67. Ibid.
68. Ibid.
69. Id. at 33.
70. Id. at 32.
71. Id. at 33.

Accordingly, the Court found that it had no jurisdiction, in the absence of Albanian consent, to adjudicate upon the Italian application.[72]

Thus, it would seem to be extremely difficult to force an unwilling State to appear as either an applicant or an intervenor.

The Anglo-Iranian Oil Co. Case

The United Kingdom was no more successful with the International Court of Justice in the *Anglo-Iranian Oil Co. Case*. The Case involved the Iranian Oil Nationalisation Act of May 1, 1951, which involved the nationalisation of the Iranian Oil industry by the Government of Dr. Mohammed Mossadegh.

The United Kingdom objected that the nationalisation violated a concession contract between the Government of Persia and the Anglo-Persian Oil Co.[73] which was concluded as a result of a settlement by the Council of the League of Nations of a dispute between the United Kingdom and Iran (which in 1933 was called Persia).

The United Kingdom suggested that the matter be submitted to arbitration under Article 22 of the concession contract. Iran rejected the proposal. There was also an attempt at diplomatic settlement but Iran rejected this too.[74]

The United Kingdom claimed that the concession contract, arising as it did from the League of Nations settlement procedure, constituted an agreement between the two States. Accordingly, the United Kingdom filed an application asking the Court to declare that the Government of Iran was under a duty to submit to arbitration, that the Iranian Oil Nationalisation Act was contrary to international law insofar as it purported to annul the terms of the agreement unilaterally and that the British Company was entitled to compensation for all acts which had already been performed pursuant to the Nationalisation Act.

Alternative relief was sought based on the principle of denial of justice, a principle of general international law. This limb of the

72. Id. at 34.
73. April 10, 1933. Application [1952] ICJ Pleadings, p. 8.
74. Id. at pp. 11-12.

United Kingdom case rested on most-favoured-nation status accorded to it by Iran in a Treaty of 1857, and a commercial convention of 1903 combined with a series of treaties between Iran and other States which provided that the nationals of those States were to be treated by Iran in accordance with the principles of international law.[75] By virtue of the most-favoured-nation clause, the United Kingdom Government felt that its nationals were entitled to the same treatment that the nationals of those other States were entitled to.

The United Kingdom based its claim to the jurisdiction of the International Court of Justice on Article 36(2) and 36(5) of the Court's Statute. The United Kingdom's Declaration was desposited on 28 February 1940.

The Iranian Declaration of 19 September 1932 was the narrower of the two. It provided:

Le Gouvernement impérial de Perse déclare reconnaître comme obligatoire, de plein droit et sans convention spéciale, vis-à-vis de tout autre État acceptant la même obligation, c'est-a-dire sous condition de réciprocité, la juridiction de la Cour Permanente de Justice internationale, conformément à l'article 36, paragraphe 2 du Statut de la Cour, sur tous les différends qui s'élèveraient àpres la ratification de la présente déclaration, au sujet de situations ou de faits ayant directement ou indirectement trait à l'application des traités ou conventions acceptés par la Perse et postéreiurs à la ratification de cette déclaration, exception faite pour:

a) les différends ayant trait au statut territorial de la Perse, y compris ceux relatifs à ses droits de souveraineté sur ses îles et ports;

b) les différends au sujet desquels les Parties auraient convenu ou conviendraient d'avoir recours a un autre mode de reglement pacifique;

c) les différends relatifs à des questions qui, d'après le droit international, relèveraient exclusivement de la juridiction de la Perse;

Toutetefois, le Gouvernement imperial de Perse se réserve le

---

75. These treaties are listed in paragraph 11 of Annex 2 of the United Kingdom Memorial, id. at pp. 150-151.

droit de demander la suspension de la procédure devant la Cour pour tout différend soumis au Conseil de la Société des Nations.

La présente declaration est faite pour une durée de six ans; à l'expiration de ce délai, elle continuera à avois ses pleins effets jusqu'a ce que notification soit donnée de son abrogation.[76]

The Government of Iran denied that the Court had competence to entertain the merits of the dispute and did not appear. The substance of the Iranian objection to the jurisdiction of the Court was that the agreement of 1933 was not a treaty, that nationalisation of the Oil Compnay was an internal matter and that the Court was excluded from consideration of the question by Article 2(7) of the United Nations Charter and paragraph (c) of Iran's Declaration of 1932.

Iran also claimed that its declaration allowed the Court to consider only those treaties which it concluded after the ratification of the Declaration. Most of the treaties relied on by the United Kingdom were concluded prior to that time. Furthermore, the treaties, even those such as the Treaty of Friendship, Establishment and Commerce Between Persia and Denmark signed on February 20, 1934, could only be invoked through most-favoured-nation clauses contained in treaties concluded between the United Kingdom Government and Persia between 1857 and 1903.

76. Id. at pp. 146-147; [1952] ICJ 93, 103.
"The Imperial Government of Persia recognizes as compulsory *ipso facto* and without special agreement in relation to any other State accepting the same obligation, that is to say, on condition of reciprocity, the jurisdiction of the Permanent Court of International Justice, in accordance with Article 36, paragraph 2, of the Statute of the Court, in any disputes arising after the ratification of the present declaration with regard to situations or facts relating directly or indirectly to the application of treaties or conventions accepted by Persia and subsequent to the ratification of this declaration, with the exception of:
(a)   disputes relating to the territorial status of Persia, including those concerning the rights of sovereignty of Persia over its islands and ports;
(b)   disputes in regard to which the Parties have agreed or shall agree to have recourse to some other method of peaceful settlement;
(c)   disputes with regard to questions which by international law, fall exclusively within the jurisdiction of Persia;
However, the Imperial Government of Persia reserves the right to require that proceedings in the Court shall be suspended in respect of any dispute which has been submitted to the Council of the League of Nations.
The present declaration is made for a period of six years. At the expiration of that period, it shall continue to bear its full effects until notification is given of its abrogation."

On June 22, 1951, the United Kingdom filed a request for interim measures of protection claiming that if the Court were to decide in favour of the United Kingdom Government, its decision could not be executed because of acts which were on the point of being committed by the Iranian Government which would irreparably injure United Kingdom interests.[77]

In a telegram dated June 21, 1951, the agent for the United Kingdom requested the President of the Court to send a telegram to the Iranian Minister of Foreign Affairs, pursuant to Article 61(3) of the Rules of Court in force at the time, suggesting the desirability of suspending the measures of constraint directed against the Anglo-Iranian Oil Co. pending the decision of the Court.[78] Such a cable was sent on June 23, 1951 by the President of the Court, Judge Basdevant.

On June 30, the Iranian Minister at The Hague delivered to the Court a reply signed by the Iranian Minister of Foreign Affairs. This statement declared that the matter was not within the Court's competence "because of the fact that exercise of the right of sovereignty is not subject to complaint".[79] It expressed the hope that: "Under these circumstances, the request for interim measures of protection would naturally be rejected".[80]

The Hearing, at which the Iranian Government was not represented, was held on June 30. The major issue before the Court was whether the Court could grant interim relief without first deciding whether it had jurisdiction to hear the merits of the dispute.

The Court said that the complaint concerned an alleged violation of international law by breach of the concession agreement and by a denial of justice:

> ... it cannot be accepted *a priori* that a claim based on such a complaint falls completely outside the scope of international jurisdiction... .[81]

Thus the Court was willing to indicate interim measures on the basis that the dispute involved a claimed violation of international

77. Request for Interim Measures of Protection, Pleadings, id. at pp. 47-48.
78. Id. at pp. 62-63.
79. Id. at p. 92.
80. Ibid.
81. *Anglo-Iranian Oil Co. Case [Interim Measures]* [1951] ICJ 89, 92-93.

law and of an international agreement. That being so, the complaint could only have been refused if jurisdiction appeared to be manifestly absent. The Court granted five measures that were almost legislative in their detail.[82]

Judges Winiarski and Badawi filed a Joint Dissenting Opinion. They did not go along with the liberal holding on jurisdiction. They felt that it was based on a presumption in favour of the competence of the Court which they did not think was in consonance with the principles of international law pursuant to which jurisdiction rested on the consent of the parties.[83] They argued that the presumption should be reversed and suggested an alternative standard:

> ... s'il existe de fortes raisons en faveur de la compétence contestée, la cour peut indiquer des mesures conservatoires; s'il existe des doutes sérieux ou de fortes raisons contra cette compétence, elle ne peut pas les accorder.[84]

Iran, still insisting that the International Court of Justice had no jurisdiction, not only refused to comply with the indication but ordered the expulsion of all British staff of the Oil Co. remaining in Iran.

On September 28, 1951, the United Kingdom complained to the Security Council under Article 94(2) of the United Nations Charter.[85] But the debate on Britain's proposed resolution was ultimately postponed to await the ruling by the International Court of Justice on the question of jurisdiction.[86] The Security Council never resumed debate on this question.

Following the granting of interim protection, the Government of Iran designated an agent, appointed a judge *ad hoc* and filed preliminary objections on February 4, 1952. It also participated in the oral arguments on jurisdiction held on June 9 to 23 and July 22, 1952.

In its judgment of July 22, the International Court of Justice

82. Id. at 93-94.
83. Id. at 96-97.
84. Id. at 97.
... if there exist weighty arguments in favour of the challenged jurisdiction, the Court may indicate interim measures of protection; if there exist serious doubts or weighty arguments against this jurisdiction such measures cannot be indicated.
85. 28 September 1951, UN Doc.S/2357.
86. 565th Mtg, 17 October 1951, pp. 2-8,

upheld Iran's preliminary objections.[87] It concluded that the declaration was limited to disputes relating to the application of treaties or conventions entered into by Iran after the date on which it was ratified.[88] The treaties containing the most-favoured-nation clauses invoked by the United Kingdom were all concluded prior to that date and consequently could not serve as a basis for the jurisdiction of the Court.[89] Furthermore, neither the concession contract of 1933 nor the League of Nations settlement constituted a treaty *"postérieur à la ratification"* of the Iranian Declaration. The concession contract was not a treaty but rather an agreement between the Government of Iran and a foreign company.[90] Hence the matter was one which was within Iran's domestic jurisdiction and not an international question. The concession contract did not in any way regulate the relations between the two Governments.[91]

The Nottebohm Case

Friedrich Nottebohm was a German national born in Hamburg in 1881. He had resided in Guatemala since 1905 as an important and successful businessman. In 1939, soon after the beginning of World War II, he asked Liechtenstein to naturalise him. On October 13, 1939, he became a national of that State pursuant to the Liechtenstein Law of Nationality of 1934.[92] Pursuant to Article 6(d) of that law,[93] the three year residency requirement was suspended in his case. According to German law, he lost his German nationality under Article 25 of the German Nationality Law of 1913.

He returned to Guatemala in January 1940 and on February 5, he was registered by Guatemalan authorities as a Liechtenstein national. He continued to reside in Guatemala until November 20, 1943. On December 11, 1941, Guatemala declared war on Germany. Throughout the whole of World War II, Liechtenstein

---

87. [1952] ICJ 93.
88. Id. at 107.
89. Id. at 109.
90. Id. at 112.
91. Ibid.
92. [1955] ICJ Pleadings, Vol. I, p. 12.
93. Id. at p. 72.

maintained a position of strict neutrality and was never at war with Guatemala.[94]

On November 19, 1943, Nottebohm was arrested and the following day, he was placed on an American vessel and interned in the United States as an enemy alien. Guatemala seized and retained his property. After the war, in 1946, he returned to Liechtenstein and became a permanent resident.

On December 17, 1951, Liechtenstein filed a unilateral application claiming that the Government of Guatemala had acted contrary to international law and incurred international responsibility by the detention, internment and expulsion of Nottebohm and by the sequestration and confiscation of his property. The application also claimed that the Government of Guatemala was bound to return Nottebohm's property and pay him compensation for both his internment and the loss of his property.[95] Liechtenstein based its application on the acceptance of the compulsory clause by Liechtenstein and Guatemala. The Guatemalan Declaration was deposited on January 27, 1947. It provided:

> The Government of Guatemala declares that, in accordance with Article 36(2) and (3) of the Statute of the International Court of Justice, it recognises as compulsory, *ipso facto*, and without special agreement, in relation to any other State accepting the same obligation, *and for a period of five years* the jurisdiction of the Court in all legal disputes... [emphasis added].[96]

On September 9, 1952, Guatemala sent the Court a communication raising objections to the Court's jurisdiction. It argued that its acceptance of the Court's compulsory jurisdiction had expired on January 26, 1952. From that date, it said, the Court could not have jurisdiciton without Guatemala's consent.[97] It further claimed that it would be contrary to the domestic laws of Guatemala to appear and contest the claim. But it stressed that this attitude was not to be considered as one of default or voluntary absence but was rather based "on great respect for the domestic

94. Id. at p. 27.
95. [1953] ICJ 111, 113.
96. Supra note 92, Vol. I.
97. Supra note 95 at p. 115.

laws in force in our country and the need for enforcing them".[98]
It further stated that the competent organs of the Guatemalan
Government were studying the desirability and terms of a new
declaration and that, as soon as the new declaration was approved
by the relevant State organs, it would be deposited. It also said
that it was perfectly willing to consider the conclusion of a special
agreement.[99]

In its Judgment of November 18, 1953, the Court recognised
the Guatemalan communication as a preliminary objection. It
noted that the Guatemalan communication itself had recognised it
as such.[100] This recognition may have been necessary. But it set an
unfortunate precedent by treating an extra-procedural communication to the Court as a form of pleading. (In the *Anglo-Iranian
Oil Case*, the Iranian Government had also communicated its views
to the Court. But at the interim measures phase of that case, it was
not necessary to treat the Iranian letter as a form of preliminary
objection.)

Liechtenstein's written statement, filed on May 21, 1953, argued that it was for the Court to decide whether the communication from the Government of Guatemala was a preliminary objection, within the meaning of Rule 62 of the Rules of Court, or a
default.[101] The Guatemalan declaration of January 26, 1947, it
said, was sufficient to confer jurisdiction on the Court to hear and
determine any case which was instituted prior to January 26,
1952. The Court had the power, in accordance with the general
principles of international law and Article 36(6) of the Statute, to
decide for itself whether it had competence.[102]

The Government of Guatemala was not represented at the hearing of November 10, 1953.[103] At the end of the hearing, the
Liechtenstein Agent stated that he would file an additional conclusion with the Registry in writing. That conclusion was:

Le Gouvernement de Liechtenstein se reserve le droit, le cas

98. Id. at 116.
99. Ibid.
100. Id. at 118.
101. Ibid.
102. Id. at 117.
103. Ibid.

> echeant, d'invoquer quant au fond du present differend des dispositions de l'article 53 du Statut de la Cour.[104]

In its Judgment, the Court first examined its power to decide on its own jurisdiction. It pointed out that Article 36(6) merely adopted, in respect of the Court, a rule consistently accepted by general international law.[105] This rule had been generally recognised since the *Alabama Arbitration*. It assumes particular force when the international tribunal is no longer an arbitral tribunal but a pre-established judicial tribunal.[106] Having thus established its competence to adjudicate on its own jurisdiction under both the Statute and general international law the Court examined Guatemala's preliminary objections.

The application had been filed at a time when Liechtenstein's and Guatemala's declarations were both in force.[107] Guatemala's contention, said the Court, was a completely new interpretation of the effect attaching to the limited period of validity of a declaration.[108] The declarations related to the period within which the Court may be seised of a dispute. Once the Court is seised, by the filing of an application, the Court must exercise its statutory powers to deal with the claim.[109] The expiration of a declaration cannot subsequently deprive the Court of its jurisdiction.[110] The Court did not consider it necessary to examine the laws of Guatemala in that connection. The Court also set time limits for the filing of a counter-memorial by Guatemala, a reply by Liechtenstein and a rejoinder by Guatemala.[111]

Guatemala then appointed an agent and a judge *ad hoc* and it filed its counter-memorial on April 20, 1954 in which it challenged the admissibility of Liechtenstein's claim, primarily on the ground that the Principality of Liechtenstein had failed to prove that Nottebohm had properly acquired Liechtenstein nationality

---

104. Id. at 118.
The Government of Liechtenstein reserve their right to invoke, should the necessity arise, the provisions of Article 53 of the Statute of the Court in relation to the merits of the present dispute.
105. Id. at 119.
106. Ibid.
107. Id. at 120.
108. Ibid.
109. Id. at 123.
110. Ibid.
111. Id. at 124.

in accordance with Liechtenstein law and even if such proof were provided, the applicable Liechtenstein law could not be regarded as being in conformity with international law.[112]

The Court held that, because of Nottebohm's lack of effective contact with Liechtenstein, Guatemala was under no obligation to recognise Nottebohm's Liechtenstein nationality and that, consequently, Liechtenstein was not entitled to extend its protection to him *vis-à-vis* Guatemala. It dismissed Liechtenstein's claim as inadmissible.[113]

The Fisheries Jurisdiction Cases

The Cases arose from a conflict over the limits of Iceland's territorial waters going back to 1958. In that year a decree by the Government of Iceland extended the limit of its territorial waters from 3 miles to 12 miles. The Federal Republic of Germany and the United Kingdom opposed the decree and continued to fish within the 12-mile limit. As a result a series of incidents occurred which was known as the "First Cod War".[114]

In 1959, the *Althing* (Icelandic Parliament) declared that Iceland had an indisputable right to a fishing limit of 12 miles and that Iceland should seek to obtain recognition of its rights to the superjacent waters of the entire continental shelf area.

As a result of the Second United Nations Conference on the Law of the Sea of 1958, the United Kingdom and Iceland reached an agreement which was embodied in exchanges of notes which were approved by the *Althing* on March 9, 1961. Under these agreements:

(a) The United Kingdom lifted its objections to the 12-mile fishing zone.

(b) The baselines were modified in a number of respects.

(c) The Parties agreed on a transitional period of 3 years in which British fishing vessels would continue to be entitled to fish in certain specified areas within the outer 6 miles of the 12-mile zone.

112. [*Second Phase*] [1955] ICJ 4, 9.
113. Id. at 26.
114. U.K. Application [1975] ICJ Pleadings, Vol. I, p. 4.

(d) The Parties recognised that the Government of Iceland would continue to work for the *Althing* Resolution ... but would be obliged to give the Government of the United Kingdom six months notice of any exclusion from any part of the 6-mile outer zone. Furthermore, the Parties agreed that in the event of any dispute in relation to such extension, the matter would, at the request of either Party, be referred to the International Court of Justice.[115]

A similar agreement was arrived at with the Federal Republic of Germany on July 19, 1961.

On July 14, 1971, the Government of Iceland issued a policy statement in which it announced that the agreements with the United Kingdom and the German Federal Republic would be terminated and the Icelandic fishing limit extended to 50 nautical miles effective September 1, 1972. At the same time, a zone of 100 nautical miles would be created for protection against pollution.[116]

On April 14, 1972, the United Kingdom and the Federal Republic of Germany filed applications with the International Court of Justice in which they asked the Court to declare that there was no foundation in international law for the new Icelandic limits.[117]

After the Government of Iceland issued regulations purporting to carry out the extension of Iceland's fishing limit,[118] the United Kingdom and the German Federal Republic on July 21, 1972, filed requests for interim measures of protection claiming that enforcement of the limit would mean immediate and irreparable damage to their fishing and associated industries which could not be made good merely by the payment of monetary compensation.[119]

The applicants based their claim to jurisdiction on the 1961 Agreements which, they said, contained very clear jurisdictional clauses.

By a letter of 29 May 1972 from the Minister of Foreign Affairs of Iceland to the Registrar, the Icelandic Government argued that

115. Id. at p. 5.
116. Id. at p. 6.
117. Id. at p. 10. Federal Republic of Germany's Application is at Vol. II at p. 11.
118. U.K. Request for Interim Measures of Protection, id., Vol. I, at p. 71.
119. Id., Vol. I at p. 72; See German Request, Vol. II at pp. 23-24.

the Agreements of 1961 were not of a permanent nature, that their objects and purposes had been fully achieved and that they had therefore been terminated. The letter also referred to "changed circumstances". Thus, it said, on April 14, 1972, there was no basis under the Statute of the Court for the Court to exercise jurisdiction. It concluded:

> The Government of Iceland, considering that the vital interests of the people of Iceland are involved, respectfully informs the Court that it is not willing to confer jurisdiction on the Court in any cases involving the fishery limits of Iceland and specifically in the case sought to be instituted by the Government of the United Kingdom of Great Britain and Northern Ireland on 14 April 1972. Having regard to the foregoing an Agent will not be appointed to represent the Government of Iceland.[120]

A similar letter was sent in respect of the German Case.[121]

On July 19, 1972, letters and telegrams were sent to the Minister for Foreign Affairs of Iceland informing him of hearings which were to be held on the requests for interim measures and inviting the Government of Iceland to present observations on the requests.[122]

The reply was by telegram on July 28. The telegrams reiterated that the 1961 Agreements had terminated and that there was no basis for jurisdiction and objected specifically to the indication of interim measures.[123] But the Government of Iceland did not appear to contest the case.

Germany and the United Kingdom denied that the Icelandic Declaration could constitute a denunciation of the agreements. They stressed that the agreements were made precisely for the situation which had arisen and that it could not possibly be inferred that it was the common understanding of the Parties that the agreements could be unilaterally denounced by one of them "at the very first instance for which its application had been envisaged".[124]

120. Id., Vol. II at pp. 375-376.
121. Id., Vol. II at pp. 380-382.
122. Id., Vol. II at pp. 385-387.
123. Id., Vol. II at pp. 388-389.
124. German Request, id. Vol. II at p. 25.

In two Orders dated August 17, 1972, the Court granted the requests of the applicants. The Orders asked the Government of Iceland to refrain from taking any measures to enforce the limits against British and German vessels engaged in fishing activities in waters around Iceland outside the 12-mile fishing zone. But it limited the annual catch which United Kingdom and German vessels could take in the disputed area.[125] The Court promised to review the Order at an appropriate time before August 15, 1973, at the request of either Party if it had not rendered its final judgment by that time. It noted the failure of Iceland to appear, but found that its own jurisprudence and the jurisprudence of the Permanent Court of International Justice demonstrated that the non-appearance of one of the parties "cannot constitute an obstacle to the indication of provisional measures, provided the parties have been given an opportunity of presenting their observations on the subject".[126]

As to jurisdiction, the Court took the position that:

> ... on a request for provisional measures the Court need not before indicating them, finally satisfy itself that it has jurisdiction on the merits of the case, yet it ought not to act under Article 41 of the Statute if the absence of jurisdiction on the merits is manifest.[127]

Citing the exchanges of notes between the parties, it concluded that:

> ... the above-cited provision as an instrument emanating from both Parties to the dispute appears to afford a possible basis on which the jurisdiction of the Court might be founded.[128]

The lone dissenter was Judge Padilla Nervo[129] who relied heavily on the Joint Dissenting Opinion of Judges Winiarski and Badawi in the *Anglo-Iranian Oil Case*.[130]

---

125. *United Kingdom v. Iceland* [1972] ICJ 12, 17-18; *Federal Republic of Germany v. Iceland* [1972] ICJ 30, 35-36.
126. Id. at 15, 32-33.
127. Id. at 15, 33.
128. Id. at 16, 34.
129. Id. at 20, 37.
130. See supra note 83-84 and accompanying text.

On August 18, 1972, the Prime Minister of Iceland sent the Registrar a telegram strongly protesting the Order and expressing "astonishment at the fact that the Court considers itself to be in a position to deliver such an order while it has not ruled on its jurisdiction in the said cases".[131] It repeated its objection to the jurisdiction of the Court.

Subsequent communications from the Government of Iceland merely noted its previous argument that the Court had no jurisdiction and informed the Court that its position was unchanged.[132]

On February 2, 1973, the International Court of Justice declared that it had jurisdiction to hear the Cases on their merits.[133] On November 13, 1973, a limited agreement was concluded between Iceland and the United Kingdom allowing a specified number of British ships to fish in the disputed waters.[134]

When, on January 8, 1974, the Registrar informed the Minister that a meeting was being convened to ascertain the views of the Parties with regard to further procedures, the Minister's reply on January 11 noted that the Third United Nations Conference on the Law of the Sea had been convened and that the principle of the Exclusive Economic Zone enjoyed very wide support. It noted the agreement of November 13 but it stated that its position with regard to the proceedings was otherwise unchanged. The Government of Iceland had no further correspondence with the Court and it took no part in the merits phase of the proceedings. Nor did it, at any time, comply with the interim measures.

On July 25, 1974, the Court gave judgment on the merits in favour of the United Kingdom and the Federal Republic of Germany.[135]

Thus, the *Fisheries Jurisdiction Cases* constitute the first situation in which a State, Iceland, persisted in its contumacy through all phases of the Cases in question. In so doing, it set a precedent for the rash of non-appearances that followed. One can sympathise with Iceland, as a small nation which is almost totally dependant upon its fisheries and on the conservation and management of its fisheries resources. But one is not debarred thereby from asking

131. Supra note 14, Vol. II at p. 399.
132. Id., Vol. II at pp. 404-405.
133. [1973] ICJ 3, 49.
134. Supra note 114, Vol. II at pp. 459-461.
135. [1974] ICJ 3, 175.

whether its failure to appear and to take any procedural actions really served that nation's interests. Nor is one permitted to ignore the probability that Iceland's behaviour resulted in irreversible damage to the cause of international adjudication.

The Nuclear Test Cases

The Cases arose out of objections by New Zealand and Australia to French nuclear weapons testing on Mururoa atoll in the Pacific.

The New Zealand application dated May 9, 1973, asked the Court to adjudge and declare that nuclear tests which give rise to radio active fall out constitute a violation of New Zealand's rights under international law.[136] The Australian application, filed on the same day, asked the Court for a judgment and a declaration that:

> ... the carrying out of further *atmospheric* nuclear tests in the South Pacific Ocean is not consistant with applicable rules of international law [emphasis added].[137]

Australia filed a request for interim measures with its Application. New Zealand filed its request several days later on May 14. The two requests again differed in that the Australian request asked that France should desist from any further atmospheric tests pending judgment in the case.[138] New Zealand asked France to desist from tests that cause radio active fall out while the Court was seised of the Case.[139]

New Zealand and Australia claimed two alternative bases for jurisdiction.[140] The first contention was that jurisdiction existed by virtue of Article 36(1) of the Statute and Article 17 of the General Act for the Pacific Settlement of International Disputes of September 26, 1928, which provides that:

136. *New Zealand v. France* [1974] ICJ 457, 460.

137. *Australia v. France* [1974] ICJ 253, 254. See also Elkind, "Footnote to the Nuclear Test Cases: Abuse of Right — A Blind Alley for Environmentalists" 9 Vand. J. Transnat'l L. 57, 58-59 (1976).

138. *Australia v. France [Interim Measures]* [1973] ICJ 99, 100.

139. New Zealand Application [1974] ICJ Pleadings, Vol. II, p. 49.

140. Id., New Zealand Application, Vol. II, p. 5; Australian Application, Vol. I, pp. 14-15.

All disputes with regard to which the parties are in conflict as to their respective rights shall, be submitted for decision to the Permanent Court of International Justice, unless the parties agree, ... to have resort to an arbitral tribunal.

It is understood that the disputes referred to above include in particular those mentioned in Article 36 of the Statute of the Permanent Court of International Justice.[141]

France, New Zealand and Australia all acceded to the General Act on May 21, 1931[142] each with a number of reservations which do not appear to have been relevant to the Cases. Thus, Article 37 of the Statute, which provides for continuity of jurisdiction between the International Court of Justice and the Permanent Court of International Justice, was invoked along with Article 36(1).

The second basis for jurisdiction claimed in the applications was the French declaration of acceptance under Article 36(2) which was signed on 16 May 1966. It excluded from the Court's competence:

1) des différends a propos desquels les parties seraient convenues ou conviendraient d'avoir recours à un autre mode de règlement pacifique;

2) des différends relatifs à des questions qui, d'après le droit international, relèvent exclusivement de la compétence nationale;

3) des différends nés d'une guerre ou d'hostilités internationales, des différends nés à l'occasion d'une crise intéressant la sécurité de la nation ou de toute mesure ou action s'y rapportant et des différends concernant des activités se rapportant à la défense nationale;

4) des différends avec un État qui, au moment où les faits ou situations donnant naissance au différend se sont produits, n'avoit pas accepté la juridiction obligatoire de la Cour internationale de justice.[143]

141. 93 LNTS 343, 351.
142. French accession 107 LNTS 529; New Zealand accession 107 LNTS 532-534; Australian accession 107 LNTS 531-532.
143. 562 UNTS 72.
(1) Disputes with regard to which the parties may have agreed or may agree to have recourse to another mode of pacific settlement;
(2) Disputes concerning questions which, according to international law, are exclusively within domestic jurisdiction;

New Zealand accepted the compulsory jurisdiction on April 8, 1940,[144] Australia on January 6, 1954.[145]

On May 16, 1973, The Ambassador of France to the Netherlands handed the Registrar of the Court a letter informing the Court that it was "manifestly not competent" to deal with the disputes and urging the Court to drop the matter from its list. An annex to that letter contained a Statement in which the French Government set out its position.[146] It argued that the disputes concerned activity "connected with the national defence" and were thus excluded by the third reservation in its declaration.

With regard to the General Act, France claimed that the General Act was an integral part of the League of Nations system and had fallen into desuetude as a result of the demise of the League.[147]

On June 22, 1973, the Court granted the New Zealand and Australian requests for interim measures.[148] The Orders were roughly similar and spoke of "tests causing radio-active fall-out" rather than atmospheric tests.[149]

The Court rejected the French contention that the absence of jurisdiction was manifest. It cited statements in both the New Zealand and the Australian arguments which demonstrated that a genuine dispute over jurisdiction existed.[150] It concluded, on the basis of those statements, "that the provisions invoked by the applicant[s] appear, *prima facie*, to afford a basis on which the jurisdiction of the Court might be founded".[151]

The various opinions, however, revealed a deep split amongst the judges as to the extent to which the Court had to satisfy itself as to its competence on the merits.

In a dissent, Judge Forster, who had voted with the majority in

---

(3)   Disputes arising out of a war or international hostilities, disputes arising out of a crisis affecting national security or out of any measure or action relating thereto, and disputes concerning activities connected with national defence;
(4)   Disputes with a State which, at the time of occurrence of the facts or situations giving rise to the dispute, had not accepted the compulsory jurisdiction of the International Court of Justice.
144. [1971-72] ICJYB, pp. 75.
145. Id. at p. 55.
146. Supra note 139 at Vol. II, pp. 347-348.
147. Id. at p. 348.
148. [1973] ICJ 99, 135.
149. New Zealand Order, id. at 142. Australian Order at 106.
150. Id. at 102, 138.
151. Ibid.

the *Fisheries Jurisdiction Cases*, urged the abandonment of the *prima facie* doctrine in light of what he called the "exceptional" nature of the *Nuclear Test Cases*.[152]

In the Judgment dealing with the Australian Case, he examined the jurisdictional issues and found that the General Act was "moribund if not well and truly dead" and secondly that the third French reservation "in terms that are crystal clear categorically exclude our jurisdiction when the dispute is concerned with the national defence...".[153] He concluded that:

> L'ordonnance de ce jour est un incursion dans un secteur français formellement interdit par la troisième réserve.... Pour en franchir la frontière, il fallait à la Cour, non point un simple probabilité, mais l'absolu certitude de sa compétence. N'étant point, personnellement, parvenue à cette certitude, je refuse d'accompagner la majorité.[154]

None of the other judges went quite so far in examining actual jurisdiction. Judge Gros felt that Article 53(2) was applicable to the interim measures phase of the case. Thus, when one of the Parties fails to appear, Article 53(2) requires the Court to satisfy itself that it has actual and not merely *prima facie* jurisdiction.[155]

Judge Petrén did not find it probable that any propositions upon which New Zealand and Australia based their claims would afford a basis for jurisdiction.[156]

Judge Ignacio-Pinto also dissented and devoted his opinion primarily to distinguishing the Cases from the *Fisheries Jurisdiction Cases*. He did not believe that the Court possessed jurisdiction. He also expressed frank confusion as to the precise rules of international law that France was supposed to have violated.[157]

On December 20, 1974, the Court dismissed the actions of New

152. Id. at 112.
153. Ibid.
154. Id. at 113.
The Order made this day is an incursion into a French sector of activity placed strictly out of bounds by the third reservation.... To cross the line into that sector, the Court required no mere probability but the absolute certainty of possessing jurisdiction. As I personally have been unable to attain that degree of certainty, I have declined to accompany the majority.
155. Id. at 115, 149.
156. Id. at 126, 161.
157. Id. at 130.

Zealand and Australia[158] on the ground that a unilateral decision by the French Government to cease atmospheric nuclear testing was sufficient to terminate the dispute. The French decision was gleaned from a number of documents such as a communiqué of June 8, 1974, issued by the Office of the President of the French Republic stating that:

> ... où en est parvenue l'exécution de son programme de défense en moyens nucléaires la France sera en mesure de passer au stade de tirs souterrains aussitôt que la série d'expériences prévues pour cet été sera achevée.[159]

Other similar communications were cited to demonstrate that France had indeed undertaken to cease atmospheric testing.[160]

The Court also examined communications by officials of the New Zealand and Australian Governments[161] to demonstrate that an assurance by France that nuclear testing in the atmosphere is finished would meet the objectives of the Parties' claims.[162]

Purporting to exercise its duty to ascertain the true subject of the dispute,[163] the Court declared that the object of the dispute was to procure termination of atmospheric nuclear tests by France.[164] This object had been achieved and therefore the Cases had become moot.[165] In doing so, it either ignored the fact that New Zealand had asked for a cessation of tests which cause radioactive fall-out or it assumed that underground tests did not cause such fall-out.

The Trial of Pakistani Prisoners of War Case

After the war between Pakistan and India in 1972, which resulted in the emergence of Bangladesh as an independent nation, the

158. [1974] ICJ 253, 457.
159. Id. at 469.
... in view of the stage reached in carrying out the French nuclear defence programme France will be in a position to pass on to the stage of underground explosions as soon as the series of tests planned for this summer is completed.
160. Id. at 469-471.
161. Id. at 464-465.
162. Id. at 466.
163. Id. at 467.
164. Id. at 465-466.
165. Id. at 475-477; *Australia v. France*, at 270-272.

leaders of the new State, allegedly with Indian encouragement, declared their intention to try 195 Pakistani prisoners of war on charges of genocide.[166] These prisoners were in Indian custody.

Pakistan claimed that, under Article VI of the Convention on the Prevention and Punishment of the Crime of Genocide, of December 9, 1948, to which Pakistan and India were both Parties, exclusive jurisdiction in respect of the prisoners was vested in Pakistan.[167]

Accordingly, it filed an application on May 11, 1973, asking the Court to declare that Pakistan had exclusive jurisdiction; that allegations against the prisoners related to acts of genocide and not to "crimes against humanity" or "war crimes"; that the transfer of custody of the prisoners from India to Bangladesh was not justified in the light of Pakistan's exclusive jurisdiction; and that the term "Competent Tribunal" in Art. VI of the Genocide Convention meant a tribunal of impartial judges applying international law and permitting the accused to be defended by counsel of their choice. It objected that such a tribunal would not be possible in view of "the atmosphere of hatred" that prevailed in Bangladesh.[168]

Pakistan also asked the Court for interim measures on the same day to the effect:

(1) That the process of repatriations of prisoners of war and civilian internees in accordance with international law, which has already begun, should not be interrupted by virtue of charges of genocide against a certain number of individuals detained in India.

(2) That such individuals, as are in the custody of India and are charged with alleged acts of genocide, should not be transferred to "Bangla Desh" for trial till such time as Pakistan's claim to exclusive jurisdiction and the lack of jurisdiction of any other government or authority in this respect has been adjudged by the Court... .[169]

Pakistan founded jurisdiction on Article XI of the Genocide Con-

---

166. Application [1973] ICJ Pleading, pp. 3-4.
167. Id. at p. 3.
168. Id. at p. 7.
169. Request, id. at pp. 7-8.

64

vention, which provided:

> Disputes between the Contracting Parties relating to the interpretation, application or fulfillment of the present Convention including those relating to the responsibility of a State for Genocide or any other acts enumerated in Article III shall be submitted to the International Court of Justice at the request of any of the parties to the dispute.[170]

It also argued that the Court possessed jurisdiction under Article 17 of the General Act, a treaty to which Pakistan voluntarily succeeded upon obtaining its independence from India.[171]

Finally, Pakistan claimed that jurisdiction could be founded on the basis of the declaration of the two countries accepting the compulsory jurisdiction of the Court under Article 36(2) of the Statute.[172] The oral hearings were held on June 4, 5 and 26.

The jurisdictional issues raised are exceedingly complex and a necessarily lengthy discussion of them here would seem to fall outside of the ambit of this work. But the way in which they were raised is of interest to us.

India did not appear. But it carried the practice of intervention by communication to a logical extreme. On May 23, 1973,[173] the Ambassador of India communicated a letter to the Registrar which set out India's objections to the proceedings in which it raised a reservation it had made to Article IX of the Genocide Convention which reservation required the consent of all the parties to the submission of the dispute to the International Court of Justice.

Pakistan responded in a letter of May 25[174] arguing that the reservation was inadmissible and of no legal effect. It also called upon India to appoint an agent and appear in the action.

On May 28, India again sent a letter which contained a "Statement of the Government of India In Support of Its Letter dated 23 May 1973 Addressed to the Registrar of the International Court of Justice"[175] in which it protested at the absence of

170. Oral Argument of Mr. Bakhtiar, Chief Counsel for the Government of Pakistan, Public Sitting June 4, 1973, id. at p. 45.
171. Id. at p. 51.
172. Id. at pp. 54-55.
173. Id. at pp. 121-137.
174. Id. at pp. 118-120.
175. Id. at pp. 139-152.

Bangladesh citing the *Monetary Gold Case.*[176] It also pointed out that Pakistan had not objected to its reservations to the Genocide Convention.

Then on June 4, just moments before the oral hearing was about to begin, the Indian Ambassador communicated another letter to the Registrar containing a 20 page "Statement of the Government of India In Continuation of Its Statement of 28 May 1973 and In Answer to Pakistan's Letter of 25 May 1973" in which it raised objections to Pakistan's claim to jurisdiction under Article 36(2) of the Statute[177] and argued that the General Act was not in force and that, at any rate, Pakistan was not a party to it.[178]

The following day, Mr. Bakhtiar, Chief Counsel for the Government of Pakistan made the following statement:

> May it please the Court, just before I addressed the Court yesterday, a further communication, bearing yesterday's date, was received from the Government of India....
> What I said to the Court yesterday, and what I shall have to say to the Court today in continuation of my address, was of course prepared before the latest Indian communication. In point of fact, what I have said and will say, touches on a number of points raised in that last communication, and I shall also comment on the previous Indian communication dated 28 May. I have already made some brief comments on their previous letter of 23 May 1973. But obviously, in the time available, it has not been possible to prepare any specific reply to this latest communication – the one dated 4 June – and I feel sure that the Court would not expect me to make one at this stage. [...]
> In our view the course being followed by India amounts to an abuse of the process of the Court. India, while declining to appear and professing to disregard these proceedings is, in fact, arguing her case virtually as fully as if she were appearing, by means of a series of communications which the Court cannot well avoid receiving or looking at, although they should strictly, in the circumstances, be regarded as out of order and irreceivable. Nor can we be in any way sure that

176. Supra note 56 and accompanying text.
177. Supra note 166 at pp. 141-143.
178. Id. at pp. 143-146.

the latest Indian communication of 4 June will be the end of the matter.

When I have completed my present address, there will be nothing to prevent India sending in a further communication, commenting on it; and if Pakistan then asks the Court for an opportunity to reply to it, and this is accorded, an Indian rejoinder to that can be expected. Such a process can go on indefinitely if the Court allowed it, and it is one which enables India to reap almost all the advantages of being party to the proceedings while simultaneously reserving the right not to recognise them.

Moreover, it is a process which seriously handicaps Pakistan in the presentation of her case. Instead of being able to deal in a straightforward way with the issue of interim measures as such, Pakistan has been sidetracked into a number of highly complex issues of jurisdiction which do not really arise now, and should be gone into at a later stage; and, even so, Pakistan has not been able to deal with these jurisdictional questions on the basis of, and by way of answer to, a completed Indian memorial or oral statement, which Pakistan would have before her for the purpose of preparing the sort of considered reply which is customary in proceedings before the Court.

The Indian arguments have come out piecemeal in successive communications, each one overtaking Pakistan in dealing with the previous one, and in the middle of the proceedings of an inherently urgent character that do not afford time for a comprehensive treatment, at this juncture, of issues that are strictly extraneous to the question of interim measures.[179]

On July 11, 1973, the Agent for Pakistan informed the Court that negotiations would soon take place between Pakistan and India on issues which were the subject of the application and asked the Court to postpone further consideration of its request for interim measures in order to facilitate those negotiations.

Holding that urgency was the essence of a request for interim measures, the Court, on June 13, held that the request for a post-

179. Id. at pp. 56-57.

ponement signified that it was no longer a matter of urgency. Indicating that the request for interim measures could be raised again at a later stage of the proceedings, the Court simply decided that written proceedings should next be addressed to the question of jurisdiction.[180]

Judge Nagendra Singh voted with the majority but claimed, in a separate opinion, that:

(a) Bangladesh and not India was the proper respondent in the case since the prisoners were to be tried in Bangladesh,
(b) that the Court had no jurisdiction with regard to Bangladesh and that,
(c) the Court lacked "all *prima facie* competence".[181]

Judge Petrén dissented because he considered that the Court should have attended to jurisdiction then and there.[182] He saw this duty arising from Article 53 of the Court's Statute. Thus, he accepted the view put forth by Judge Gros in the *Nuclear Test Case*.[183] He also felt that it was improper to conclude that Pakistan had withdrawn its request for interim measures in the absence of a specific statement to that effect.[184]

On December 14, the Court received a letter from the Agent for Pakistan informing it that negotiations with India had resulted in an agreement between them and requesting that proceedings be discontinued. This was done in an Order dated December 15, 1973.

The Aegean Sea Case

The dispute involved Turkish exploration for petroleum over portions of the continental shelf lying off the coast of a number of Greek Islands. Turkey contended that the area constituted a natural prolongation of the Anatolian coast and that, rather than having a continental shelf of their own, the Islands were situated on the Turkish continental shelf.

Greece's claim was based[185] on Article 1, paragraph (b) of the

180. [1973] ICJ 328, 330.
181. Id. at 332.
182. Id. at 334.
183. Supra note 155 and accompanying text.
184. Supra note 180 at 336.
185. Greek Application, Annex II [1980] ICJ Pleadings at p. 21.

Geneva Convention on the Continental Shelf 1958,[186] pursuant to which islands are recognised to have continental shelves of their own; and on Article 6, paragraph 1 of that Convention which provided that the rule for delimitation of states opposite each other in narrow waters was the "equidistance" rule which involved finding the median line between the two States. Greece had acceded to that treaty on November 6, 1972. Turkey was not a party to it. But Greece relied on the Convention as a codification of customary international law.[187] The Turkish Government expressed its willingness to seek agreement on a solution in conformity with international law.[188]

On January 27, 1975, the Government of Greece addressed a note to the Government of Turkey proposing that the difference be referred to the International Court of Justice.[189] The Turkish reply on February 6 stated that the Turkish Government favoured the idea in principle.

On May 17-19 the Foreign Ministers of the two States met with their advisers. The Greek Government submitted the draft text of a *compromis*. The Turkish representatives replied that they were not ready to discuss it and argued that substantive negotiations were required first. The communiqué issued on 19 May, at the end of their meeting, stated that questions regarding the Aegean Sea Continental Shelf had been discussed and a preliminary study of the text of a *compromis* concerning submission of the dispute to the Court had taken place.[190]

On May 31, the Prime Ministers of the two countries met in Brussels and issued a further communiqué to the effect that:

> Ils ont décidé ... que ces problèmes doivent être résolus ... pacifiquement par le voie des négotiations et concernant le plateau continentale de la mer Égée par la Cour internationale de La Haye.[191]

186. 29 April 1958, 499 UNTS 311, entered into force 10 June 1964.
187. Supra note 185 at pp. 21-22.
188. Id. at pp. 23-25.
189. Id. Annex II at pp. 29-30.
190. Id. at pp. 30-31.
191. Id. Annex II at p. 33.
They decided ... that those problems should be solved ... peacefully by means of negotiations and as regards the continental shelf of the Aegean Sea by the International Court of Justice at The Hague.

In its Application of August 10, 1976, the Greek Government asked the Court to adjudge and declare that the Greek Islands were entitled to a continental shelf under international law; that Greece was entitled to exercise sovereign and exclusive rights over its continental shelf as regards exploration and exploitation of its natural resources; that Turkey was not entitled to explore and exploit those areas without the consent of Greece; that its activities in doing so infringed Greek sovereignty; and that Turkey should cease its activities. The Greek Government also asked the Court to declare the boundary or boundaries under international law between portions of the continental shelf appertaining to Greece and Turkey in the Aegean Sea.[192] The Greek Government viewed the Brussels Joint Communiqué as a "special agreement" under Article 36(1) of the Statute. The other basis for jurisdiction claimed by the Greek Government was again Article 17 of the General Act to which both Greece and Turkey were parties.[193]

Turkey, following a now, well-established pattern, refused to appear or appoint an agent. Instead, it filed with the Registrar of the Court a document entitled *"Observations du Gouvernement de la Turquie sur la demande en indication de mesures conservatoires présentée par le Gouvernement de la Grèce"* (hereinafter "Turkish Observations") dated August 10, 1976. In these observations, it contended that the General Act was no longer in force[194] and that, in any event, jurisdiction was precluded by a Greek reservation to Article 17 excluding:

a) Les différends nés de faits antérieurs, soit à l'adhesion de la Grèce soit à l'adhésion d'une autre Partie avec laquelle la Grèce viendrait à avoir un différend;

b) les différends portant sur des questions que le droit international laisse à la compétence exclusive des États et, notament, les différends ayant trait au statut territorial de la Grèce, y compris ceux relatifs a ses droits de souveraineté sur ses ports et ses voies de communication.[195]

192. *Aegean Sea Continental Shelf Case [Interim Measures]* [1976] ICJ 4.
193. Greece acceded to the General Act on September 14, 1931, 111 LNTS 414; Turkey acceded on June 26, 1934, 152 LNTS 297.
194. Turkish Observations, para. 18, supra note 185 at p. 73.
195. *Aegean Sea Continental Shelf Case [Jurisdiction]* [1978] ICJ 3, 20.
(a) disputes resulting from facts prior either to the accession of Greece or to the accession of another Party with whom Greece might have a dispute;

Greece's request for interim measures arose from the fact that Turkish exploratory vessels were accompanied by warships and that Turkey threatened to do more of the same. The request was filed on the same day as the Greek application and it asked the Court to direct both Governments to refrain from exploration activity or scientific research in the area and to "refrain from taking further military measures which may endanger their peaceful relations".[196]

The Court, in an Order of September 11, 1976, denied Greece's request for interim measures of protection. The reason given by the Court was that it was unable to find a risk of irreparable prejudice sufficient to grant provisional measures.[197]

It is interesting to note that the Court actually quoted the Turkish Observations to the effect that:

> Exploration by Turkey of the kind of which the complaint is made by Greece cannot be regarded as involving any prejudice to the existence of any possible rights of Greece over continental shelf areas in the Aegean Sea. The sovereign rights over the continental shelf (including the exclusive right to exploration) that exist are not taken away or diminished by exploration.[198]

No expert witnesses were presented by Turkey and no inquiry was undertaken. The Turkish Observations were simply cited.

As to jurisdiction, the split on the Court was even wider than in the *Nuclear Test Cases*. Although the Court voted overwhelmingly to deny the request, the separate opinions revealed very different approaches to the jurisdictional question.

President Jiménez de Aréchaga took the position that Article 41 is an autonomous grant of jurisdiction and that jurisdiction to entertain the merits of the dispute is "but ... one among the cir-

---

(b) disputes concerning questions which by international law are solely within the domestic jurisdiction of States, and in particular disputes relating to the territorial status of Greece, including disputes relating to its rights of sovereignty over its ports and lines of communication."
196. Supra note 192 at 4-5.
197. Id. at 11.
198. Id. at 10 citing Turkish Observations, supra note 185, para. 18, at p. 12.

cumstances which the Court has to take into account in deciding whether to grant the interim measures.[199]

Judges Nagendra Singh[200] and Morozov[201] adopted Judge Gros' view that the non-appearance of one of the parties imposes upon the Court a special burden under Article 53 of the Statute to satisfy itself that it has jurisdiction. Judge Morozov took exception to the idea that Article 41 was a jurisdictional provision[202] as did Judge Tarazi.[203] Judge Lachs felt that the Court was under an obligation to consider the issue of jurisdiction *proprio motu.*[204]

Judge Ruda[205] and Judge Mosler[206] both supported the *prima facie* test although Judge Mosler disagreed with the view that substantive jurisdiction was merely one circumstance to be taken into account in considering the necessity for interim measures. He regarded it rather as a precondition to the "examination of whether such circumstances exist". The issue of jurisdiction had to be considered in a cursory manner when deciding whether to grant interim protection. But even on cursory examination he was unable to form a conclusion that there was a *prima facie* basis for jurisdiction in the Case.[207]

The Greek Judge *Ad Hoc* Stassinopolous felt that the Court only needed to satisfy itself on an "extremely summary examination" that it had *prima facie* jurisdiction.[208]

On December 19, 1978, the Court found that it was without jurisdiction to entertain the Greek application.[209]

With regard to the General Act, it noted that Article 59 of the Statute says that "the decision of the Court has no binding force except between the parties and in respect of that particular case. Since any pronouncement of the Court as to the status of the General Act might have implications for States other than the parties,[210] it refrained from deciding on that question preferring

199. Id. at 16.
200. Id. at 17.
201. Id. at 21-22.
202. Id. at 21.
203. Id. at 32.
204. Id. at 19-20.
205. Id. at 23.
206. Id. at 24.
207. Ibid.
208. Id. at 39.
209. Supra note 195.
210. Supra note 192 at 16-17.

instead to hold that the Greek reservation barred its jurisdictional claim because the dispute related to the territorial status of Greece.[211]

It also held that the Brussels Communiqué "was not intended to and did not constitute an immediate commitment by the Greek and Turkish Governments ... to accept unconditionally the unilateral submission of the present dispute to the Court".[212]

It noted that the Turkish Government was not represented at the hearings and that it did not file preliminary objections or take any steps in the proceedings. "But", it said:

> there is no provision in the Rules of Court which excludes the submission of written observations on a request for interim measures; nor is there any provision which excludes the raising of questions of jurisdiction in written observations submitted on the indication of provisional measures. On the contrary, in view of the urgency of a request for interim measures, written communications not submitted through an agent but either directly or through the Ambassador in The Hague have invariably been admitted by the Court; while one of the very purposes of such communications has commonly been to raise questions as to the competence of the Court with respect to the particular case... ."[213]

It cited, in this respect the *Anglo-Iranian Oil Case*, the *Fisheries Jurisdiction Cases*, the *Nuclear Test Cases* and the *Pakistani Prisoners Case*. Thus, in the procedural circumstances of the Case the Court had before it an invocation by Turkey of the Greek Reservation (b) which conformed to the provisions of the General Act and to the Rules of Court and it was entitled to take cognizance of that Reservation "duly invoked in *limine litis* in the proceedings on the request for interim measures".

To fail to consider a reservation which respondent "properly" brought to its notice in earlier proceedings would be a failure to discharge its duty under Article 53.[214] Thus the Court appears to

211. Id. at 37.
212. Id. at 44.
213. Id. at 19.
214. Id. at 20.

have given sanction to extra-procedural communications, arguably only at the interim protection phase. But matters which are properly raised at that stage, can be considered at a later stage.

The Hostages Case

The *Case Concerning United States Diplomatic and Consular Staff in Tehran* involved the invasion of the United States Embassy compound in Tehran on November 4, 1979, the detention of United States diplomatic and consular staff and the subsequent ratification of those actions by the effective Government of Iran at the time. The Case also involved the U.S. *Chargé d'Affaires* who was able to take sanctuary at the Iranian Ministry of Foreign Affairs with two others but was offered no safe conduct.

The United States tried indirect and direct negotiations to no avail. On November 29, 1979, the United States appealed to the Security Council and, at the same time, filed an application with the International Court of Justice asking it to declare that Iran had violated provisions of the Vienna Convention on Diplomatic Relations of April 18, 1961;[215] the Vienna Convention on Consular Relations of April 24, 1963;[216] the Convention on the Prevention and Punishment of Crimes Against Internationally Protected Persons Including Diplomatic Agents, of December 14, 1973;[217] The Treaty of Amity, Economic Relations and Consular Rights between the United States and Iran of August 15, 1955;[218] and Articles 2(3), 2(4), and 33 of the United Nations Charter. It also asked the Court to declare that Iran was under an obligation to secure the release of the hostages, pay compensation and punish those responsible.[219]

The Vienna Conventions contain a host of provisions detailing the treatment of diplomatic and consular personnel and providing that their *personae* and property are to be treated as inviolate and are to be immune from criminal jurisdiction in the receiving State.

215. Entered into force April 24, 1964, 500 UNTS 95.
216. Entered into force March 19, 1967, 596 UNTS 261.
217. Done at New York, 14 December 1973. For text, see Annex GA Res. 3166 (XXXVIII) GAOR Twenty-eighth Session, supplement No. 30 (A/9030).
218. 284 UNTS 93.
219. United States Application, pp. 12-13.

Other provisions ensure the inviolability of diplomatic premises, documents and archives.[220]

The Convention on Internationally Protected Persons obliges its Parties to cooperate in the prevention of crimes against the official premises and staff of embassies, to take all practicable measures to prevent preparation in their territory for the commission of such crimes and to submit to competent authorities for the purpose of prosecution all persons who have been engaged in committing such crimes.[221]

Finally, the Treaty of Amity, Economic Relations and Consular Rights placed Iran specifically under an obligation to ensure that nationals of the United States received "the most constant protection and security" within the territory of Iran. United States Nationals were to receive reasonable and humane treatment if placed in custody and the United States was to have an opportunity to safeguard their interests and they were to have full access to United States consular officials and services.

Along with its application, the United States asked the Court for interim measures of protection aimed at securing the hostages' immediate release and restoration of the premises to the United States. It was also concerned to prevent the threatened trial of the hostages on charges of espionage and to protect their lives, safety and well-being.[222]

The United States claim to jurisdiction was based on Article 36, paragraph 1 of the Court's Statute relating to "treaties and conventions in force". Both the Vienna Conventions have optional protocols concerning the compulsory settlement of disputes[223] allowing disputes arising out of their application or interpretation to be brought to the Court by unilateral application.[224]

The Treaty between the United States and Iran also provides for submission to the Court of disputes concerning its provisions which are not satisfactorily adjusted by diplomacy or submitted to some other means of pacific settlement.

The Convention on Internationally Protected Persons provides

220. Id. at pp. 8–10.
221. Id. at p. 10.
222. United States Request, pp. 4-5.
223. The Protocol to the Diplomatic Convention is found at 500 UST 241, the Consular Convention at 596 UST 487.
224. Supra note 219 at p. 6.

for disputes to be submitted to arbitration. But if, within six months from the date of the request for arbitration, the Parties are unable to agree on the organisation of the arbitration, any one of them may refer the dispute to the Court.[225]

On December 4, 1979, the United Nations Security Council unanimously passed Resolution 457 which called .for immediate release of the hostages.

Iran did not appoint an agent or appear at the proceedings, but on December 9, 1979, its Government addressed a letter to the Court asking the Court not to take cognizance of the Case or indicate interim measures. The letter set out the Iranian arguments opposing the jurisdiction of the Court. The legal points raised by the letter are not very clear but it has been suggested that the overall thrust of the communication was to attack the justiciability of the dispute.[226] Shorn of its rhetoric, the letter can be summarised as follows: The case represented only a marginal and secondary aspect of a problem involving 25 years of American interference in the internal affairs of Iran. The problems involved not merely the application and interpretation of treaties but much more fundamental and complex issues. Hence the Court could not consider the problem divorced from its proper context which was the whole political dossier of relations between Iran and the United States over a period of 25 years. The request for interim measures was an attempt to secure a judgment on the substance of the Case. Finally, provisional measures, in that they are intended to protect the interests of the parties could not be unilateral.[227]

In its Order of December 15, 1979, the Court unanimously granted the interim measures sought by the United States.[228] The Court set aside its differences over the question of jurisdiction and accepted the *prima facie* test.[229] Actually the two Protocols relied on by the United States provided a stronger than *prima facie* basis for jurisdiction. "It is", said the Court, "manifest ... that the provisions of these Articles furnish a basis on which the jurisdiction of the Court might be founded".[230]

225. Id. at p. 8.
226. Gross, "The Case Concerning United States Diplomatic and Consular Staff in Tehran Phase of Provisional Measures", 74 AJIL 395, 396-397 (1980).
227. C.R. 79/1, Public Sitting, Monday December 10, 1979, p. 31, Discussed by Gross, id. at 404-405.
228. [1979] ICJ 7.
229. Id. at 13.
230. Id. at 14.

The Court did not find it necessary to consider the other two treaties on which the claim to jurisdiction was based.[231]

Commenting on Iran's letter, the Court said:

> ... however important, and however connected with the present case, the iniquities attributed to the United States Government by the Government of Iran in that letter may appear to be to the latter Government, the seizure of the United States Embassy and Consulate and the detention of internationally protected persons as hostages cannot, in the view of the Court, be regarded as something "secondary" or "marginal" having regard to the legal principles involved....[232]

The Court also dismissed the other Iranian contentions.[233]

Iran continued to hold the hostages despite the Security Council Resolution and the Order of the Court. On December 29-31, 1979, the Security Council met to consider further measures. It passed a Resolution calling upon Iran to comply with the earlier Resolution and with the Order of the International Court of Justice.[234] It also stipulated that the Security Council would reconvene the following week to consider sanctions. However, when it reconvened, a proposed resolution[235] authorising sanctions failed because of a veto by the U.S.S.R. on the ground that the situation was not a threat to international peace and security.[236]

Iran continued to ignore the Court and on April 24, 1980, the United States tried unsuccessfully to rescue the hostages by means of an Entebbe type operation in Iranian territory.

Iran did not participate in the second phase of the Case which dealt with both jurisdiction and the merits of the Case. Either the Court thought that the jurisdictional issues were so clearcut that a separate phase was not warranted or perhaps the Court was unwilling to treat the Iranian letter as a genuine preliminary objection. Possibly both considerations played a part.

231. Id. at 14-15.
232. Id. at 15.
233. Id. at 16-17, 20.
234. SC Res. 461 (1979) (31 December 1979), S/RES/461 (1979).
235. S/13735.
236. S/PV. 2192 (12 January 1980).

The Judgment of May 24, 1980, held that the Optional Protocols[237] of the two Vienna Conventions and the Treaty of Amity, Economic Relations and Consular Rights[238] supported its jurisdiction.

On the merits, the Court, by a lopsided vote, decided that Iran was in violation of obligations owed by it to the United States, that these violations engaged its international responsibility to the United States and that it was under an obligation to make reparation to the United States.[239] It decided unanimously that Iran was under a duty to release the hostages, to give them the necessary means to leave the country and to place the premises, archives and documents of the United States in the hands of the protecting power. It also said that no diplomatic or consular staff might be kept in Iran or be subjected to any form of judicial proceedings or participate in them as a witness.[240]

On January 20, 1981, the hostages were released and flown home to the United States. One of the terms of the Agreement leading to their release was an undertaking by the United States to drop its suit before the International Court of Justice. Although the hostages were released, Iran did not agree to pay compensation, nor were their captors punished nor was the Embassy compound restored to the United States.

237. [1980] ICJ 3, 24-26.
238. Id. at 26-28.
239. Id. at 44-45.
240. Ibid.

CHAPTER 3

"DEFAULT" BEFORE THE
INTERNATIONAL COURT OF JUSTICE

INTRODUCTION

The study of non-appearance in municipal systems in Chapter 1 may assist us to understand the question of default or non-appearance before the International Court of Justice. The Statute of its predecessor, the Permanent Court of International Justice, was drafted with the laws of procedure in municipal systems very much in mind.[1] They could have no other model except perhaps the various procedural rules of *ad hoc* international arbitral tribunals. But the drafters of the PCIJ Statute were concerned to establish a permanent judicial tribunal in the nature of a court.

It may be convenient at this point to draw a distinction between "default" and "non-appearance". The terms are often used interchangeably, but we have seen in Chapter 1 that not all defaults stem from non-appearance. Most municipal jurisdictions recognize two types of default, default for failure to appear (*défaut faut de comparaître*) and default for failure to plead (*défaut faut de conclure*).

In a French judicial dictionary the word "*défaut*" is defined in the following way:

> ... situation d'une partie qui, dans un procès régulièrement engagé ou sur un point de ce procès demeure volontairement étrangère au debat, lequel ne peut revêtir ainsi le caractère contradictoire.
>
> ... on distingue le — contre avoué ou — faut de conclure et le

---

1. See e.g. *Procès verbaux*, 28th Mtg., Annex 2 at p. 607.

contre partie ou — faut de comparaître; s'emploie aussi pour designer le jugement rendu contre le non — comparante.[2]

But not all instances of failure to appear necessarily constitute a default. Jowitt's *Dictionary of English Law* defines default as:

> ... omission of that which a man ought to do; neglect; non-appearance in court... .[3]

It then goes on to explain:

> When a defendant neglects to take certain steps in an action which are required by the rules of court, the court may thereupon give judgment against him by default. ...[4]

Thus, the concept of default involves the failure of a duty of some sort so that those who want to say that a non-appearing party is in default must first establish that the proceedings are duly constituted and that the non-appearing party has a duty to appear.

There are a number of important distinctions that must be made between the International Court of Justice and its predecessor on the one hand and municipal tribunals on the other. These relate to the relative compulsory powers of the institutions.

The International Court of Justice cannot execute its judgments. Nor does it have the power to compel the attendance or punish the non-attendance of States who do not choose to submit to its authority. It cannot order the arrest of non-appearing States nor can it levy fines against them, attach their property,[5] or out-

---

2. Huigeman, Steiner, Piccard & Thilo, *Dictionnaire juridique — Français — Allemand* (1939), p. 157.
   [describes] the situation of a party who, while involved in a duly constituted proceeding or with regard to an issue in this proceeding chooses not to involve himself in the debate which thereby loses its contested nature.
   ... a distinction is made between "counter-solicitor" or -failure to plead and "counter-party" or -failure to appear; the term is also used for a judgment rendered against a non-appearing party.
3. (1977) Vol. I, p. 578 citing Co. Litt. 259b.
4. Ibid.
5. A State which has a judgement against another State may be able to attach assets of that State which are located in its territory. The United Kingdom examined the possibility of seizing Albanian property in the United Kingdom to satisfy the judgement of the ICJ in the *Corfu Channel* [*Assessment of Damages*] *Case* [1949] ICJ 244, but there was no Albanian property under the control of the United Kingdom at the time. See Rosenne, *The International Court of Justice* (1957) p. 98. See supra Ch. 1, notes 58-75 and accompanying text.

law defaulting States. Its jurisdiction is based on the consent of States.

This principle is often stated without qualification. In a joint dissenting opinion in the *Anglo-Iranian Oil Case*, Judges Winiarski and Badawi said:

> En droit international c'est le consentement des parties qui confère juridiction à la Cour; la Cour n'a compétence que dans la mesure où sa juridiction a été acceptée par les parties.[6]

Stated in this unqualified form, the principle of consent has been used to justify the non-appearance of States before the International Court of Justice.

In the *Nuclear Test Cases*, the French statement[7] said of the General Act for the Pacific Settlement of Disputes:

> ... le statut actuel de l'Acte général d'arbitrage et l'attitude à son égard des parties intéressées, en premier lieu de la France, interdisent de considérer qu'il existerait sur ce fondement, de la part de la France, cette volonté clairement exprimée d'accepter la compétence de la Cour que celle-ci selon une jurisprudence constante, estime indispensable, pour exercer sa juridiction.[8]

As we have seen,[9] its position was that the General Act, as an integral part of the League of Nations system, had fallen into desuetude as a result of the demise of the League.

Iceland too, in its letter of May 29, 1972 in the *Fisheries Juris-*

6. [1951] ICJ 89, 97.
In international law it is the consent of the parties which confers jurisdiction on the Court; the Court has jurisdiction only in so far as that jurisdiction has been accepted by the parties.
7. See Ch. 2, note 146 and accompanying text.
8. Annex to letter of 16 May 1973, [1974] ICJ Pleadings, Vol. II, p. 348.
... the present status of the General Act of Arbitration and the attitude towards it of the interested parties, and in the first place of France, render it out of the question to consider that there exists on that basis, on the part of France, that clearly expressed will to accept the competence of the Court which the Court itself according to its constant jurisprudence deems indispensable for the exercise of its jurisdiction. Translated "White Paper on French Nuclear Tests" published by the French Government, Annex B.X., p. 93.
9. Supra, Ch. 2, note 147 and accompanying text.

diction Case informed the Court that the agreement constituted by the Exchange of Notes of 11 March 1961:

> ... was not of a permanent nature, that its object and purpose had been fully achieved, and that it was no longer applicable and had termianted; that there was on 15 April 1972 no basis ... to exercise jurisdiction in the case; and that the Government of Iceland ... [was] not willing to confer jurisdiction on the Court.[10]

This position was supported by Eisemann writing in the *Annuaire Français de droit international*:

> ... toutes ces instances furent introduites par voie de requêtes unilatérales. Astreints à se presenter devant la Cour contre leur gré, au nom de clauses compromissoires oubliées ou contestées, l'Islande, la France et l'Inde purent y voir une violation de la règle du consensualisme qui depuis toujours donne seule compétence au juge international.[11]

But this unqualified statement of the principle of consent is an inaccurate statement of the law.

CONSENT AND JURISDICTION

The Advisory Committee of Jurists, established by the League of Nations Covenant to draft the Statute of the Permanent Court of International Justice, originally envisaged that the Court was to exercise compulsory jurisdiction on the Members of the League of Nations. Compulsory jurisdiction was first proposed by Dr. B.C.J. Loder of the Netherlands.[12] M. Francis Hagerup of Norway asked

10. [1972] ICJ 12, 17.
11. Eisemann, "Les effets de la non comparution devant la Cour Internationale de Justice" (1973) 19 *Annuaire Français de droit international* 351, 352.
... each of these cases was introduced by a unilateral application. Compelled to appear before the Court against their will on the basis of compromissory clauses that were forgotten or disputed, Iceland, France and India interpreted this as a violation of the rule of consent which has always been the sole basis for the competence of the international judge.
12. Supra note 1 at p. 229.

Dr. Loder if he held this view even when plaintiff was not a Member of the League of Nations.[13] Dr. Loder replied in the negative.[14] Mr. Elihu Root of the United States supported Dr. Loder's proposal. He pointed out that the principle of compulsory jurisdiction had been accepted in 1907 and in numerous treaties since then.[15]

He was referring to the fact that, at the Second Hague Conference in 1907, an attempt had been made to establish a "Court of Arbitral Justice". The project was enthusiastically supported by both the great and the small powers and the principle of compulsory arbitration was unanimously accepted. The attempt to establish the Court then failed because of disagreement over the appointment of judges. The great powers insisted on their own permanent national judges. The small powers demanded equality.[16]

The one member of the Advisory Committee to dissent from the proposal for compulsory jurisdiction was M. Mineichiro Adatci of Japan who objected to compulsory jurisdiction on the ground that it was contrary to Article 14 of the League of Nations Covenant which provided:

The Council shall formulate and submit to Members of the League for adoption plans for the establishment of a Permanent Court of International Justice. The Court shall be competent to hear and determine any dispute of an international character which the parties thereto submit to it.....

He felt that this provision limited the competence of the Court to disputes which were voluntarily submitted.[17]

The members who supported compulsory jurisdiction were reluctant to retreat from the principle which, in view of the unanimous support it had received at the Hague Conference of 1907, they felt was an idea whose time had come. In a memorandum to the Advisory Committee, Dr. Loder explained his position:

13. Ibid.
14. Ibid.
15. Id. at p. 229-230.
16. Fachiri, *Permanent Court of International Justice*, (2nd ed. 1932), p. 3.
17. Supra note 1 at p. 231.

A quoi bon, autrement, créer cette Cour? Pour constituer une doublure de la Cour d'Arbitrage? Pour conserve un état de choses déplorable, et continuer à ne faire justice entre deux adversaires qu'après avoir obtenu leur consentement mutuel, leur accord sur la formule de grief et le choix des juges? Cela n'en valait pas la peine. On ne sait que trop comment ceux qui se sentent coupables aux yeux du droit et de la justice savent profiter de leur situation, n'approuvant jamais rien, et font servir à leurs fins les exceptions et les subterfuges.

La différence entre arbitrage et justice ne se trouve pas dans la nature de la décision rendue. Dans les deux cas le droit et l'équite peuvent être sauvegardés, M. le Président l'a très bien démontré dans son discours au début de nos discussions. Mais dans l'arbitrage, il faut le consentement de la partie adverse pour que justice soit faite et son concours pour la définition du point en litige, ainsi que pour le choix des juges qu'elle peut récuser s'ils n'ont pas l'heur de lui plaire. L'arbitrage, c'est un combat avant le combat.

Le Pacte n'a pas voulu abolir l'arbitrage, mais il a désiré placer à côté de lui une Cour de Justice.

Elle doit être permanente, et laisser la porte ouverte à ceux qui se présenteront pour lui demander de régler tous les différends qui rentrent dans les limites de sa compétence, mais le concours gracieux de l'adversaire n'est plus requis; on s'arrangera sans lui.

Le traité de Paix démontre que tel est bien réellement le sens, la signification de la nouvelle institution. Au cours des débats actuels, l'attention des membres du Comité s'est fixée sur différents articles qui renvoient à la décision de la Cour — sans compromis ou rien qui y ressemble.

En 1907 on a vainement essayé de créer une Cour de Justice.

C'était toujours une Cour de Justice Arbitrale. Comment aurait-il pu en être autrement? Le lien entre les Etats manquait.

Ce n'est que par l'avènement de la Société des Nations que la possibilité de l'existence d'une vraie Cour de Justice fut créée, une Cour où le demandeur n'aura plus à attendre le bon vouloir de son adversaire. C'est une telle Cour que le Pacte a voulu, et non point une doublure inutile.

Ce serait à mon avis lui faire manquer son but, que de suivre toujours l'ancien sillon, que de s'attacher indéfiniment à l'interprétation d'un article qui, pris dans son sens naturel, ne prête a aucune équivoque.

Le Pacte a voulu faire ce pas en avant, qui constitue un réel progrès. Notre collègue Mr. Root l'a clairement démontré. Et à mon avis il faut déclarer ouvertement que le pas est fait. Je m'associe à la proposition de Mr. Root d'inserar au projet de ce Comité l'article 21 des cinq États.

Quelques-uns de nos collègues pretendent que c'est inutile parce qu'il ferait double emploi avec l'article 14 du Pacte. Je crois que ce n'est pas exact, mais quand il le serait, ce ne serait pas une raison pour nous de nous abstenir de statuer sur ce qui rentre dans notre projet, par la nature même du sujet qu'on y traite.[18]

18. Id. at 12th Mtg., Annex No. 1, pp. 250-251.

Otherwise, why create this Court? In order to duplicate the Court of Arbitration? To conserve a deplorable state of affairs and administer justice between two contesting parties only after having obtained their mutual consent, and their agreement on the wording of the complaint, and the choice of judges? That is not worth the trouble. It is only too well known that those who feel themselves offenders in the eyes of the law and of justice know how to profit by their position; they never agree to anything, and many exceptions and subterfuges serve their ends.

The difference between arbitration and justice is not to be found in the nature of the decision rendered. In both, law and equity may be protected. The President has shown this very clearly in his speech at the beginning of our discussion. But in arbitration the consent of the opposing party is necessary before justice can be done; his concurrence on the definition of the disputed point is necessary, as well as his agreement to the choice of judges which he may rule out if by chance they do not please him. Arbitration means a combat before the combat.

The Covenant did not intend to abolish arbitration, but it wished to place beside it a Court of Justice.

The latter must be permanent, it must be open to all who present themselves before it for a decision in all cases which come within the bounds of its competence. The gracious consent of the adversary is no longer required: one can do without him.

The Treaty of Peace shows that such is really the meaning of the new institution. During the present discussions the attention of the members of our Committee has been directed to various articles which refer to decision by the Court, without compromise or anything resembling it.

In 1907 a vain attempt was made to create a Court of Justice.

It was still a Court of Arbitral Justice. How could it have been otherwise? The bond between the States was lacking.

It was only the institution of the League of Nations that made possible a real Court of Justice, a Court where the plaintiff would no longer have to wait upon the good will of his opponent. It is such a Court that is intended in the Covenant, and not a useless duplication.

In my opinion it would cause the Covenant to miss its goal, to follow always in the old track, to adopt a vague interpretation of an article which taken in its natural meaning was unmistakable.

The Advisory Committee of Jurists opted for compulsory jurisdiction. The first scheme was submitted by Lord Phillimore with amendments by M. Hagerup:

> In the absence of any Convention to the contrary between the parties the Permanent Court of International Justice shall be deemed to be the Court of Arbitration mentioned in Article 13 of the Covenant, and shall have jurisdiction in all cases of disputes between States, which involve:
> (a) the interpretation of a Treaty;
> (b) any question of International Law;
> (c) the existence of any fact, which, if established, would constitute a breach of any international obligation;
> (d) the extent or nature of a reparation to be made for any such breach;
> (e) the interpretation of its own judgments.
> The Court shall also have jurisdiction in the several cases which are referred to it by the Treaty of Versailles, and also in cases in which the Parties have bound themselves by a Convention to submit to the International Court, either all disputes arising between them or a special dispute.
> In all the cases above mentioned, the Parties shall be deemed to have agreed to submit the dispute to the Court, so that the Court will be competent to hear and determine it according to the terms of Article 14 of the Covenant; and either of the Parties may require the Court to exercise jurisdiction without any further assent on the part of the other party. Consequently, if one of the Parties does not enter an appearance in the Court, or abstains in any other way from stating its intentions in the case, the other Party may demand that the case shall be tried by the Court of International Justice upon the basis of the statement of facts supplied by the later Party,

---

The intention of the Covenant was to take this step which would constitute a real progress. Our colleague, Mr. Root, has shown it clearly. In my opinion, we must openly declare that this step forward has been taken. I agree with the proposal of Mr. Root to insert in the Committee's plan article 21 of the Five Powers.
Some of our colleagues think that it is useless, because it would duplicate article 14 of the Covenant. I do not think this is correct, but even if it were so, it would not be a reason for us to abstain from putting into our project a point which ought to be there from the very nature of the subject dealt with.

provided that this statement is not contrary to proofs submitted to the Court or to common knowledge.[19]

The proposal on jurisdiction that the Advisory Committee eventually adopted, however, was submitted by Baron Descamps.[20]

Article 34 of the Draft Statute submitted by the Advisory Committee to the Council of the League of Nations provided:

> Between States which are members of the League of Nations the Court shall have jurisdiction [and this without any special conventions giving it jurisdiction] to hear and determine cases of a legal nature... .[21]

When this provision reached the League of Nations Council, Lord Balfour, the representative of Great Britain, took the lead in urging the rejection of the compulsory jurisdiction provision. He agreed with M. Adatci that the draft exceeded the authority granted by Article 14 of the Covenant.[22]

Article 36 of the Statute of the PCIJ finally adopted by the League of Nations represented a compromise between the ideal of compulsory jurisdiction and the principal of consent by making the compulsory jurisdiction optional:

> The jurisdiction of the Court comprises all cases which the parties refer to it and all matters specially provided for in Treaties and Conventions in force.
>
> The Members of the League of Nations and the States mentioned in the Annex to the Covenant may, either when signing or ratifying the protocol to which the present Statute is adjoined, or at a later moment, declare that they recognize as compulsory *ipso facto* and without special agreement, in relation to any other Member or State accepting the same obligation, the jurisdiction of the Court in all or any of the classes of legal disputes concerning:

19. Id., 11th Mtg., Annex No. 3, p. 253.

20. Id., 12th Mtg., Annex No. 1, p. 272. See infra Ch. 4, note 26 and accompanying text.

21. Scott, *The Project of a Permanent Court of International Justice and Resolution of the Advisory Committee of Jurists* (1920), p. 95.

22. *Documents Concerning the Action Taken by the Council of the League of Nations under Article 14 of the Covenant and the Adoption of the Statute of the Permanent Court of the International Justice* (1921), p. 38 [hereinafter *Documents*].

(a) the interpretation of a Treaty;

(b) any question of international law;

(c) the existence of any fact which, if established, would constitute a breach of an international obligation;

(d) the nature or extent of the reparation to be made for the breach of an international obligation.[23]

In 1945, another attempt was made to institute compulsory jurisdiction for the new International Court of Justice. The Committee of Jurists which was charged with drafting the ICJ Statute preferred two alternative texts on jurisdiction. One of them repeated the optional clause. The other one provided that the Court was to have compulsory jurisdiction over all legal disputes between States.[24]

The great majority of States at the San Francisco Conference were in favour of compulsory jurisdiction. But the U.S. and the U.S.S.R. were opposed. The United States delegate even threatened that the United States would refuse to be a party to the Statute if compulsory jurisdiction were adopted. Since the Statute was to be an integral part of the United Nations Charter, insistence on compulsory jurisdiction might have excluded the U.S. and the U.S.S.R. from the United Nations.[25] The optional system was maintained.[26]

Article 36 of the Statute of the International Court of Justice is very similar. Paragraphs (1) and (2) provide:

(1) The jurisdiction of the Court comprises all cases which the parties refer to it and all matters especially provided for in the United Nations Charter or in treaties or conventions in force.

(2) The States Parties to the present Statute may at any time declare that they recognise as compulsory *ipso facto* and without special agreement, in relation to any other State accepting the same obligation, the jurisdiction of the Court in all legal disputes concerning... .

23. Hudson, M. (1934) 1 World Court Reports 34. Article 36 is referred to alternately as the Compulsory Clause and the Optional Clause.

24. 14 UNCIO, pp. 667-668.

25. Report of the Rapporteur of Committee IV/1, 13 UNCIO, pp. 390-392.

26. See Rague, "The Reservation Power and The Connally Amendment", 11 NYUJIL & Pol. 323, 337 (1978); Waldock, H., "Decline of The Optional Clause", (1955-56) 32 BYIL 244, 245-246.

The remainder of the Article is identical to the second sentence of the PCIJ Statute. Article 36(6) says:

> In the event of a dispute as to whether the Court has jurisdiction, the matter shall be settled by the decision of the Court.

The statement that the jurisdiction of the Court is based on the consent of the parties is therefore inaccurate in so far as it creates the impression that consent must be obtained from the respondent in each specific case. That would be compatible only with the first part of Article 36(1), jurisdiction by special agreement, and if that were the only way to get into Court, a unilateral application would not be possible.

The words "without special agreement in relation to any other State accepting the same obligation" indicate that Article 36(2) recognises that a continuing consent to compulsory jurisdiction may be expressed by filing a declaration recognising it. Continuing consent may also be expressed by ratifying a treaty which provides for the submission of a certain class of dispute to the Court. States *do* conclude such treaties and they *do* file declarations under Article 36(2).[27] Yet, when other States have the temerity to invoke those instruments, respondent States take refuge behind the principle that jurisdiction is based on consent. If States persist in this attitude they may ultimately render any form of compulsory jurisdiction unworkable.

In fact many States may revoke their acceptance of the Compulsory Clause virtually at will.[28] But if they conclude a treaty which provides for the submission of certain classes of disputes to the International Court of Justice, will they refuse to see themselves as bound by it?

---

27. In Ch. 4, we will show that the ratifications of the United Nations Charter also amounts to an acceptance of the Court's jurisdiction *rationae personae*.

28. In 1974, France terminated its Declaration under Article 36(2) as a result of the *Nuclear Test Cases*. It also denounced the General Act for the Pacific Settlement of International Disputes without prejudice to its contention that the Act was no longer in force. Perhaps the only situation where a State may not revoke a declaration which it has specifically declared to be revocable upon notice is after a Unilateral Application has been filed against it invoking that Declaration. See *Nottebohm Case [Preliminary Objections]* [1953] ICJ 111, 122.

Article 40, paragraph 1 of the Statute provides that:

Cases are brought before the Court, as the case may be, either by the notification of the special agreement or by a written application addressed to the Registrar. In either case the subject of the dispute and the parties shall be indicated.

Article 42 says:

1. The parties shall be represented by agents.
2. They may have the assistance of counsel or advocates before the Court.

Article 38 of the present Rules of Court says:

1. When proceedings before the Court are instituted by means of an application ... the application shall indicate the party making it, the State against which the claim is brought and the subject of the dispute.
2. The application shall specify as far as possible the legal grounds on which the jurisdiction of the Court is said to be based; it shall also specify the precise nature of the claim, together with a succinct statement of the facts and grounds on which the claim is based.[29]

Article 40, paragraph 2 of the Rules states:

When proceedings are instituted by means of an application, the name of the agent for the applicant shall be stated. The respondent, upon receipt of the certified copy of the application, or as soon as possible thereafter, shall inform the Court of the name of its agent.[30]

29. (1978) 17 ILM 1286, 1293.
30. Ibid.

But some of the cases which we have been discussing were decided under the regime of earlier rules. Article 35(2) of the Rules of 1972 said:

> When a case is brought before the Court by means of an application, the application must ... indicate the party making it, the party against whom the claim is brought and the subject of the dispute. It must also, as far as possible, specify the provisions on which the applicant founds the jurisdiction of the Court, state the precise nature of the claim and give a succinct statement of the facts and grounds on which the claim is based, those facts and grounds being developed in the Memorial, to which the evidence will be annexed.[31]

Article 38, paragraph 3 said:

> The party against whom the application is made and to whom it is notified shall, when acknowledging receipt of the notification, or failing this, as soon as possible, inform the Court of the name of its agent.[32]

These provisions repeated and carried forward Articles 32(2) and 35(3) of the 1946 Rules.[33]

So the first act that can be regarded as an act of appearance on the part of the respondent is the appointment of an Agent.

Article 31 of the Statute provides that if one of the parties to a dispute has a judge of its nationality on the bench, the other State may appoint a judge *ad hoc*. If neither party has a judge of its nationality on the bench, then both parties may appoint judges *ad hoc*.

Article 35 of the Rules says:

> 1. If a party proposes to exercise the power conferred by Article 31 of the Statute to choose a judge *ad hoc* in a case, it shall notify the Court of its intention as soon as possible....

31. 67 AJIL 195, 204 (1913).
32. Id. at 207.
33. *Acts and Documents Concerning the Organization of the Court* (2nd. ed. 1947), p. 54.

2. If a party proposes to abstain from choosing a judge *ad hoc*, on condition of a like abstention by the other party, it shall so notify the Court which shall inform the other party... .[34]

Article 3 of the 1946 and 1972 Rules was more specific. It said that the Party had to notify the Registrar of the Court of its intent to exercise the right to appoint a judge *ad hoc* within the time-limit fixed for the filing of the memorial or counter-memorial, as the case may be, or, in the case of summary proceedings the time-limit fixed for the filing of the corresponding pleadings. There was no equivalent to Article 35(2).

So the notification of an intent to appoint a judge *ad hoc* is another way in which to appear in the action.

Article 79 of the present Rules provides for preliminary objections to jurisdiction:

1. Any objection by the respondent to the jurisdiction of the Court or to the admissibility of the application, or other objections the decision upon which is requested before any further proceedings on the merits, shall be made in writing within the time-limit fixed for the delivery of that party's first pleading.
2. The preliminary objections shall set out the facts and the law on which the objection is based, the submissions and a list of the documents in support; it shall mention any evidence which the party may desire to produce. Copies of the supporting documents shall be attached.
3. Upon receipt by the Registry of a preliminary objection, the proceedings on the merits shall be suspended and the Court, or the President if the Court is not sitting, shall fix the time-limit within which the other party may present written statements of its observations and submissions; documents in support shall be attached and evidence which it is proposed to produce shall be mentioned.
4. Unless otherwise decided by the Court, the further proceedings shall be oral.
5. The statements of fact and law in the pleadings referred to

34. *Supra* note 29 at pp. 1292-1293.

in paragraphs 2 and 3 of this Article and the statements and evidence presented at the hearings contemplated by paragraph 4 shall be confined to those matters that are relevant to the objection.

6. In order to enable the Court to determine its jurisdiction at the preliminary stage of the proceedings, the Court, whenever necessary, may request the parties to argue all questions of law and fact, and to adduce all evidence, which bear on the issue.

7. After hearing the parties, the Court shall give its decision in the form of a judgment, by which it shall either uphold the objection, reject it, or declare that the objection does not possess, in the circumstances of the case, an exclusively preliminary character. If the Court rejects the objection or declares that it does not possess an exclusively preliminary character, it shall fix time-limits for the further proceedings.[35]

The Article relating to preliminary objections in the 1972 Rules was Article 67. In the 1946 Rules, it was Article 62.

We can see that the Rules provide their own means for objecting to the jurisdiction of the Court. Such an objection has the effect of suspending the proceedings on the merits and preliminary objections are heard and argued as a separate phase of the case and are dealt with in a separate judgment.

The language of Article 42 of the Statute would seem to require a respondent to appoint an agent.

Indeed, the appointment of an agent facilitates communication between the Court and the respondent. But the question is whether failure to do this is a default which invalidates all further proceedings on the part of the respondent.[36]

In fact the practice of the Court does not treat the appointment of an agent as essential. As we have seen in Chapter 2,[37] the Court has accepted communication by post, communication by telegraph and communication handed to it by diplomatic representatives who have not been designated as agents.

35. Id. at p. 1299.
36. This was the criterion of Counsel for Pakistan in the *Trial of Pakistani Prisoners of War Case*, C/R 73/9 [1973] ICJ Pleadings, pp. 57-58.
37. See supra Chapter 2, notes 146-147, 173-179, 194, 226 and accompanying textual material.

94

Notionally, France's statement, Turkey's Observations and Iran's letter could have been delivered to the Court through an agent without any of those parties agreeing to appear in the case. But perhaps proceeding in accordance with the Court's Statute was too redolent of submission to its jurisdiction.

Eisemann accepts that the designation of an agent answers a clear practical purpose of facilitating relations between the Court and a pleader. But he does not think that the appointment of an Agent is mandatory.[38] He arrives at this conclusion by a rather close interpretation of Article 42 of the Statute. The imperative character of Article 42 attested to by the use of the present indicative, he reasons, does not envisage the obligation to designate an agent but rather, it signifies that, when a State wishes to be represented, it can only be by an agent and not by some other category of representative with limited rights and powers.

Eisemann then turned to Article 38 of the 1972 Rules in force at the time of his article which appeared to him to impose a more precise obligation on the parties. But he interpreted it as imposing a greater obligation on the applicant than on the respondent. The claimant "must" designate an agent in order to seise the Court.

By contrast, under the present Rules the respondent must designate an agent for the purpose of receiving the communication of the request. Despite its imperative language, the Rule does not indicate any sanctions for non-compliance.

Rosenne, however, is of the opinion that the specific duty under the Statute to appoint an agent is "equally obligatory" for both Parties.[39] But he does not suggest that failure to appoint an agent ought to have any adverse consequence for the respondent.

Judge Jessup feels that the Rules of Court require the respondent to appear and file preliminary objections to the jurisdiction of the Court. "The telegraphic or postal substitute for a memorial have frequently contained arguments of a substantive nature." In his view, the Court should not refer to and answer such "evasive pleadings" although he notes that the Court's practice of accepting them arises from the fact that it has been traditionally mindful that the parties are sovereign States and entitled to some latitude in procedural matters.[40]

38. Supra note 11 at p. 366. Citing Guyomar, *Le défaut des parties à un différend devant les juridictions internationale* (1960), p. 150.
39. Rosenne, *The Law and Practice of the International Court*, Vol. II (1965), p. 150.
40. Elkind, *Interim Protection: A Functional Approach* (1981), pp. XI-XII.

Eisemann seems to feel that a refusal to entertain such communications would amount to treating the objectives of the non-appearing State in a cavalier fashion.

The Court would have to examine any possible objection to jurisdiction on its own if necessary. But usually these objections will be raised by the complainant himself, if only to combat them.[41]

Eisemann quotes from the *Mavromatis Palestine Concessions Case* to the effect that, in exercising international jurisdiction the Court is not bound to attach the same importance to matters of form as in municipal law.[42]

The Court must take a position which reflects the equality of the States involved whether they appear or not. The absent State must be free to utilise other methods of making its views known to the Court.[43]

The documents submitted in these situations in fact appeared to conform to the Rules of Procedure in certain respects. Article 67(2) of the 1972 Rules required the objections to contain a statement of law upon which the objections were based along with conclusions. Eisemann claims that the postal and telegraphic communications in fact did this and in his position was subsequently supported by the Court in certain respects. In the *Agean Sea Case [Jurisdiction Phase]*, the Court noted that the Turkish Government had not been represented and did not file a preliminary objection or take any steps in the proceedings. "But", it said:

> ... there is no provision in the Rules of Court which excludes the submission of written observations on a request for provisional measures nor is there any provision which excludes the raising of questions of jurisdiction in written observations submitted in proceedings on the indication of provisional measures. [...]
>
> In the procedural circumstances of the case it cannot be said that the Court does not now have before it an indication by Turkey of reservation (b) which confirms the provisions of the General Act and of the Rules of Court. Nor can it be said

41. Supra note 11 at pp. 362-363.
42. [1924] PCIJ, Ser. A, No. 2, p. 12 at p. 34.
43. Supra note 11 at p. 363.

that the Court substitutes itself for the Turkish Government if it now takes the cognisance of a reservation duly invoked in *limine litis* in the proceedings on the request for interim measures. It would not discharge its duty under Article 53 of the Statute if it were to leave out of its consideration a reservation, the invocation of which by the Respondent was properly brought to its notice earlier in the proceedings.[44]

In short, such communcations amount to pleading without appearing.[45]

Eisemann does feel however that India's repeated communications in the *Trial of the Pakistani Prisoners of War Case* carried this right too far. What is regrettable about such a practice is that the Court risks losing control of the direction of the debate. Since the Judges have taken account of the respondent's argument, they cannot refuse to allow the applicant to reply to it. This interrupts the entire direction of the proceedings. He felt that the Court should adopt a rule whereby every new document submitted after the termination of the written phase of the proceedings should be submitted to the adverse Party who must agree to its being distributed to members of the Court. To make this possible, it would be necessary for the Court to fix a deadline after which written documents will no longer be received directly by it.[46]

In order to explain non-appearance, Judge Jessup has suggested that the refusal to appear in Court or to appoint an agent as required by the Rules may be due to fears on the part of States that the Court might extend its use of the doctrine *forum prorogatum* and hold that the act of appearing amounts to a consent to jurisdiction.[47]

He traces this attitude, which he describes as "overly cautious", to language used by the Permanent Court of International Justice in the *Rights of Minorities in Polish Upper Silesia (Minority Schools) Case*:

And there seems to be no doubt that the consent of a State to the submission of a dispute to the Court may not only

44. [1976] ICJ 3, 19-20.
45. Id. at p. 355.
46. Id. at pp. 365-366.
47. Supra note 40 at p. XII.

result from an express declaration, but may also be inferred from acts conclusively establishing it. It seems hard to deny that the submission of arguments on the merits, without making reservations in regard to the question of jurisdiction, must be regarded as an unequivocal indication of the desire of a State to obtain a decision on the merits of a suit... .[48]

It would seem fairly clear that what constituted an acceptance of the jurisdiction of the Court was the failure of Poland to state its objections to jurisdiction.[49] But Ambassador Shabbatai Rosenne argues that this *dictum* made it possible to conceive of proceedings being instituted by an application which does not have to indicate the consensual element upon which the jurisdiction would rest.[50]

Judge Jessup noted a suggestion made to the Court that, in order to avoid fears of *forum prorogatum*, the Rules which deal with preliminary objections might be amended to include a provision to the effect that a preliminary objection limited to the question of the jurisdiction of the Court will not be considered as an acceptance or recognition of the jurisdiction within the meaning of Article 36 of the Statute.[51]

United States law recognises the institution of a "Special Appearance" made specifically for the sole purpose of objection to the jurisdiction of the court without such an appearance being considered a submission to that jurisdiction. This right has been abolished by statute in some States. But where it has not been abolished, it is almost universally recognised[52] although it is usually subject to the requirement that leave of the court be first obtained.

This practical proposal aimed at putting States more at ease about appearing to contest jurisdiction was not taken up by the Court in its preparation of the 1978 Rules.

In the view of the present author, the question of whether the

48. [1928] PCIJ, Ser. A, No. 15, p. 4 at p. 24.
49. Supra note 40.
50. Supra note 39, Vol. 1 at p. 348. See also Jenks, *The Prospects of International Adjudication* (1964), p. 134.
51. Supra note 40 at pp. III-XIII.
52. 6 *Corpus Juris Secundum* § 5; *Baker v. Gotz*, 408 F. Supp. 238 (D.Del. 1976); *Regents of the University of New Mexico v. Superior Court of Los Angeles*, 125 Cal. Rptr. 413, 52 Cal. App. 3d 964 (1975); *Boyce v. Mellerup*, 229 NW 2d 719 (Ia. 1975); *Maner v. Maner*, 189 So. 2d 336, 279 Ala. 652 (1966).

Court should receive telegraphic or postal communication is subject to the one section of the Statute which provides specifically for non-appearance. Article 53 provides:

> 1. Whenever one of the parties does not appear before the Court, or fails to defend his case, the other party may call upon the Court to decide in favour of its claim.
> 2. The Court must, before doing so, satisfy itself, not only that it has jurisdiction in accordance with Articles 36 and 37, but also that the claim is well founded in fact and law.

Thus, in the event of non-appearance, the Court is under a duty to ascertain the issues and to decide those issues for itself. To this end, it will have the assistance of the appearing applicant who will, perforce, be required to anticipate the respondent's case in order to rebut it. But it would seem inconsistent with the Court's duty in this regard to reject information, however irregular, which will assist it to perform this duty. It should refrain however from treating these communications as official and from citing them in its judgment as it did in the *Aegean Sea Continental Shelf Case.*[53] It should also be careful to give such communications the weight they merit as less than full written or oral argumentation.

Eisemann rejects the contention that receipt of telegraphic or postal information is governed by Article 53. Citing Guyomar,[54] he says that non-appearance in any of the phases of the case which precede the definitive determination of jurisdiction cannot lead to a default in the technical sense of the term.[55] As long as the Court has not ruled positively on the question of its competence to hear the case, a party cannot be considered to have defaulted. Its behaviour constitutes a simple non-appearance and no law, except perhaps a rule of courtesy, requires it to present itself before the Court.[56] Appearance is thus not required either during the interim protection phase (if there is one) or at the preliminary objections phase:

> ... au lendemain d'une décision affirmant la compétence l'affaire sera en état d'être jugée par défaut.[57]

53. [1976] ICJ 4, 10. Citing Turkish Observations, para. 18 (10 August 1976).
54. Supra note 38 at p. 20 note 26.
55. Supra note 11 at p. 356.
56. Id. at p. 358.
57. Id. at p. 357. ... following a decision upholding competence the case will be subject to a default judgment.

Thus, of all the non-appearing parties, only Iceland was in default by virtue of its continued refusal to appear after the Court actually ruled that it had jurisdiction in the *Fisheries Jurisdiction Cases*.[58]

On the other hand Iran (in the *Anglo-Iranian Oil Case*), France (in the *Nuclear Test Cases*) and India (in the *Pakistani Prisoners of War Case*) were not in default.

(One wonders what he would have made of the *Hostages Case* where the Court dealt with jurisdiction and with the merits in the same phase of the case.)

Article 53 is normally regarded as the "default" provision. Thus, Eisemann feels that it cannot govern such cases since the parties cannot be in default.[59] He discerns a *jurisprudence constante* supporting his view, in that the Court did not cite Article 53 in any of the above cases. He found the duty of the Court to receive and consider postal and telegraphic communications, not in Article 53 of the Statute, but rather in Article 66(8) of the 1972 Rules which said:

> The Court shall only indicate interim measures of protection after giving the parties an opportunity of presenting their observations on the subject. The same rule applies when the Court revokes or modifies a decision indicating such measures.[60]

In the *Agean Sea Case*, the Court has now given a clear indication that it sees its duty to consider such communications as arising under Article 53 of the Statute.[61]

The jurisdictional basis for interim measures of protection will be dealt with in Ch. 4. But, pending that discussion, the following comments may be made about Eisemann's analysis.

He seems primarily concerned to avoid attaching the label "defaulter" to Iran, Iceland, France and India. Whether they can be called defaulters seems to be beside the point. Article 53 simply states the duty of the Court in the event of the non-appearance of one of the parties. The term "default" or "defaulter" is nowhere

58. Id. at p. 358.
59. Id. at p. 357.
60. Supra note 31 at 216.
61. See supra note 44 and accompanying text.

used. We are dealing with the effect of non-appearance whether one chooses to label the non-appearing party a defaulter or not. The duty of the Court would seem clear in any event. The Court, before deciding in favour of the applicant, must first satisfy itself *both* that it has jurisdiction and that the claim is well-founded in fact and law. To say that Article 53 does not apply at the phase of the case devoted to jurisdiction would make nonsense of the words.

Failure to appoint an agent or to file the relevant papers or to make preliminary objections may, on the basis of an analogy with the municipal law examples cited in Chapter 1, be regarded as a failure to enter an appearance. In municipal jurisdictions such a failure can be cured at any time before judgment and, in some cases, a default judgment may be reopened.

THE DRAFTING HISTORY OF ARTICLE 53

An examination of the Drafting History of Article 53 may help to cast some light on its purpose and interpretation.

Some of the draft schemes originally submitted to the Advisory Committee of Jurists contained proposals dealing with the non-appearance of one of the parties. However the question of non-appearance was considered premature because the Committee had not yet considered the question of the Court's jurisdiction.[62] The issue depended, at least in part, on whether the Statute was to provide for compulsory jurisdiction.

We have seen how the compulsory jurisdiction of the Court was emasculated when the question came before the League Council.[63] But Article 36 still involves situations in which actions may be brought by the unilateral application of a State. Hence the question of non-appearance remained an issue even after the Council's action.

At the 28th meeting of the Advisory Committee a memorandum was tendered by M. Hagerup of Norway in which he contrasted the Continental procedure of the time, in which the plaintiff's allegations of fact were taken as admitted[64] in the event of non-

62. Supra note 1, 11th Mtg. at p. 247.
63. Supra note 22 and accompanying text.
64. See supra Ch. 1, note 62 and accompanying text.

appearance, with the English procedure of the time, in which the plaintiff was called upon to prove his case in so far as the burden of proof lay with him.[65] Modern expert opinion generally recommended the Continental system. M. Hagerup preferred it also because the English system placed the plaintiff under the disadvantage of having to prove facts which the defendant would have disputed had he presented himself before the Court.[66] But the Advisory Committee as a whole preferred the English system.[67]

M. Ricci-Busatti of Italy objected that, if the powers of the Court were to be exactly the same in cases of judgments by default as they were to be when both parties appeared, the provision would be quite useless. To his way of thinking, the inclusion of a special provision would be justified only if it were to operate in the interests of the plaintiff and to punish the other party for its dereliction in failing to come to the Court. Since such a provision was not practicable in international affairs, he proposed suppression of the Article.[68]

Mr. Root of the United States countered that judgments by default were necessary and that such judgments should contain a full statement of the reasons.[69]

Thus Article 52 of the Advisory Committee's Draft was very similar to Article 53 of the current ICJ Statute.[70] It took its final form at the Fifth Meeting of the Third Committee of the First Assembly.[71]

From this we may draw the conclusion that the intent of the drafters, in the event of the non-appearance of one of the parties was that the applicant should be held to the same standard of proof that it would be held to if the defendant did appear.

Reference to the *British Whitebook* and to American Inter-State cases in Chapter 1 show us that, in these jurisdictions, non-appearance by the defendant does not mean that the plaintiff automatically wins his case. But he is not saddled with a greater burden of proof than he would have if the defendant had appeared. He has to prove his cause of action — an onus which lies with the plaintiff. A non-appearing defendant makes two pro-

---

65. Id. note 108 and accompanying text.
66. Supra note 1, 28th Mtg., Annex 2 at p. 607.
67. Id. at p. 569.
68. Ibid.
69. Ibid.
70. Supra note 21 at p. 124.
71. Supra note 22 at p. 136.

cedural sacrifices. He (or she) sacrifices the opportunity to rebut the evidence of the plaintiff and also the opportunity to establish an affirmative defence. The duty to prove a cause of action in municipal systems means that the court must be satisfied that the claim is well-founded in fact and law in these too.

This means that, before the International Court of Justice, the applicant has the onus of proof. But that onus does not extend to beyond the normal burden of establishing legally and factually a cause of action and the Court must see to it that the burden is satisfied. It should be no greater than that which would rest with the applicant if the respondent had appeared.

If we apply this to the *Aegean Sea Case*[72] we can see that the onus of alleging and proving irreparable injury belonged to Greece. Demonstrating that the interests sought to be protected were subjective or incapable of pecuniary ascertainment should have satisfied that onus. But at that point, the burden of coming forward with the evidence to negate the claim of irreparable injury should have shifted to Turkey. In Turkey's absence, no evidence to the contrary was presented and the Court should have held that the case for irreparable injury was established. The Court should not have merely cited the Turkish Observations to the effect that the exploration by Turkey cannot be regarded as involving any prejudice to Greek rights over the continental shelf.[73]

Neither does Article 53 require the Court to raise defences *proprio motu*.

The standard which is to be adopted is that which is appropriate to the phase of the case which is in progress. The drafting history of Article 53 and the law from which it is drawn indicate that it is erroneous to interpret that Article as requiring a higher standard if the respondent fails to appear.

72. See supra Ch. 2, notes 197-198 and accompanying text.
73. See supra Ch. 2, note 198 and accompanying text. For a more detailed discussion of the point see Elkind, supra note 40 at pp. 209-219

CHAPTER 4

INTERIM PROTECTION AND NON-APPEARANCE

INTRODUCTION

Most of the instances in which a defendant State failed to appear before the International Court of Justice alleging that the Court had no jurisdiction to try the cause were characterised by the fact that the claimant had filed, with the Court, a request for interim measures of protection.

Article 41 of the Statute of the International Court of Justice provides that:

> (1) The Court shall have the power to indicate, if it considers that circumstances so require, any provisional measures which ought to be taken to preserve the respective rights of either party.
> (2) Pending the final decision, notice of the measures suggested shall forthwith be given to the parties and to the Security Council.

In the *Anglo-Iranian Oil Company Case*, the contention of the non-appearing party was borne out by a decision of the International Court of Justice which ultimately held that it did not, in fact, possess jurisdiction.[1]

One writer, Eisemann sees a certain measure of justification for the practice of staying away at the interim protection phase. He denies that it constitutes a default:

1. [1952] ICJ 93.

Un dernier argument decisir empêche de considérer l'attitude de l'Islande, de la France et de l'Inde comme équivalent à un défaut. Le statut oblige le juge à verifier l'existence de sa compétence avant d'adjuger ses conclusions au demandeur car il ne saurait se prononcer en l'absence d'accord lui attri-buant exprèssement compétence. C'est le corollaire du prin-cipe du consensuallisme qui régit le recours au règlement juri-dictionnel des différends dans l'ordre international contem-porain.[2]

Thus, none of the phases prior to the definitive establishment of jurisdiction by a court can give rise to a default in the technical sense of the term. Only after a decision by the Court upholding its competence will the non-appearing State be in default. Thus, he says, of all the interim protection cases, the only defaulting party was Iceland in the *Fisheries Jurisdiction Cases* when it continued to ignore the proceedings even after the Court found that it had jurisdiction.[3] As long as the Court has not ruled positively on the question of its competence to hear the case, a party cannot be said to have defaulted. Its actions constitute, what he calls *"un simple non comparution"* and the only law which requires its appearance is perhaps the law of courtesy.[4]

The difficulty stems from a certain confusion about the jurisdic-tional authority of the Court to entertain a request for the indica-tion of interim measure of protection. The problem is, may a court, which might not have jurisdiction, make a provisional order preserving the rights of a party before it has had an opportunity to decide whether it has jurisdiction. Since the *Anglo-Iranian Oil Case*, many judges and scholars have been timid about the Court's power to indicate interim measures without sufficient assurance that the Court actually had jurisdiction to hear the merits of the case. Many States have viewed this uncertainty as a justification

---

2. Eisemann, *"Les effets de la non comparution devant la Cour Internationale de Justice."* (1973) 18 *Annuaire français de droit international* 351, 356.
One final decisive argument precludes us from considering the attitude of Iceland, France and India as equivalent to default. The Statute requires the judge to verify the existence of his jurisdiction before giving his decision on the claims of the applicant since he could not pronounce judgment in the absence of an agreement expressly giving him competence. This is the corollary which governs recourse to jurisdiction in dispute settlement in the modern international order.
3. [1973] ICJ 49. The merits phase is reported at [1974] ICJ 3.
4. Supra note 2 at 358.

for staying away at least from the interim measures stage. In the *Hostages Case*, in which Iran did not participate, there was no separate phase on the issue of jurisdiction. The Judgment of May 24, 1980 dealt both with the Court's jurisdiction to hear the Case and with the merits of the Case itself.[5]

In both the *Nuclear Test Cases* and the *Aegean Sea Continental Shelf Case* the judges were sharply divided. An incomplete understanding on the part of the judges as to the statutory basis for jurisdiction has led to a conflict over the question of the extent to which the Court must satisfy itself that it has jurisdiction to hear the merits of the case before it can grant interim measures. This question has been canvassed more extensively in a recent book on interim protection.[6] It will be useful here to briefly summarise some of the points made in that book.

THE BASIS OF JURISDICTION

The most popular assumption is that the jurisdiction of the Court to grant interim measure is granted in Article 36(1) and (2) which are normally regarded as the provisions of the Statute through which consent to the Court's jurisdiction is expressed. But the suggestion has also been made that Article 41 is, in itself, a jurisdictional provision.[7] In addition, Judge Elias has suggested that Article 36(6) may give the Court an authority to grant interim measures.[8]

Another possible solution stems from the view that the power to indicate interim measures is an inherent part of the judicial function. On this view, the power to prevent Parties from prejudicing the outcome of the dispute is part of the power to adjudicate. It is thus part of the Court's incidental jurisdiction.[9]

Under paragraphs (1) and (2) of Article 36, there are normally three roads to the Court: special agreement; treaties or conventions in force (where there are no reservations that would exclude

5. [1980] ICJ 3.
6. Elkind, *Interim Protection: A Functional Approach* (Martinus Nijhoff 1981), Chapter 7.
7. *Aegean Sea Continental Shelf Case* [1974] ICJ 4, 15 [D.O. Jiménez de Aréchaga].
8. Elias, "The International Court of Justice and the Indication of Provisional Measures of Protection" (Gilbert D'Amado Memo.ial Lecture, 1978), p. 9.
9. *Northern Cameroons Case* [S.O. Fitzmaurice] [1963] ICJ 15, 103. See also Stone, *Legal Control of International Conflicts* (1954), p. 132; Elias, ibid.; Eisemann, supra note 2 at 258.

the jurisdiction of the Court in a particular case) or; declarations (by both parties) under Article 36(2) (the Optional Clause) without reservations that would exclude the jurisdiction of the Court in a particular case. Thus, the issue of jurisdiction, under these provisions, may turn on the validity or force of the agreement,[10] the validity or force of the treaty or convention,[11] the interpretation of reservations made in respect of the pertinent treaty or convention[12] or the interpretation of reservations to the acceptance of the Optional Clause.[13] These objections have been canvassed by the Court even where the objecting party has not appeared.[14] Article 53 prevents the Court from hearing the merits of the case until it has satisfied itself that it has jurisdiction to do so.[15]

Paragraph 6 of Article 36, on the other hand is said to be a basis for the Court's jurisdiction to grant interim measures on the ground that it makes the Court the sole judge of its jurisdiction. But Article 36(6) does not appear to confer any jurisdiction on the Court. In deciding whether it has jurisdiction under Article 36(6), the Court must still refer to some authority outside of Article 36(6) to support its decision.[16]

In recent years, the view that Article 41 is an autonomous grant of jurisdiction has attracted the judicial support only of Judge Jiménez de Aréchaga in the *Aegean Sea Case*.[17] The view is open to the objection that even jurisdiction to indicate interim measures must be based on the consent of States.

The view that Article 41 reflects an inherent power was also expressed by Judge Nagendra Singh in his declaration in the *Nuclear Test Cases*.[18] But he appears to have retreated from this view in the *Aegean Sea Case*.[19] This view still leaves open the question of how a State's consent to such jurisdiction is expressed. Interim protection is almost always contested and normally requires

10. *Aegean Sea Case*, supra note 7.
11. *Nuclear Test Cases* [1973] ICJ 99, 457; *Aegean Sea Case*, ibid.
12. *Trial of Certain Pakistani Prisoners of War Case* [1963] ICJ; *Aegean Sea Case*, ibid.
13. *Nuclear Test Cases*, supra note 11; *Norwegian Loans Case* [1957] ICJ 9; *Interhandel Case* [1957] ICJ 105.
14. See supra Ch. 2.
15. See supra Ch. 3.
16. Supra note 6 at p. 169.
17. Supra note 1.
18. *Australia v. France* [1973] ICJ 99, 108-109.
19. Supra note 1 at 17.

separate written and oral proceedings. So, again we are left with the necessity of determining how the parties consent to jurisdiction to indicate interim measures.

CATEGORIES OF JURISDICTION

Questions of jurisdiction may be separated into four categories: *ratione personae, ratione materiae, ratione temporis* and *ratione loci*. Since the International Court of Justice is a "world court", jurisdiction *ratione loci* is really not applicable.[20]

When a court or tribunal has jurisdiction *ratione personae*, the court has jurisdiction with respect to the parties to the dispute before it. There are two basic aspects of jurisdiction *ratione personae*. The first involves the access of the plaintiff or applicant to the court. The second involves the authority of the court over the defendant or respondent.

In municipal law, the access of the plaintiff to the court is generally treated as a question of standing to sue (*locus standi*) and involves the interest of the plaintiff in the subject matter of the dispute.[21] In most municipal jurisdictions authority over the defendant is linked with jurisdiction *ratione loci*. It may be exercised where a defendant is caught even fleetingly within the territorial competence of the court.[22] In almost all of these jurisdictions, persons over whom the court does not otherwise have jurisdiction may voluntarily consent to it.[23] In criminal law, courts may have jurisdiction over a defendant if he or she is apprehended in the territory of the prosecuting State.[24]

Jurisdiction *ratione materiae* refers to the jurisdiction of the court with regard to the subject matter of the dispute. In France, it is called *compétence d'attribution*. It refers to the type of cases

20. Jurisdiction *ratione loci* is vital to municipal courts and relevant to such international tribunals as the European Court of Human Rights, the Court of Justice of the European Communities and the Inter-American Court of Human Rights.

21. England. See *Attorney-General v. Independent Broadcasting Authority* [1973] 2 WLR 344 (CA) France. See Carbonnier, *Droit civile* (5th ed. 1954) Vol. 1, p. 63.

22. England. See *Maharanee of Baroda v. Wildenstein* [1972]2 QB 283. U.S. See *Restatement (second) of Conflict of Laws*, § 28 (1971) p. 271: "(Presence) A State has power to exersize judicial jurisdiction over an individual who is present within its territory whether permanently or temporarily". Germany. See *ZPO* §§ 12-37.

23. France, *C. Civ. art.* 111. Germany *ZPO* §§ 39.

24. The *Lotus Case* [1927] PCIJ, Ser. A, No. 10, p. 4.

a court is authorized to decide. For instance, in France the *tribunaux commercials* and in Austria the *Handelsgerichte* are authorised to apply only commercial law.

Article 38 of the Statute places the International Court of Justice under similar restrictions with respect to the law which it is to apply. It provides that the Court's function is to decide disputes in accordance with international law. Other limitations on jurisdiction *ratione materiae* include maximum or minimum jurisdictional amounts.

Interim protection resembles preliminary injunctive relief. In most municipal jurisdictions this sort of relief is based on jurisdiction *ratione personae.*[25]

DRAFTING HISTORY

In the preparation of the Statute of the Permanent Court of International Justice, a draft of an article dealing with jurisdiction *rationae materiae* to be submitted to the Committee of Jurists was presented to the Committee by Baron Descamps. It followed the language of Article 13, paragraph 2 of the League of Nations Covenant:

> The Permanent Court of International Justice is competent decide disputes concerning cases of a legal nature, that is to say those dealing with:
> (a) the interpretation of a treaty;
> (b) any question of international law;
> (c) the existence of any fact which, if established, would constitute a breach of any international obligation;
> (d) the extent and nature of any reparation to be made for the breach of an international obligation;
> (e) the interpretation of any sentence to be rendered by the Court.[26]

25. (a) Roman Law. See J. Cambell, *A Compendium of Roman Law* (2nd ed. 1982), p. 149 for a discussion of the Interdict; (b) English Law. See F. Maitland, *Equity* (2nd ed. reprinted 1944), p. 322; Kerr, *A Treatise on the Law and Practice of Injunctions* (1878), p. 8; (c) United States. See *Restatement (second) of Conflict of Laws*, supra note 22 at p. 103; (d) Germany. See Cohen, E.J., *Manual of German Law*, Vol. III (1971), p. 247; (e) France. See Carbonnier, supra note 18 at p. 65.

26. *Procès verbaux*, 13th Mtg. Annex No. 1, Art. 1, at p. 272. Sub para (e) was later dropped.

Later, Lord Phillimore noted that this was a project concerning material competence. He offered to submit one concerning personal competence.[27]

The formula which he proposed was: "Any State signing the present Act, is considered as having agreed to submit to the Permanent Court any dispute between itself and another signatory State, as described in Article 1".[28]

Thus, the distinction between jurisdiction *ratione personae* and jurisdiction *ratione materiae* was clearly recognised by the drafters. The former was expressed through consent by adherence to the Act. The latter dealt with the type of case that the Court was authorized to decide.

The two primary jurisdictional provisions which ultimately emerged from the Committee were Article 32 and 34 of its draft. Article 32, as adopted by the League of Nations Council became Article 35 of the Statute of the Permanent Court of International Justice.

It provided that the Court would be open to Members of the League and other States mentioned in the Annex to the Covenant. The League of Nations Council was to set conditions under which the Court would be open to other States subject to special conditions contained in treaties in force. But the provisions forbade any Party to be placed in a position of inequality before the Court.

States were to adhere to the Statute by means of a Protocol of Signature. As soon as the Protocol was ratified by a majority of Members of the League, the Court would then be able to sit in a dispute between those States to which the Court was open under Article 35, paragraph 2 of the Statute.

However, the League of Nations Council rejected the provision for compulsory jurisdiction in Article 34 of the Committee's draft and substituted what is now Article 36 of the Statute with its provisions for optional acceptance of compulsory jurisdiction. This introduced an element of jurisdiction *ratione personae* into Article 36. Thus, the Court has jurisdiction over States (*personae*) under Article 36 but with regard to "cases" which the parties refer to it, "matters" provided for in the Charter or in treaties and conventions in force and "legal disputes" under the Optional Clause.

27. Id. at p. 290.
28. Id. Annex No. 4 at p. 276.

The provision of the PCIJ Statute which was specifically intended to deal with jurisdiction was Article 35. But Judge Hudson, in his Treatise noted that, even though Article 35 created the impression that a Party to the Protocol conferred jurisdiction on the Court, if that Party did not come within Article 36(1) or (2), its acceptance of the Court's jurisdiction under Article 35 meant that its consent "that an institution which it helped maintain may exercise the contentious jurisdiction conferred by other States and the advisory jurisdiction conferred by Article 14 of the Covenant."[29]

But he saw the Protocol as providing a basis for incidental jurisdiction. He included in this the Court's power to allow intervention by third States and the power of the Court to indicate interim measures of protection "even in advance of its determination whether jurisdiction has been conferred upon it to deal with the merits of the case, under Article 36 of the Statute".[30]

Thus, when a State becomes a party to the Statute, it consents to the operation of the Statute and to such incidental jurisdiction as is necessary to the performance of the Court's judicial functions.

Today, Article 35(1) of the Statute of the International Court of Justice simply provides that "the Court shall be open to States Parties to the present Statute". But the Statute of the International Court of Justice is a part of the United Nations Charter and the Court is an organ of the United Nations.

Article 35 of the Statute must be read with Article 93 of the United Nations Charter which provides that all Members of the United Nations are *ipso facto* parties to the Statute of the Court although the General Assembly, on recommendation of the Security Council may lay down conditions by which a non-member may become a party. Most States became Parties to the Statute when they ratified the United Nations Charter. There was no need for a subsequent protocol of signature.

As in municipal law, where interim remedies are usually founded on jurisdiction *ratione personae*, Article 35 of the Statute

29. *A Treatise on the Permanent Court of International Justice* (1934), pp. 359-360.
30. Id. at p. 360.

and Article 93 of the Charter can be said to provide the jurisdictional basis for the indication of interim protection.[31]

PROBABILITY OF JURISDICTION

Quite a variety of attitudes have emerged from the jurisprudence
of the Court and scholarly writing on the subject. They are:

1. Substantive jurisdiction is irrelevant to a request for interim
   measures.[32]
2. Only manifest absence of jurisdiction can preclude the Court
   from indicating interim measures.
3. Article 41 is an autonomous grant of jurisdiction.
4. The Court must have *prima facie* jurisdiction.
5. There must be weighty arguments in favour of jurisdiction.
6. The Court must fully satisfy itself that it has jurisdiction.
7. Substantive jurisdiction is one among a number of circumstances which the Court can consider.

There does not seem to be much support for the first view in the
sense that the probability of substantive jurisdiction need not be
considered at all at the interim protection stage. If, however, one
sees Article 41 as giving the Court only very limited procedural
powers, as one commentator has suggested,[33] then substantive
jurisdiction would not need to be considered at all.

The "manifest absence" view was the view of the Court in the
Anglo-Iranian Oil Co. Case.[34]

The autonomous grant theory would seem to be related to the
"manifest absence" theory although Judge Jiménez de Aréchaga
felt that it was more akin to the seventh view, that jurisdiction
was merely a circumstance which the Court should consider in
deciding whether to indicate interim measures.[35]

The *prima facie* view has attracted the support of the majority

31. Support for the distinction made herein between Article 35 and Article 36 can
be found in Gross, "The International Court of Justice: Consideration of Requirements
for Enhancing Its Role in the International Legal Order", 65 AJIL 253, 306-307 (1971).
32. Identified by Merrills, "Interim Measures of Protection and the Substantive
Jurisdiction of the International Court" (1977) 36 CLJ 86, 90.
33. Hammerskjöld, A., "Quelques aspects de la question des mesures conservatoires
en droit internationale positif" in *Zeitschrift für ausländisches öffentliches Recht und
Völkerrecht* (1935), p. 25.
34. Supra note 1 at 92-93.
35. Supra note 1 at 15.

112

of the Court in recent cases. But, as a test, it appears to be rather difficult to apply. In the *Nuclear Test Cases*, the majority felt that a *prima facie* basis existed.[36] But Judge Forster[37] and Ignacio-Pinto[38] applying the same test, denied that such jurisdiction existed.

The "weighty arguments" approach was first suggested by Judges Winiarski and Badawi in the *Anglo-Iranian Oil Case.*[39] This view has been criticised as too stringent and as inconsistent with the expeditious nature of the remedy. It is likely to prejudice any rights which might be in jeopardy.[40]

The view that the Court must fully satisfy itself as to its jurisdiction was advanced in the *Nuclear Test Cases* by Judge Forster.[41] Judge Gros has suggested that Article 53 requires the Court to fully satisfy itself that it has jurisdiction when one of the parties fails to appear.[42] In the *Aegean Sea Case*, Vice President Nagendra Singh[43] and Judge Morozov[44] accepted this latter view.

The general view that the Court must satisfy itself that it has jurisdiction is open to the objection that it is inconsistent with the urgent nature of the remedy.

The view of Judge Gros has been criticised by Eisemann on a number of additional grounds:

> En première lieu, on ne peut pas dire que la France soit "en défaut" à ce stade de la procédure. En second lieu, il fait abstraction du caractère très particulier de l'intervention du juge s'agissant de mesures conservatoires.[45]

Eisemann notes that Judge Gros expressed a desire to find an equi-

---

36. *Australia v. France* [1973] ICJ 99, 102; *New Zealand v France* [1973] ICJ 135, 138.
37. Id. at 148.
38. Id. at 129-130.
39. Supra note 1 at 96. See Merrills, supra note 32 at 877-890; Mendelson, "Interim Measures of Protection in Cases of Contested Jurisdiction" (1972-73) 46 BYIL 259, 301.
40. Merrills, id. at 103.
41. Supra note 11 at 148.
42. Id. at 149.
43. Supra note 7 at 17.
44. Id. at 22.
45. Supra note 2 at p. 361. But see supra Ch. 3, note 61 and accompanying text.
In the first place, one cannot say that France was "in default" at that stage of the proceedings. In the second place, his reasoning did not take account of the highly particular nature of judicial intervention in considering measures of protection.

librium between the two notions of jurisdiction and urgency.[46] But he feels that the *prima facie* test is the better, perhaps the only way to strike that balance.[47]

Judge Gros' view has also been criticised on the grounds that (a) it provides States with a powerful disincentive to appear in interim protection cases and (b) if the Article 53 argument is carried to its extreme, it would seem also to require the Court to first find in an applicant's favour on the merits since Article 53 says not only that the Court must satisfy itself that it has jurisdiction under Articles 36 and 37, but also that the claim is well-founded in fact and law.

Furthermore, as we have seen in Ch. 3, the drafting history of Article 53 shows quite clearly that this is not what was intended since, under Article 53, the applicant is under no greater burden than he would have to sustain if the respondent appeared.

In the *Hostages Case*, the Court unanimously repaired to the *prima facie* test.[48] Judge Gros, Vice President Nagendra Singh and Judge Morozov all participated in the decision. Despite the references to the *prima facie* test, they must have felt fully satisfied that the Court had jurisdiction, since the Court moved on to the merits without even having a separate phase on jurisdiction.

Actually, the view that the Court must fully satisfy itself of its jurisdiction is a quarrel with the practice of hearing the request for interim measures as a separate phase, independent of the preliminary objecton phase. It has been described as a *guerre d'escalade* mounted by Judges since 1951 with the ultimate objective of restoring the Court to a more modest role in the interpretation of its powers with respect to interim protection.[49]

But the implementation of such a proposal would require a change in the Rules of Court which still, even after the 1978 alterations, permit the indication of interim measures at any stage of the proceeding[50] and which still provide that a decision on interim measures shall be treated as a matter of urgency.[51] It would seem that the Court did not opt for such a change in its

46. Supra note 11 at 20 and 155.
47. Supra note 2 at p. 361.
48. [1979] ICJ 6, 13.
49. Arbour, "Quelques réflexions sur les mesures conservatoires indiquées par la Cour Internationale de Justice", (1975) 16 *Cahiers de Droit* 532, 569.
50. Rule 73(1).
51. Rule 74(2).

last revision. Therefore, the siege ought to be lifted. The Judges are obliged to decide cases in accordance with the Rules currently in force.

The view that substantive jurisdiction is one among a number of circumstances which the Court may consider has been proposed by M.H. Mendelson[52] and accepted by Judge Jiménez de Aréchaga[53] as a way out of the Court's impasse. It involves balancing the likelihood of jurisdiction against the hardship which the respondent might suffer in complying with the order and which the applicant may suffer if the order is not granted.

One author has criticised this approach[54] on the ground that probability of success on the question of jurisdiction is not logically related to the hardship which respondent may suffer in complying with the order or which the applicant might suffer if the order was not granted. Respondent's threatened action may be unlawful and may seriously threaten the applicant with irreparable harm even though the likelihood of success on jurisdiction is minimal. In such a case no order can be granted.

CONCLUSION

This considerable confusion over the extent to which the Court needs to assure itself that it has jurisdiction under Article 36 before it can grant interim measures has almost certainly been a chief cause in the tendency of States to absent themselves from interim protection proceedings. A State which does appear is under a considerable cloud as to the extent to which it has to sustain claims to jurisdiction under Article 36 or rebut them as the case may be. The applicant must, of course, appear and make the best argument it can. Respondents however, seem inclined to abstain from the exercise and let the applicant and the Court struggle with the problem.

Confusion is easily dispelled however if we accept the view that the real basis for jurisdiction to indicate interim measures is Article 35 of the Statute and Article 93 of the United Nations Charter. It would seem, in the light of this, that the most logical

---

52. Supra note 39 at p. 321.
53. Supra note 7 at 15.
54. Supra note 6 at p. 238.

test is the "manifest absence" test. The Court cannot completely ignore the probability of jurisdiction under Article 36, but it need only assure itself that the claimed jurisdiction under Article 36 is not frivolous.

CHAPTER 5

THREE KINDS OF SELF JUDGMENT

INTRODUCTION

The principle *nemo judex in sua causa*[1] (no one may be a judge in his own cause) is recognised as a fundamental principle of dispute settlement. In international law, it is recognised as a "general principle of law recognised by civilised nations".[2]

In Professor Bin Cheng's view, the application of the principle extends not only to judicial procedures but to disputes settlement in general.[3] He cites as an example the *Case on Interpretation of Article 3, Paragraph 2, of the Treaty of Lusanne (Frontier Between Iraq and Turkey)* in which the Permanent Court of International Justice held that representatives of States on the Council of the League of Nations should abstain from voting in disputes between themselves. In so holding, it said:

> The well-known rule that no one can be a judge in his own suit holds good.[4]

The Report on the Project Concerning the Establishment of the Proposed International Court of Arbitral Justice stemming from the Second Hague International Peace Conference 1907, also cited the rule as a universally accepted doctrine.[5]

1. Or any of its various Latin formulations.
2. Cheng, *General Principles of Law as Applied by International Court and Tribunals* (1953), Ch. 13; Lauterpacht, *The Development of International Law by the International Court* (1958), pp. 158-164.
3. Id. at p. 279.
4. [1925] PCIJ, Ser. B, No. 12, p. 6 at p. 32.
5. *IIe Conférence international de paix*, 1 *Actes et Documents* (1907), p. 307.

But international law appears to recognise an exception to this principle. Where a treaty imposes obligations but does not provide any authoritative means for interpreting them, it is understood that the parties to the treaty will have the power to interpret their obligations for themselves. This is called "autointerpretation".[6] It is said to be a creation of the doctrine of sovereignty.[7]

A corollary of this principle is the canon of international law, noted in Chapter 3,[8] that the jurisdiction of international tribunals must be voluntarily accepted by States[9] although as we have seen in that Chapter, consent may be expressed in a variety of ways. But:

> It does not follow from the principle of voluntary submission to procedure for pacific settlement nor does it follow from the doctrine of sovereignty "that the State is in principle the sole judge of the existence of any individual rule of law".[10]

This is so because any State which claimed to be the sole judge of the existence of rules of international law would, in effect, subject other States to its judgment.

The principle of autointerpretation operates on the assumption that, if a State is arbitrary or unreasonable in interpreting its obligations towards other States, then those other States will object. In the end, the interpretation of such a treaty or other norm of international law will be worked out by negotiation between the States concerned. But where a treaty provides that there is to be an authoritative means of settling disputes concerning its interpretation, it creates a duty born of consent, to submit disputes to such a settlement procedure and failure to do so is a violation of the terms of the treaty.[11]

6. Gross, "States as Organs of International Law and the Problems of Autointerpretation" in Lipsky (ed.), *Law and Politics in the World Community* (1953), p. 59; Watson, "Autointerpretation, Competence and the Continuing Validity of Article 2(7) of the UN Charter", 71 AJIL 60 (1977); see also Watson, "Legal Theory, Efficacy and Validity in the Development of Human Rights Norms in International Law" (1969) U. Ill. Law Forum 609, 625. Cheng, "Epilogue on the Nature and Sources of International Law" in Cheng (ed.), *International Law Teaching and Practice* (1982), pp. 211-212.

7. Lauterpacht, *The Function of Law in the International Community* (1933), p. 3.

8. See Ch. 3, notes 2-8 and accompanying text.

9. See supra note 7 at p. 4.

10. Gross, supra note 6 at p. 77; quoting Lauterpacht, id. at p. 3.

11. *Interpretation of Peace Treaties with Bulgaria, Hungary and Rumania [Second Phase]* [1950] ICJ 65, 70-71.

The power of a tribunal to determine its own competence or *compétence de la compétence* is also a fundamental principle of judicial dispute settlement and a "general principle of law recognised by civilised nations".[12] In the *Case of Interpretation of the Greco-Turkish Agreement of December 1, 1926 (Final Protocol Article IV)* the Permanent Court of International Justice had to interpret a provision which said:

> Les questions de principe présentant quelque importance et qui pourraient surgir au sein de la Commission mixte à l'occasion des attributions nouvelles que lui confère l'accord signé ce jour et qu'elle n'avait pas à la conclusion de ce dernier sur la base des actes antérieurs fixant sa compétance, seront soumises à l'arbitrage du président du Tribunal arbitral grèco-turc, siégeant à Constantinople. Les sentences de l'arbitre seront obligatoires.[13]

The article contained no express provision designed to settle the question of by whom and when the matter was to be referred to the President of the Tribunal. The Court felt that the very silence of the article made it "possible and natural to deduce" that the power to refer the matter rested with the Mixed Commission:

> ... there can be no doubt that only questions arising in the course of deliberations of the Commission are contemplated. But, that being so, it is clear — having regard amongst other things to the principle that, as a general rule, any body possessing jurisdictional powers has the right in the first place to determine the extent of its jurisdiction — that questions affecting the extent of the jurisdiction of the Mixed Commission must be settled by the Commission itself without action by any other body being necessary.[14]

12. Cheng, supra note 2 at pp. 275-278.
13. [1928] PCIJ, Ser. B, No. 16, p. 4 at pp. 19-20.
Any questions of principle of importance which may arise in the Mixed Commission in connection with the new duties entrusted to it by the Agreement signed this day and which, when that Agreement was concluded, it was not already discharging in virtue of previous instruments defining its powers, shall be submitted for arbitration to the President of the Greco-Turkish Arbitral Tribunal sitting at Constantinople. The arbitrator's awards shall be binding.
14. Id. at p. 20.

It would also seem to be the essence of compulsory jurisdiction that the competence of the tribunal cannot be successfully opposed by one of the parties after the dispute has arisen.[15] As to the International Court of Justice itself, Article 36, paragraph 6 of its Statute gives the Court competence to determine its own jurisdiction.

Despite this provision, States which fail to appear normally cite, as a reason for their non-appearance, their perception that the Court lacks jurisdiction to decide the case. They purport to decide the issue of jurisdiction for themselves. Thus non-appearance is one form of self-judgment. This Chapter will study non-appearance in terms of the phenomenon of self-judgment.

Basically there are three types of self-judgment, implicitly self-judging reservations, explicitly self-judging reservations and non-appearance. Judge Lauterpacht and others have suggested that certain legal consequences flow from self-judging reservations. But, as will be demonstrated, self-judging reservations are a somewhat equivocal form of self-judgment and strong arguments can be made for avoiding the consequences proposed by Judge Lauterpacht and others. Non-appearance on the other hand is unequivocal and therefore, in the case of non-appearance, these consequences should not be avoided.

SELF-JUDGING RESERVATIONS

One way to exclude the jurisdiction of the International Court of Justice is by including within the declaration of acceptance of the Optional Clause (Article 36(2)) a reservation to the effect that the declarant does not accept the compulsory jurisdiction of the Court in certain classes of disputes.[16] Some reservations such as Reservation (b) of the United States Declaration purport to reserve to the declarant State the right to decide whether the Court has jurisdiction. This Reservation excludes from the competence of the Court in:

---

15. Borel, E. and Politis, N., *"L'extension de l'arbitrage obligatoire et la compétence de la Cour Permanente de Justice International"* (1927-II) 18 *Annuaire de l'Institut de Droit International* 675. See also *Nottebohm Case [Preliminary Objections]* [1953] ICJ 111, 119-120.

16. Reservations may also be made to treaties and conventions in force mentioned in Article 36(1). See supra Ch. 4, note 13 and accompanying text.

Disputes with regard to matters which are essentially within the domestic jurisdiction of the United States of America as determined by the United States of America.[17]

The last eight words of this Reservation were added by an amendment introduced in the United States Senate by Senator Tom Connally of Texas[18] and are popularly known as the "Connally Amendment".

Such reservations have been given a variety of names. The most popular is "self-judging",[19] but they have also been called "automatic",[20] "peremptory"[21] and "subjective".[22]

Judge Lauterpacht used the term "automatic" because:

That description expresses the automatic operation of that reservation in the sense that, by virtue of it, the function of the Court is confined to registering the decision made by the defendant Government and not subject to review by the Court.[23]

Of these, "subjective" is probably the most accurate term. The terms "automatic" and "peremptory" prejudge the questions which we will consider below, whether such reservations leave any residuum of decision-making power to the Court.

The term "self-judging" is not entirely without problems. For the uninitiated, the term "self-judging reservation" might raise the picture of a reservation which judges itself. But we will use it in this discussion since it involves the fundamental problem of a State attempting to judge for itself whether the Court has jurisdiction in apparent conflict with the principle *nemo judex in sua causa*.

But not all self-judging reservations are the same. We may note two basic types. There are reservations which are implicitly self-judging and reservations which are explicitly self-judging.

17. [1980-1981] ICJYB, p. 88.
18. 92 Cong. Rec., p. 10763 (August 1, 1946).
19. Larsen, "The Self-Judging Clause and Self Interest", 46 APAJ 729 (1960).
20. *Case of Certain Norwegian Loans* [1957] ICJ 9, 34 [D.O. Lauterpacht].
21. Briggs, "The United States and the International Court of Justice", 53 AJIL 301, 306 (1959).
22. Waldock, H., "Decline of the Optional Clause" (1955-1956) 32 BYIL 244, 271.
23. Supra note 20.

Implicitly self-judging reservations

A reservation may not state in so many words that the declarant shall have the power to determine whether a case falls within its ambit. But it may nonetheless deal with an area of the law in which a State's assessment of its own requirements is generally held to be a major if not the sole criterion for assessing its content.

The third paragraph of the French Declaration of May 20, 1966 may provide us with an example. That paragraph excluded, *"différends concernant les activités se rapportant a la défense nationale."*[24]

That reservation was not self-judging on its own terms. The French Government claimed, however, that it was self-evident that the reservation excluded from the jurisdiction of the Court the question of whether atmospheric nuclear tests were unlawful.[25] Mr. Ellicott, the Solicitor-General of Australia argued for Australia that:

> ... in any event the mere existence of the French reservation upon the assumption that it has an objectively definable content, cannot be taken as creating a situation in which the court is now manifestly without jurisdiction under Article 36(2) ... .[26]

If, however, the defence reservation was to be regarded as self-judging then, argued Mr. Ellicott, it was void as being contrary to the fundamental policy of the Statute of the Court.[27]

The Court accepted Mr. Ellicott's view as indicating that a dispute over jurisdiction existed:

> Whereas in its oral observations the Government of Australia maintained *inter alia* ... that if the reservations in paragraph 3 of the French declaration of 20 May 1966 relating to "disputes concerning activities connected with the national defence" is to be regarded as one having an objective content, it is questionable whether nuclear weapon development falls

24. "... disputes concerning activities connected with the national defence."
25. [1974] ICJ Pleadings, Vol. I, P.S. 21, May 1973, p. 208.
26. Ibid.
27. Ibid.

within the concept of national defence; that if this reservation is to be regarded as a self-judging reservation, it is invalid, and in consequence France is bound by the terms of that declaration unqualified by the reservations in question; ....[28]

Thus, the Court found that it was not manifestly incompetent and granted the interim measures sought by New Zealand and Australia.[29] But the following year, it dismissed the Case on other grounds.[30] So it never did adjudicate upon the content of this reservation.

The defence reservation was not self-judging on its own terms. It would have been self-judging only if the Court had been willing to accept the view that it endowed France with such an unlimited margin of appreciation as to what its defence needs were that the matter was incapable of objective assessment by anyone else. That was the basis of the French argument and it was apparently supported by Judges Forster[31] and Ignacio-Pinto.[32] Other judges refrained from addressing themselves to the validity or meaning of the defence reservation.

A reservation of matters connected with national security or *ordre publique* might also fall into the category of implicity self-judging reservations.

But the power to determine the extent of the margin of appreciation enjoyed by a declarant remains with the Court. The Court might have decided in the end that it would not question France's appreciation of its own defence needs. On the other hand, the Court might have said that the reservation did not leave France with the margin of appreciation which it claimed for itself. But either way it would have been a decision of the Court. So to this extent, the self-defence reservation is wholly consistent with Article 36(6) of the Statute. Thus, there is a fundamental distinction between reservations which may be implicitly self-judging and those which purport to be explicitly self-judging.

---

28. *Nuclear Test Case [Australia v. France]* [1972] ICJ 99, 102.
29. [1973] ICJ 99 and 135.
30. [1974] ICJ 253 and 457.
31. Id. at 112-113.
32. Id. at 129-130.

Explicitly self-judging reservations

United States policy prior to Connally. The Connally Reservation did not spring newborn from the United States Senate like Minerva from the head of Jove. It was rather a consistent practice of the United States Senate to attach self-judging reservations to American legal obligations. Examples have been provided by Judge Lauterpacht in the *Interhandel Case.* [33] Often these stipulations took the form of a requirement that any "special agreement" concluded pursuant to an Arbitral Treaty would itself require the advice and consent of 2/3 of the United States Senate.

Perhaps the most notorious example of a U.S. self-judging reservation was the Lodge Reservation to the Treaty of Versailles. Approved by the Senate on November 13, 1919, it reserved to the United States "exclusively the right to decide what questions are within its domestic jurisdiction". [34]

In 1926, the question of adherence to the Protocol of Signature of the Permanent Court of International Justice came before the United States Senate. On January 27 of that year, the Senate passed a Resolution [35] advising and consenting to the Protocol of Signaure. It did not accept the Optional Clause. It also formulated the additional reservation that recourse to the Court should not "imply a relinquishment by the United States of its traditional attitudes toward purely American questions". [36]

Even though the Protocol of Accession drawn up in Geneva in 1929 endeavoured to meet the Senate's conditions, the Senate did not consider it until 1935 at which time the resolution failed to receive the necessary two-thirds vote. [37]

Chapter VIII, Section A, paragraph 7 of the Dumbarton Oaks proposals provided that arrangements pertaining to pacific settlement of disputes by the United Nations shall not "apply to situa-

---

33. [1959] ICJ 5, 107-111 [D.O. Lauterpacht]. See also Finch, E.H., "United States Policy Regarding Compulsory Arbitration", 46 ABAJ 852 (1960); Preuss, "The International Court, The Senate and Matters of Domestic Jurisdiction", 40 AJIL 720, 722-723 (1946).
34. *Interhandel*, id. at 109.
35. S. Res. 5, 69th Cong. 1st Sess. (January 27, 1926).
36. 20 AJIL Supp. 73, 74 (1926).
37. Hudson, "The United States Senate and the World Court", 29 AJIL 301, 304 (1935).

tions or disputes arising out of matters which by international law are solely within the domestic jurisdiction of the state concerned".

Neither the United States nor the U.S.S.R. were willing to allow either the United Nations or the International Court of Justice to require them to resort to judicial settlement of matters which they believed lay essentially within their jurisdiction.[38]

This reluctance found expression in Article 2, paragraph 7 of the United Nations Charter and in their resistance to proposals to make the jurisdiction of the International Court of Justice compulsory.[39]

Article 2, paragraph 7 of the United Nations Charter says:

> Nothing contained in the present Charter shall authorise the United Nations to intervene in matters which are *essentially* within the domestic jurisdiction of any State or shall require the Members to submit such matters to settlement under the present Charter; but this principle shall not prejudice the application of enforcement measures under Chapter VII [emphasis added].

This provision may be contrasted with Article 15, paragraph 8 of the League of Nations Covenant which spoke of disputes *"solely* within the domestic jurisdiction" of parties to a dispute. The word "solely" was repeated in the Dumbarton Oaks proposal.

Senate debates on the Connally Amendment. A resolution to accept the compulsory jurisdiction of the International Court of Justice was originally introduced by Senator Wayne Morse of Oregon on July 28, 1945, the day on which the Senate approved the United Nations Charter and the Statute of the Court.[40] It contained a domestic jurisdiction reservation excluding from the competence of the Court "disputes with regard to questions which by international law fall exclusively within the jurisdiction of the United States". But it was not considered by the Senate in that Session.

---

38. Padelford, "The Composition of the International Court of Justice: Background and Practice" in K. Deutsch and S. Hoffman (eds.), *Relevance in International Law: Essays in Honour of Leo Gross* (1968), p. 219 at p. 223.
39. Supra Ch. 3, notes 24-25 and accompanying text.
40. S.Res. 160, 91 Cong. Res. 8164.

On November 28, 1945, Senator Morse reintroduced his resolution with bipartisan support. Reservation (b) excluded "disputes with regard to matters which are essentially within the domestic jurisdiction of the United States". Presumably the word "essentially" replaced the word "exclusively" to bring the resolution into line with Article 2(7) of the United Nations Charter.[41]

The resolution was referred to the Committee on Foreign Relations. On June 12, 1946, the Chairman, Senator Tom Connally, appointed a Subcommittee under the Chairmanship of Senator Thomas of Utah[42] which held hearings on July 11, 12 and 15 with Senator Morse and a large number of other witnesses appearing and testifying.

The Subcommittee had before it a "Memorandum of John Foster Dulles concerning Acceptance by the United States of the Compulsory Jurisdiction of the International Court of Justice of July 10, 1946".[43] Mr. Dulles pointed out that it would be unnecessary "to stipulate who decides what is domestic" if the proposed declaration said that the Court could not decide a case involving the United States unless the law to be applied was based on a treaty to which the United States was a party or unless the parties agreed in advance on what principles of international law should be applied by the Court. Thus:

> With cavalier disregard for the institutional developments of 75 years in the judicial settlement of international legal disputes, Mr. Dulles favoured turning the clock back to the *Alabama Arbitration* of 1872 as a precedent, where the parties first negotiated a treaty establishing the law to be applied before going to Court.[44]

A proposal before the Committee to allow the United States to accept or reject the Court's jurisdiction on a case by case basis

---

41. See supra note 21 at 306.
42. *Hearings Before a Subcommittee of the Committee on Foreign Relations, U.S. Senate*, 79th Cong., 2d Sess. on S.Res. 196, July 11, 12 and 15, 1946.
43. Printed id. at pp. 43-45. Mr. Dulles was not yet United States Secretary of State. He was appointed by President Eisenhower in 1953.
44. Supra note 21 at 312. See also Hudson, M.O., "The World Court: America's Declaration Accepting Jurisdiction", 32 ABAJ 832, 895-896 (1946).

was unanimously rejected by all members of the Committee including Senator Connally.[45] A self-judging reservation (similar to
the Connally Amendment) proposed by Senator Austin of
Vermont was also rejected.[46] On July 17 and 24 the Subcommittee reported its findings to the Senate Foreign Relations Committee. By a unanimous vote on July 24, the Committee reported
the Bill back to the Senate for favourable action. The Report of
the Foreign Relations Committee said:

> The Committee therefore decided that a reservation of the
> right of decision as to what are matters essentially within the
> domestic jurisdiction would tend to defeat the purposes
> which it is hoped to achieve by means of the proposed dele-
> gation as well as the purposes of article 36, paragraphs 2 and
> 6 of the Statute of the Court.[47]

On August 1, 1946, Senator Thomas asked for the unanimous consent of the Senate that the Senate proceed to consideration of
S.Res.196.[48] There were no objections and the Senate did so.

In the course of his introductory remarks, Senator Thomas
noted an inconsistency between the jurisdiction of the Security
Council and the Court:

> Under the terms of the Charter the Council is authorised to
> take cognizance of any dispute or situation which is likely to
> endanger peace and security. In a sense it may be said that its
> jurisdiction over political disputes is compulsory and no state
> can refuse a summons by the Council to appear before it. The
> court, on the other hand has jurisdiction only over those legal
> cases which the parties, of their own volition, refer to it for a
> settlement. *A state may thus ignore the summons of the
> court* [emphasis added]. It may say, in effect, "we believe in
> the process of judicial settlement, but in this particular case
> our arguments are weak. Since the chance of securing a
> favourable opinion are not good, we would prefer not to sub-

---

45. Rhyne, "An Effective World Court is Essential", 46 ABAJ 749, 750 (1960).
46. Supra note 18 at p. 11624.
47. Ibid.; Senate Report No. 1835 to accompany S.Res. 196; 79th Cong. 2d Sess.,
pp. 4-5.
48. Id. at p. 10613.

mit to the jurisdiction of the court". [...]

To be sure, the United States has been a member of the court ever since the United Nations Charter went into effect. But membership in itself is only a half hearted beginning. If the member states can flout the court and can refuse to submit their differences to it, a regime of law in the international community can never be realised.[49]

The tenor of his remarks and the circumstances of his making them seem to indicate that he viewed the Optional Clause as a means by which States could relinquish their ability to flout the Court.

He also pointed out that the compulsory jurisdiction of the Court was limited to the four categories of dispute mentioned in Article 36(2).

He assured the Senators that:

The declaration would not confer upon the court jurisdiction over matters which are essentially within the domestic jurisdiction of the United States. This limitation is in conformity with the principle expressed in article 2 of the Charter....[50]

He noted that concern had been expressed that the Court might be given jurisdiction over controversies involving domestic issues such as immigration and trade barriers.

These are vital matters over which the sovereign state has traditionally exercised complete control and we certainly would not want the court or any other international agency to order us to admit twenty or fifty million additional immigrants to our shores.[51]

"The resolution" he said "clearly safeguards our national interests on this point":

Moreover, I would remind you, Mr. President, that it is the function of the court, under the compulsory jurisdiction

49. Id. at p. 10614.
50. Id. at p. 10615.
51. Ibid.

clause, to decide cases in accordance with the rules of international law. Clearly, therefore, it would be impossible to act since there is no international law dealing with the subject of immigration. That is a matter which we have often dealt with in the Senate and we have never had to take account of the international rights and duties of other states.[52]

The tariff is another case in point. There would only be international law on the subject if the United States were to deliberately enter into a treaty about the matter.

The question of who is to judge whether a dispute is essentially domestic was first raised by Senator Donnell of Missouri. After a speech by Senator Wiley of Wisconsin supporting the Declaration, Senator Donnell asked him:

> Suppose that the court itself should take the position that a specific question presented to it was not a matter essentially within the domestic jurisdiction of the United States. Is it the judgment of the Senator that ... article 36 of the statute of the court ... can be interpreted as meaning that the court could decide whether or not the specific matter in controversy were one which was essentially within the domestic jurisdiction of the United States, or whether the United States itself could undertake to make that determination? [...]
> My question is this: If a particular question comes before the court and the United States says that the matter involved is essentially within the domestic jurisdiction of the United States, does the Court of International Justice, ... have the right to determine whether the matter is or is not one essentially within the domestic jurisdiction of the United States?[53]

Mr. Wiley responded by reading Article 2(7) of the United Nations Charter. He felt that the words "Nothing contained in the present Charter ... shall require the members to submit such matters to settlement" would justify the United States in taking the position that it was not compelled to submit the controversy:

52. Ibid.
53. Id. at pp. 10621-10622.

My personal opinion is that if the question were a close one
and the United States pleaded that the court did not have
jurisdiction, the question would be presented of whether or
not we would abide by the judicial process. ... If the court
held against the United States then the question of what
power the court had to enforce its judgment would arise.[54]

This point of view was amplified by Senator Austin. In a statement, which Lawrence Preuss described as "typically Austinian"[55]
he said:

Mr. President, this court does not have a sheriff and does not
have the power of execution. The only power this court has
is moral power, and if the situation should arise to which the
distinguished Senator from Wisconsin has alluded, that a
state, a party, has been ruled against when it raised the question of jurisdiction, and that state has held up its head and
said, "Notwithstanding the decision we know from our history, and our experience, and existing conditions that this is
a question which is purely domestic, and that we will disregard the decision of the court," that state has the final
decision instead of the court. The court cannot execute its
judgment. What that state has done by the convention is to
say that it will agree to the decisions of the court that are
within the four corners of the convention, and one of those
corners is that the court has no jurisdiction of domestic
affairs, and that a state may stand up in all honour and say,
"we will not carry out the decision of the court on a matter
that is purely domestic".[56]

Senator Connally ratified this proposed contumacy:

I have more or less enjoyed the remarks of the Senator from
Vermont to the effect that in case the court should decide
that a question which the United States considered to be
domestic was nondomestic and international we would be

54. Id. at p. 10622.
55. Supra note 33 at 722, note 9.
56. Supra note 18 at p. 10624.

justified as I agree, in defying the court. I submit an amendment to settle this question.[57]

The amendment which he then submitted was the one which we are discussing.

Senator Austin pointed out that this was the very amendment which he, Senator Austin, had offered in the Subcommittee and which had not been accepted.[58]

Senator Donnell asked Senator Connally if he disagreed with the observation of the Foreign Relations Committee to the effect that this provision would tend to defeat the purpose of Article 36(2).[59]

He replied:

> I do not agree with that. I think we have the right to adhere 100 per cent, if we choose, and we have the right not to adhere at all. Therefore, as between those two extremes, we have a perfect right to adopt an amendment of this character, because the Charter provides that domestic questions may not be considered. The Charter provides that the United Nations have no jurisdiction over domestic questions. But under the Charter the court might decide that immigration was an international question. It might decide that tariffs were an international question. It might decide that navigation of the Panama Canal was an international question. It is pretty close to it. It might decide that the regulation of tolls through the Canal was an international question.[60]

Senator Millikin of Colorado asked Senator Thomas whether he considered the Connally Amendment to be consistent with the provisions of the Charter.[61] He replied:

> Mr. President, the amendment offered by the Senator from Texas will have to be changed. As it is worded, I think it would be inconsistent with our resolution. I have already

57. Ibid.
58. Ibid.
59. Supra note 47 and accompanying text.
60. Supra note 18 at p. 10624.
61. Id. at p. 10625.

stated that for us to adopt an amendment which would be inconsistent with the Charter would cause us to go back upon our pledged word — and that would be a very bad thing to do of course.

The question of the jurisdiction of the court in the case of domestic issues is very important and very broad. The amendment of the Senator from Texas should it be adopted, would go so far as to cause a political institution such as the Government of the United States or the Congress of the United States, if it spoke on this question, to make a political decision in regard to what is purely a legal matter, then of course the amendment would be out of harmony with the fundamental principles relating to the way in which the court operates. For example, if the court does not have jurisdiction as to questions which are purely legal, then of course the court is not a court of justice, but it becomes a political institution — the very thing we are opposed to having it be.[62]

He felt that the principle that "a political institution does not interfere with a legal prerogative" was "the grandest principle of the United States Government".[63]

Senator Millikin then asked him whether the Amendment was a valid one.[64] He replied that he thought it would be a contradiction of compulsory jurisdiction itself.[65]

Senator Morse opposed the Amendment. He wanted it clearly understood:

that giving the court jurisdiction to determine whether an issue is an international-law issue is exactly what the resolution proposes to do.[66] [...]
Why should we fear the Court's jurisdiction? I submit that its jurisdiction is clearly limited by the United Nations Charter.[67]

Although he was opposed to the amendment, he was adamant that

62. Id. at pp. 10625-10626.
63. Id. at p. 10626.
64. Ibid.
65. Ibid.
66. Id. at p. 10629.
67. Id. at p. 10630

even if it were adopted "great progress would have been made by the United States in accepting the resolution".[68]

The debate continued on August 2. Senator Morse repeated his insistence that the Connally Amendment would not cripple the Declaration.

But he revealed that he too was not above refusing to abide by the decisions of the International Court of Justice:

> ... if the resolution ... is adopted by the Senate, without including the amendment proposed by the Senator from Texas, and the World Court should, in a given case, render a decision which involved not a question of international law but a domestic issue, the United States would have the right under article 94 of the United Nations Charter to raise that point and refuse to abide by the decision of the World Court.[69]

Article 94 provides:

> (1) Each Member of the United Nations undertakes to comply with the decision of the International Court of Justice in any case in which it is a party.
> (2) If any party to a case fails to perform the obligatons incumbent upon it under a judgment rendered by the Court, the other party may have recourse to the Security Council, which may, if it deems necessary, make recommendations or decide upon measures to be taken to give effect to the judgment.

Article 94 appears to constitute a clear prohibition of contumacy. It says that the decisions of the Court shall be complied with not that they shall be complied with if the parties agree. Yet Senator Morse seemed to be relying on the fact that the United States veto power could be used to frustrate any enforcement action which the Security Council might contemplate.[70]

Senator Millikin objected that a United States veto power over its judicial commitments would stultify its commitment to be

68. Ibid.
69. Id. at p. 10684.
70. Id. at p. 10689.

134

ruled by law rather than by political decisions.[71] Senator Morse
said that reference to the Security Council was a form of appeal. It
was not the sort of appeal that lawyers usually think of but:

> ... if article 94 means ... there is guaranteed to the Signato-
> ries the right to say to the Security Council; "A decision has
> been rendered against us, but see how bad the decision is. It
> is over a clear domestic issue, and not an international issue"
> — in that sense it is a court of appeal.[72]

Senator Millikin insisted that there was nothing in the Court's
Statute which contemplated a political reversal of its decision
which would be the effect of a Security Council reversal of a
decision of the Court.[73]

In this exchange Senator Millikin, a supporter of the Connally
Amendment and, as we shall see, an even more stringent amendment, had very much the better of the argument. Article 94 does
not contemplate a reversal of the Court's decision even though it
does allow a Permanent Member of the Security Council to
frustrate enforcement by means of a veto. He might have added,
that if it was a form of appeal, it was one which was available only
to some litigants — permanent Members of the Security Council.

Senator Millikin's remarks and the remarks of Senator Connally
in introducing the Amendment indicate that the Amendment was
viewed as an alternative to contumacy.[74]

Nevertheless, Senator Millikin overlooked the fact that allowing
the United States Government to determine that a matter is essentially one of domestic jurisdiction would also amount to placing
responsibility for a legal decision in the hands of a political body.
The only difference between his view and Senator Morse's was
that he would have the political body preempt, rather than review
the legal decision. Senator Morse had made that point himself in
an earlier speech.[75]

Later, Senator Donnell asked Senator Morse point blank
whether the Connally Amendment violated Article 36(6) of the

71. Ibid.
72. Ibid.
73. Ibid.
74. See supra note 57 and accompanying text.
75. Supra note 18 at p. 10684.

Statute. Senator Morse replied that he thought that it was not a violation of "any section, paragraph, sentence, clause, word, comma or period" of the United Nations Charter:

> In my judgment there would not be any conflict because I think article 36 of the Charter makes very clear that there is reserved to the individual signatories the right to file a so-called obligatory declaration or not to file it, according to their discretion, and that inherent and implied in that right on the part of the signatories, when they do file a declaration accepting the obligatory jurisdiction of the court, to place on the jurisdiction such conditions as they see fit to place. [...]
> In other words, it can go all the way, or 75 per cent of the way, or 15 per cent of the way or zero.[76]

But perhaps Senator Morse's belief that the Connally Amendment would not wreck the Declaration rested more than anything else on his confidence in the good faith of the United States:

> ... it is inconceivable that this country would ever hide behind a subterfuge or alibi and claim an international law issue to be a domestic issue.
> The United States will never take the position that an issue which clearly is not a domestic issue shall not be determined by the World Court once we accept the obligatory jurisdiction of the World Court over purely international law issues. If we should take such an unconscionable position, it is perfectly clear that the good faith of this country would be clearly challenged by the other nations of the world.[77]

But he did warn that, because of the principle of reciprocity, the Connally Amendment could work to the detriment of the United States.[78]

Other Senators, such as Senator Ferguson of Michigan simply could not see the Amendment as being inconsistent with Article 36(6):

76. Id. at p. 10690.
77. Id. at p. 10685.
78. Id. at p. 10691. See also Gambrell, "The World Court and the Connally Amendment", 47 ABAJ 57, 59-60 (1961).

... we are saying clearly and without equivocation exactly what we are accepting, and as domestic matters are not covered by the jurisdiction of the court we can leave no doubt that we are going wholeheartedly into the court; that we are submitting all matters of international relations, as provided for in section 36 of the Statute establishing the court; but that we have no intention of submitting, and it is not even the intention of the court, to have us submit, purely domestic questions.[79]

As Preuss points out, he apparently assumed that matters of domestic jurisdiction could be infallibly recognised and excluded from the competence of the Court without a preliminary legal examination as to whether the subject matter of a dispute actually is within the exclusive jurisdiction of the State concerned.[80]

The most eloquent opponent of the Connally Amendment was Senator Pepper of Florida. He pointed quite clearly to its inconsistency with the principle *nemo judex in sua causa*:

... to add [a reservation] that the United States Government is to be the sole judge of its own interest in the matter, it seems to me flies, first into the very teeth of the purpose and concept of the court, and in the second place, into violent conflict with subparagraph 6 of article 36.... [...]
Mr. President, it did not say, "It shall be settled by the State which is a signatory power to the Charter and has given compulsory jurisdiction to the Court".
Not only that, but if there is anything fundamental in the law, it is that one cannot be a judge in his own cause. Yet here we are laying down in one reservation that the World Court shall not have jurisdiction in domestic matters, and in the second place that we will decide whether or not a matter is domestic.[81]

He also warned that other nations would wish to modify their adherence to the compulsory jurisdiction of the Court in the same way.[82]

79. Id. at p. 10696.
80. Preuss, supra note 33 at 726.
81. Supra note 18 at p. 10692.
82. Id. at p. 10694.

He concluded:

> America withheld its assent to the World Court a decade or
> more ago, and we have paid in blood and treasure for that
> mistake. The United States of America tried to place reserva-
> tions in the League treaty, and we have paid in broad rivers
> of blood and uncountable treasure for those reservations. We
> have thus far gone forward so magnificiently, and have
> entered so wonderfully into the spirit of this great new enter-
> prise for peace that, in my judgment we should give the
> world encouragement, confidence and hope by extending full
> faith and credit to this great court. We should not be the first
> nation to write the insidious question mark above its author-
> ity, and the first to violate the fundamental concept of any
> law, that no litigant shall decide his own case.[83]

The Connally Amendment was passed by a vote of 51-12-33.[84]

After the vote, Senator Millikin introduced another Amendment essentially incorporating proposals in the Dulles Memorandum to the effect that the United States would only agree to the
jurisdiction of the Court in disputes where the law necessary for
decision was found in existing treaties and conventions to which
the United States was a party or where it had agreed to the applicable principles of international law.[85] This proposal was notionally even more offensive to the Statute than the Connally Reservation in that it purported to restrict the law which the court was to
apply. It was defeated by a vote of 11-49-36.[86]

The Declaration was passed by the Senate on August 2, 1946 by
a vote of 60-2-34.[87] It was promulgated by President Truman on
August 14, 1946.[88]

If we may draw any conclusions from the legislative history of
the Connally Amendment, we may observe that, while the Senators were aware of Article 36(6), a great many of them including
Senator Morse did not believe that the reservation was inconsistent

---

83. Ibid.
84. Id. at p. 10697.
85. Id. at p. 10698.
86. Id. at p. 10705.
87. Id. at pp. 10705-10706.
88. TIAS No. 1598; See Collier, "Judicial World Supremacy and The Connally
Reservation", 47 ABAJ 68 (1961).

with that Article. Many of them were seeking to erect safeguards against a possible bad faith decision by the Court in which it would somehow decide that a purely domestic matter was an international dispute. Even Senator Morse, possibly to reassure the distrustful, was prepared to play this game by suggesting that the United States could defy the Court and veto its decision in the Security Council using the Council as a sort of Court of Appeal.

Supporters of the Connally Amendment viewed it as an alternative to contumacy and displayed an equal, if not greater, distrust in the Court's good faith.

Generally, the Senate's distrust of the Court can be characterised in the words of Sir Hersch Lauterpacht as "a vague apprehension of danger as exhibited in this nervous quest for security from the law"[89] when he prophesied in 1930 that such reservations might put declarant States in the position of substituting their judgment for that of the Court.[90]

By contrast, the Senators displayed a touching confidence in the good faith of the United States Government. They seemed certain that the United States Government would make an almost judicial decision on whether a dispute was domestic or international. But however honourable a Government might be, when the scope of such a reservation is left to unilateral determination, political realities may make it difficult to concede jurisdiction.[91] "[N]ationalist sentiment or the dogma of sovereignty"[92] are likely to prevail.

Furthermore, judicial impartiality requires the Court to treat a declaration on its face and not to make background assumptions about the way in which the United States or any other State with a similar reservation will exercise its self-assumed power of unilateral determination.

Reaction to the Connally Amendment was mixed. As predicted, the example of the United States was followed by France and Mexico in 1947, Liberia in 1952, South Africa in 1955, India in 1956, Pakistan.and The Sudan in 1957, Malawi in 1966 and the

89. "The British Reservations to the Optional Clause" (1930) 10 Economica 137, 159.

90. Id. at 148-155.

91. Rogers, "United States 'Automatic' Reservation to the Optional Clause Jurisdiction of the ICJ" (1958) 7 ICLQ 758, 760.

92. See Hudson, M.O., "The New Arbitration Treaty with France", 22 AJIL 371 (1938).

Philippines in 1971. In 1958, the United Kingdom filed a Declaration with a different sort of explicity self-judging reservation. It excluded:

> ... questions which in the opinion of the Government of the United Kingdom affect the national security of the United Kingdom or any of its dependent territories.

Opposition was expressed at the highest levels. On April 29, 1954, the *Institut de Droit International* unanimously passed a *voeu* expressing the hope that States filing declarations accepting compulsory jurisdiction would leave it to the Court to decide whether the reservation is applicable.[93]

In the United States, President Eisenhower called for the repeal in successive State of the Union Messages in 1959[94] and 1960.[95] In 1959, Senator Humphrey of Minnesota introduced a resolution calling for its withdrawal[96] which received the support of the American Bar Association House of Delegates.[97]

But in hearings on the Resolution, Senator Connally continued to express his fear that such matters as the Panama Canal, immigration and tariffs might be considered "international" by the Court.[98] Ultimately, Senator Humphrey's attempt was unsuccessful.[99]

In the late 1950s and early 1960s three cases involving explicit self-judging reservations came before the International Court of Justice.

The Norwegian Loans Case

The *Norwegian Loans Case* involved Norwegian laws suspending the "gold clauses" in certain bonds which the Government of Norway had sold to French nationals.

93. (1954-II) 45 *Annuaire de l'Institut de Droit International* 197, 300.
94. 105 Cong. Rec. p. 362 (1959).
95. 106 Cong. Rec. p. 144 (1960).
96. S.Res. 94, 86th Cong. 1st Sess. (1959).
97. Ober, "The Connally Reservation and National Security", 47 ABAJ 63 (1961).
98. Senate Hearings on S.Res. 94 before the Senate Foreign Relations Committee, 86th Cong., 2d Sess. 303-304 (January 20, 1960).
99. For a fuller discussion see Ragg, "The Reservation Power and the Connally Amendment", 11 NYUJIL & P 323, 350-355 (1978).

140

The French Application of July 5, 1955, instituted proceedings on behalf of those nationals.[100]

On the merits, France asked the Court to adjudge and declare that the loans were international loans which could only be discharged by payment in gold value at the date of repayment[101] and that express conditions of performance in an undertaking with foreign nationals could not be unilaterally modified by a State without consultation with those nationals.[102] The French Government also objected that Danish and Swedish bondholders were receiving more favourable treatment than French bondholders.[103] The Norwegian Government insisted that the bondholders' claims were solely within the jurisdiction of the Norwegian Courts and involved solely the interpretation of Norwegian law.[104]

The Norwegian Declaration of November 16, 1946, read:

> Au nom du Gouvernement norvégien, je déclare que la Norvège reconnaît comme obligatoire de plein droit, et sans convention spécial, à l'égard de tout autre État acceptant la même obligation, c'est-à-dire sous condition de réciprocité, la juridiction de la Cour International de Justice, en application de l'article 36, paragraphe 2, du Statut de la Cour, pour un période de dix ans à dater du 3 octobre 1946.[105]

It contained no domestic jurisdiction reservation. The French Declaration of March 1, 1949, read in pertinent part:

> Cette déclaration ne s'applique pas aux différends relatifs à des affaires que relèvent essentiellement de la compétence nationale telle qu'elle est entendu par le Gouvernement de la République français.[106]

100. [1957] ICJ 8, 11.
101. Id. at 20.
102. Id. at 16.
103. Id. at 15.
104. Id. at 20.
105. Id. at 21. "I declare on behalf of the Norwegian Government that Norway recognizes as compulsory *ipso facto* and without special agreement, in relation to any other State accepting the same obligation, that is to say, on condition of reciprocity, the jurisdiction of the International Court of Justice in conformity with Article 36, paragraph 2, of the Statute of the Court, for a period of ten years as from 3rd October 1946."
106. Ibid. This declaration does not apply to differences relating to matters which are essentially within the national jurisdiction as understood by the Government of the French Republic.

It was an explicitly self-judging clause.

Norway interposed four Preliminary Objections. The second and third related to jurisdiction *ratione temporis*. The fourth related to non-exhaustion of local remedies. The first one was summarised by the Court as:

> L'objet du différend tel qu'il est dans la requête du Gouvernement français ..., relève du droit interne et non du droit international, alors que la juridiction obligatoire de la Cour vis-à-vis des parties en cause est limitée, par leurs declarations ..., aux différends de droit international.[107]

In explaining Objection No. 1, the Norwegian Government said of its contention that the question was a matter of domestic jurisdiction:

> Aucun doute n'est possible sur ce point. S'il en pouvait cependant subsister, le Gouvernement norvégien se prévaudrait des réserves formulées par le Gouvernement français dans sa déclaration... . En vertu du principe de réciprocité consacré par l'article 36, No 2, du Statut de la Cour, et précisé dans la declaration norvégienne..., le Gouvernement norvégien ne peut être lié, en effet, vis-à-vis du Gouvernement français, par des engagements plus étendus ou plus rigoreux que ceux qui ont été pris par ce dernier.[108]

The Court chose to see the first Norwegian Objection as consisting of two parts. The first simply maintained that the subject matter of the reservation was within the exclusive domain of Norwegian Municipal Law. But the second part involved the French Declaration, on the basis of reciprocity, in order to bar the French claim.

107. Id. at 13. The subject of the dispute, as defined in the Application of the French Government, ... is within the domain of municipal law and not of international law, whereas the compulsory jurisdiction of the Court in relation to the Parties involved is restricted, by their Declarations ... to disputes concerning international law.
108. Id. at 23; [1957] ICJ Pleadings, p. 129. "There can be no possible doubt on this point. If, however, there should still be some doubt, the Norwegian Government would rely upon the reservations made by the French Government in its Declaration of March 1st, 1949. By virtue of the principle of reciprocity, which is embodied in Article 36, paragraph 2, of the Statute of the Court and which has been clearly expressed in the Norwegian Declaration, ... the Norwegian Government cannot be bound, *vis-à-vis* the French Government, by undertakings which are either broader or stricter than those given by the latter Government."

France objected that:

> ... entre la France et la Norvège, il existe un traité qui fait du règlement de toute dette contractuelle un affaire relevant du droit international. Les deux États ne peuvent donc en cette matière parler de compétence nationale.[109]

The treaty referred to was the Second Hague Convention of 1907 on the limitation of force for the recovery of contract debts.

Ironically, in the light of later developments,[110] France also referred to the General Act for Pacific Settlement of Disputes of 1928 to which Norway was also a party. But it did not attempt to found the jurisdiction of the Court on that treaty. In the Court's view, if France had intended to proceed on that basis it would have said so.[111]

The Court proceeded to consider the second ground of the first preliminary objection. It felt that when there were two unilateral declarations, it had jurisdiction only to the extent that the declarations coincided in conferring it. Thus the Court had to rely on the narrower acceptance expressed by France[112] and it dismissed the French application.[113]

But it is important to note that the Court explicitly refrained from deciding whether the French Reservation was consistent with *"le fait d'assumer une obligation juridique"* and whether it was compatible with Article 36(6) of the Statute.[114] It noted that the validity of the reservation had not been questioned by Norway and could not be questioned by France. Without prejudging the question the Court gave effect to the reservation as it stood and as the parties considered it.[115] Thus the Court accomplished the neat trick of applying the reservation without ruling on its validity.

Vice President Badawi felt that the dispute was in the domain

109. Id. at 24; [1957] ICJ Pleadings, p. 178. "Between France and Norway, there exists a treaty which makes the payment of any contractual debt a question of international law. In this connection the two States cannot therefore speak of domestic jurisdiction."
110. See Ch. 2, note 147 and accompanying text.
111. Supra note 100 at 24-25.
112. Id. at 23.
113. Id. at 27. See Schlesinger, "The Connally Amendment – Amelioration By Interpretation", 48 Va.L.Rev. 685, 688 (1962).
114. Id. at 26.
115. Id. at 27.

of municipal law. Hence the Court should not have used the self-judging reservation, a reservation which he did not like because it was a subjective attempt to settle what he considered to be an objective question.[116]

Judge Sir Hersch Lauterpacht concurred in the result. Therefore his famous opinion was technically a Separate Opinion but he strongly dissented from the Court's reasoning. He agreed that the Court was incompetent to decide on the merits of the case. But because of the self-judging reservation he found that the French Declaration was invalid. That, he claimed, was the true reason why the Court had no jurisdiction.[117]

He thought that this particular dispute was indeed related to international law. National legislation, even currency legislation can be contrary to international obligations where it involves the property rights of aliens:

> It is not enough for a State to bring a matter under the protective umbrella of its own legislation, possibly of a predatory character, in order to shelter it effectively from any control by international law.[118]

He thought that the only Norwegian Preliminary Objection that had any validity was the one relating to the exhaustion of local remedies.[119] But the French Reservation was "an instrument incapable of producing legal effects" for two reasons:

a. It was contrary to the Statute of the Court, and

b. The existence of the obligation was dependent upon the determination by the Government accepting the Optional Clause, consequently it did not amount to the acceptance of a legal obligation.[120]

> The French reservation is ... not only contrary to one of the fundamental principles of international — and national — jurisprudence according to which it is within the inherent power of a tribunal to interpret the text establishing its juris-

116. Id. at 79.
117. Id. at 34.
118. Id. at 37.
119. Id. at 43.
120. Id. at 44.

diction. It is also contrary to a clear specific provision in the Statute of the Court as well as to the general Articles 1 and 92 of the Statute and of the Charter respectively which require the Court to function in accordance with its Statute.[121]

The French Reservation was simply an attempt to unilaterally alter the Court's Statute. "What would be the position" he asked, "if the Court were to exclude the operation of Article 36(6) not only with regard to one reservation but with regard to all reservations?" What if it were to exclude other provisions by requiring oral proceedings to be in secret or providing that the Court's judgment would only be binding if it were unanimous? What if judges of a certain nationality or nationalities were to be excluded?[122] What if the Court were allowed to apply only "treaties and customs[123] in the sense that it shall not be authorised to apply general principles of law as recognised by civilised States"?[124]

As to the general validity of the Reservation, an obligation which purports to operate only to the extent that the obligor considers that it does, is, in effect, no obligation because a valid instrument must "evidence an intention to create reciprocal rights and obligations".[125] He called this principle "self-evident as a matter of juridical principle as well as a general principle of law recognised by civilised nations".

Norway, in its Preliminary Objections, had advanced the view put by M. Maurice Bourquin, Professor of Law at the University of Geneva:

> Il est certain que pareille réserve doit être interprétée de bonne foi et qu'un gouvernement qui se retrancherait derrière elle pour dénier compétence à la Cour dans un cas où il ne s'agirait manifestement pas d'une "affaire relevant essentiellement de la compétence national" commettrait un abus de droit, devant lequel la Cour ne serait pas désarmée.[126]

121. Ibid.

122. Is this not the effect of the Chamber selected to decide the *Case of Delimitation of the Maritime Boundary in the Gulf of Maine Area*? See ICJ Communique 82/2 (January 27, 1982).

123. See the proposed Millikin Amendment supra notes 84 and 85 and accompanying text.

124. Supra note 100 at 44-45.

125. Id. at 48-49.

126. Id. at 53; Pleadings, supra note 108 at p. 131. Of course, such a reservation must

Judge Lauterpacht disagreed. He thought that the Court "would be arrogating to itself a power which has been expressly denied it".[127] Furthermore, he did not feel that it was certain, in most cases, that a State would be violating the canons of good faith if it were to decide that a dispute came within its domestic jurisdiction.

He canvassed a number of alternatives to treating the entire acceptance as tainted with invalidity; a) severance of the offending words and b) severance of the particular reservation.

The option of severing the reservation only "needed to be mentioned in order to be dismissed". It would mean that the State in question would be deemed not to have made a valid reservation with regard to matters within the domestic jurisdiction.

As to the severance of the particular words, he noted that this would have a somewhat startling outcome in the case in question because it would favour France at Norway's expense.[128] But, what he thought was more important, was that, on examination of its history, the declaration showed that self-judgment was "one of crucial limitations — perhaps the crucial limitation of the obligation".[129]

He criticised the Court for refusing to consider the validity of the French Reservation. He felt that the declaration was invalid *ab initio*.[130]

In a dissent, Judge Basdevant agreed that Norway was entitled to invoke the French Reservation by reason of reciprocity. But he felt that Norway had waived that right by attempting to prove to the satisfaction of the Court that the matter lay within the domestic jurisdiction.[131] Furthermore, he thought the Court should have considered whether the General Act for the Pacific Settlement of Disputes conferred jurisdiction on the Court.[132]

Judge Guerrero agreed that the reservation had to be considered as devoid of all legal validity both because it conflicted with

---

be interpreted in good faith and should a government seek to rely upon it with a view to denying the jurisdiction of the Court in a case which manifestly did not involve a 'matter which is essentially within the national jurisdiction' it would be committing an *abus de droit* which would not prevent the Court from acting.

127. Id. at 52-53.
128. Id. at 55-56.
129. Id. at 58.
130. Id. at 61.
131. Id. at 76.
132. Id. at 74.

Article 36(6) and because it voided France's main undertaking. Compulsory jurisdiction ceases to be compulsory if it is France and not the Court which holds the power to determine whether the Court has jurisdiction.[133] The problem was whether the unilateral will of one State or the will of the parties before the Court was to prevail over the collective will of States expressed in the Statute of the Court.[134] He concluded that he could not agree that the Court was without jurisdiction when its lack of jurisdiction was founded on an instrument which was contrary to the spirit and letter of the Statute. Although he did not say so, he appeared to favour severance of the offending words.[135]

Judge Read objected that the Norwegian Objection was a highly technical one and that Norway did not rely on it to any significant extent. It had simply made a bald statement that it was convinced that the dispute was "within the domestic jurisdiction" and had then used 134 pages in the rejoinder to argue the international questions involved in the merits of the dispute. Thus, while it did not formally abandon its objection, it could no longer seriously assert that it understood the dispute to be purely domestic.[136]

It was not sufficient for Norway to pretend that it understood or declare that it understood. To maintain its position, it would have to explain the basis for this understanding.[137] Norway itself had taken the position that an attempt to deny the jurisdiction of the Court in a case which manifestly involved an international question would be an *abus de droit*. The issue of discrimination between French nationals and other foreign nationals was clearly a question of international law[138] as was the issue of extraterritoriality.[139]

Practically speaking, it was not possible for an international tribunal "to examine a dispute between two sovereign States on the basis of either good or bad faith". But the basis principle ad-

133. Id. at 68-69.
134. Id. at 69.
135. Id. at 70. But, in a separate essay, Judge Guerrero expressed the opinion that States making self-judging reservations should not be considered as having accepted the compulsory jurisdiction of the Court. Guerrero, "*La Qualification Unilatérale de la Compétence Nationale*", in Constantopouls, et al (ed.), *Grundprobleme des Internationalen Rechts, Festschrift für Jean Spiropoulos* (1957), pp. 207-212.
136. Id. at 93.
137. Id. at 91.
138. Id. at 88.
139. Id. at 95.

vanced by Norway should be accepted. The wording of the declaration means that the respondent State must establish that there is a genuine understanding. It must be reasonably possible to reach the understanding that the dispute was essentially domestic.[140] He conceded that an interpretation which would give the respondant an arbitrary power to settle questions of jurisdiction by simply announcing that it understands the matter to be domestic without regard to the truth or falsity of the assertion would indeed lead to the conclusion that the declaration violated Article 36(6) and was consequently null and void. But such a construction would be absurd or unreasonable.[141] It ran counter to established principles of treaty interpretation that "the words of a treaty must be interpreted in a sense which they would normally have in their context unless such an interpretation would lead to something unreasonable or absurd".[142]

Examining the essential character of the dispute, he concluded that:

> I find it impossible to reach the conclusion that Norway could have reasonably understood that the case was essentially within the Norwegian jurisdiction.[143]

Following the *Norwegian Loans Case* and undoubtedly as a result of the Judgment in the case, France withdrew its self-judging reservation and filed a new declaration on July 10, 1959 replacing the self-judging reservation with an ordinary domestic jurisdiction reservation.[144] India at first withdrew its acceptance entirely. But on September 14, 1959, it filed a new declaration with an ordinary domestic jurisdiction reservation but terminable on notice. On November 26, 1958, the United Kingdom withdrew its self-judging reservation.[145]

---

140. Id. at 94.
141. Id. at 94-95.
142. *Polish Postal Service in Danzig* [1925] PCIJ, Ser. B, No. 11, p. 6 at p. 39; *Competence of the General Assembly Regarding Admission of a State to the United Nations* [1950] ICJ 4, 8. Cf. Vienna Convention on The Law of Treaties, Arts. 31 and 32, UN Doc.A/Conf. (1969); Reprinted 63 AJIL 375 (1969); 8 ILM 679 (1969).
143. Supra note 100 at 95.
144. "International Court of Justice: Optional Clause: Withdrawal of Automatic Reservation by France" (1959) 8 ICLQ 735. On January 2, 1974, following the *Nuclear Test Cases*, France withdrew its acceptance of the Optional Clause completely. [1973-74] ICJYB, p. 149.
145. [1958-59] ICJYB, p. 205.

148

The Interhandel Case

This case involved the right of the United States Government under the U.S. Trading With the Enemy Act of 1917 to seize and sell the shares of the General Aniline and Film Corporation, a company established in the United States by the Swiss firm, Interhandel, which in turn, had been under the control of I.G. Farbenindustrie in Frankfurt. The Swiss Government claimed that German control of Interhandel had ceased. It requested that the United States Government release Interhandel's assets citing a financial agreement, the Washington Accord, between Switzerland, the United States, France and the United Kingdom by which the allies agreed to unblock Swiss assets in return for investigation and liquidation of German assets in Switzerland and for the settlement of the "looted gold" problem.[146]

U.S. authorities refused to comply with a request for release of the shares in GAF.[147] The Swiss Government tried to negotiate a friendly settlement, but the United States claimed that the matter lay exclusively within United States jurisdiction.

The Swiss Government relied on Article 1 of the Treaty of Arbitration and Conciliation between Switzerland and the United States of February 16, 1941 which provided that in the event of disputes between the Contracting Parties, they would resort either to arbitration or conciliation if ordinary diplomatic proceedings between them failed.[148]

Article 5 of the Washington Accord also provided for arbitration in the case of differences of opinion with regard to its application which could not be settled in any other way.[149]

The Swiss Government filed an Application on October 2, 1957 asking the International Court of Justice to adjudge and declare:

1. Que le Gouvernement des États-Unis d'Amérique est tenu de restituer les avoirs de ... [Interhandel] à cette société;
2. Subsidiairement que le différend est de nature à être soumis à la juridiction, à l'arbitrage ou à la conciliation dans les conditions qu'il appartiendra à la Cour de determiner.[150]

146. Swiss Application [1959] ICJ Pleadings, p. 9.
147. Id. at p. 11.
148. Id. at p. 47.
149. Id. at p. 13.
150. Id. at p. 15.

The first two Preliminary Objections of the United States related to jurisdiction *ratione temporis*, the third related to non-exhaustion of local remedies. The fourth objection was divided into two parts:

(a) that the question of the sale and disposition of the shares of GAF had been determined by the United States to be a matter essentially within its domestic jurisdiction;

(b) that matters relating to the seizure and retention of the shares were, according to international law, matters within the domestic jurisdiction of the United States.[151]

Thus the United States invoked the Connally Amendment with respect to the "sale and disposition" of the shares. But, with regard to the seizure and retention of shares, it was willing to allow the Court to decide whether the claim fell within its domestic jurisdiction. The purpose of this was to demonstrate that the United States would not automatically determine, in every case, that the matter was within the domestic jurisdiction. Paradoxically, it weakened Counsel's argument in that it demonstrated that, as far as seizure and retention of the shares was concerned, the United States was prepared to maintain some doubt on the matter. Hence Reservation 4(b) took on the appearance of a question rather than an assertion.

In the Court's order of October 24, 1957, it denied a request by Switzerland for interim measures of protection[152] primarily on the ground that the situation was not sufficiently urgent. But the Court virtually ignored the argument that it had no jurisdiction to indicate interim measures because the United States had unilaterally determined that questions involving the sale and disposition of the shares were within its domestic jurisdiction. The Court simply said that if that contention were maintained, it would hear arguments on the merits.[153]

Judge Wellington Koo, in a Declaration, agreed with the deci-

---

1. that the Government of the United States of America is under an obligation to restore the assets of ... (Interhandel) to that company;
2. in the alternative, that the dispute is one which is fit for submission for judicial settlement, arbitration or conciliation under the conditions which it will be for the Court to determine.
151. [1959] ICJ 5, 11.
152. [1957] ICJ 105.
153. Id. at 109.

sion of the Court. But he was unable to agree with the Court's reasoning. He considered that the United States objection based on the Connally Amendment was well founded. Accordingly, he would have denied the measures on the ground that the Court lacked jurisdiction.[154]

Judge Klaestad was of essentially the same opinion. He felt that, *prima facie*, the Court had no jurisdiction. But he cautioned that such a *prima facie* finding should not prejudge the question of jurisdiction which the Court would have to go into at a later stage.[155]

Judge Lauterpacht, consistently with his position that an automatic reservation is not an acceptance of the Court's jurisdiction, felt that there was no jurisdiction either to indicate provisional measures or to hear the merits of the case.[156]

The Connally Amendment was not the only limitation in the United States Declaration which, we recall, was filed on August 26, 1946. It accepted the jurisdiction only with respect to "disputes hereinafter arising".[157] The Swiss Declaration contained no reservations. The only limitation was a provision that it might be abrogated subject to one year's notice.[158] The Court rejected the first[159] and second[160] Preliminary Objections.

The Court then noted that the Third Objection was an objection to admissibility. It therefore proceeded to consider part (b) of the Fourth Objection which related to the jurisdiction of the Court to consider the case.[161]

Here, the Court, citing the *Case of Nationality Decrees Issued in Turnis and Morocco,*[162] declined to assess the validity of the grounds invoked by the Swiss Government since that would have involved entering the merits of the dispute. It confined itself to considering whether questions relating to the validity and interpretation of those grounds were questions of international law.

It concluded that the matter was one which had to be decided

154. Id. at 113.
155. Id. at 115-116.
156. Id. at 118-119.
157. Supra note 151 at 14.
158. Id. at 15.
159. Id. at 21-22.
160. Id. at 23.
161. Id. at 23-24.
162. [1923] PCIJ, Ser. B, No. 4, p. 7.

in the light of the principles and rules of international law governing the relations between beligerants and neutrals in time of
war.[163] It rejected Preliminary Objection 4(b) by 14–1.[164]

With regard to Preliminary Objection 4(a), Loftus Becker,
Agent for the United States, had argued:

> This determination by the United States is not subject to
> review or approval by any tribunal. It operates to remove
> definitively from the jurisdiction of the Court the matter
> which it determines.[165]

Professor Paul Guggenheim, Co-Agent for the Swiss Government
and Professor at the Law Faculty of the University of Geneva argued:

> Les limites d'une application normale de la réserve dite auto-
> matique sont certes dépassées lorsqu'un État l'invoque dans un
> domaine qui est totalement étranger, au domaine réservé.[166]

Thus the legal issue concerning the Court's powers under the
Connally Amendment was clearly drawn. But the Court ducked
the issue. It decided not to examine Objection 4(a) in the light of
the decision which it was about to render on Objection 3.[167]

This was indeed fine footwork when we consider that the Court
had earlier decided that the proper way to proceed was to consider
questions of jurisdiction before questions of admissibility.[168]

It decided by 10–5 that it was not necessary to adjudicate on
Objection 4(a).[169] The Court upheld the Third Preliminary Objection relating to non-exhaustion of local remedies by 9–6.[170]

Judge Sir Percy Spender, in a Separate Opinion took the Lauterpacht position that the Court had before it no valid acceptance by
the United States and therefore it was without competence to
entertain the dispute.

163. Supra note 157 at 24-25.
164. Id. at 30.
165. [1959] ICJ Pleadings, p. 320.
166. Id. at p. 579. The limits for a normal application of the so-called "automatic"
reservation are definitely exceeded when a State invokes it in an area which is wholly
foreign to the reserved domain.
167. Supra note 151 at 26.
168. See supra note 161 and accompanyin₆ text.
169. Supra note 151 at 29.
170. Ibid.

152

Commenting on the Court's Judgment, he acknowledged that there was "more than a little practical wisdom to recommend this as a course to follow".[171] The issues concerned not only the interests of the United States and Switzerland but those of other States as well. If the Court had struck down the U.S. Reservation, it would, in effect, have been questioning the validity of the declarations of Mexico, Liberia, the Union of South Africa, the Sudan and possibly the United Kingdom.[172]

He would have preferred to adopt the attitude of the Court, but after considerable reflection he decided that this course was not open to him because it would leave unanswered "questions which strike at the very roots of the Court's jurisdiction".[173]

He felt that the Court should have ruled on Objection 4(a) which related to jurisdiction before it decided on the admissibility question in Objection 3.[174]

Turning to the U.S. declaration he said:

> It is in no way relevant to assume, as assume I do, that the United States would seek to use its reservation with prudence and reason.[175]

The U.S. reservation was invalid. But the consequences of its invalidity depended upon whether it was severable, either wholly or in part from the rest of the declaration. He did not feel this was possible because the words represented the core of the obligation. He also remarked that recourse to the Senate Debate on the reservation "would not be necessary or profitable".[176]

As to whether the declaration left it to the Court to decide whether the determination was reasonable, such an interpretation would disregard the terms of the reservation.[177]

It is interesting that he thought that the French reservation in *Norwegian Loans* might have been open to the "reasonableness" interpretation and that Judge Read might have been correct that

171. Id. at 54.
172. Briggs, "Interhandel: The Court's Judgment of March 21, 1959, On the Preliminary Objections of the United States", 53 AJIL 547, 558 (1959).
173. Supra note 151 at 54.
174. Ibid.
175. Id. at 56.
176. Id. at 57.
177. Ibid.

the words "as understood by the Government of the French Republic" could have left to the Court the power to decide that this understanding was unreasonable. The words "as determined" in the U.S. Declaration left no room for such a determination.[178]

(With respect, it would seem that exactly the opposite view of the two reservations is possible. An "understanding" would seem to relate to a subjective view of the matter which cannot be questioned. A "determination" is a more objective, almost a judicial process, which might well be open to review.)

He concluded that the "good faith" argument would amount to construing the words as if they contained the additional proviso "provided it is so determined by the United States of America in good faith".[179]

Judge Lauterpacht quite naturally agreed with Judge Spender about the invalidity of the U.S. Declaration. In this case, he filed his opinion as a dissent because:

> As the Court has decided, at least provisionally to proceed on the basis that the Declaration of Acceptance of the United States is a valid legal instrument cognizable by the Court, I considered it my duty to participate in the formation of the Court's Judgment.[180]

Domestic jurisdiction reservations served no purpose. States are, in any case fully protected against interference in their domestic affairs. If a matter is essentially within the domestic jurisdiction and is unaffected by any obligation "stemming from a source of international law as formulated in Article 38 of its Statute, then the Court must inevitably reject the claim as being without foundation in international law".[181] But that would be a defence on the merits and not a defence to a claim of jurisdiction.

His view on automatic or self-judging reservations was expressed in the *Norwegian Loans Case*. To avoid repetition, he referred generally to his Separate Opinion in that Case for a more detailed exposition of the grounds for his conclusions.[182] On those

178. Id. at 59.
179. Ibid.
180. Id. at 119.
181. Id. at 122.
182. Id. at 102.

154

grounds, he felt that there was no valid declaration before the Court.

He did not feel that it was of decisive legal or practical importance that the United States had invoked the reservation in respect of the "sale and disposition" but not the "seizure and retention" of the shares. The questions raised by the Swiss Applcation, were whether the United States was under an obligation to "restore the assets of Interhandel". It could not do so if it sold the shares.[183] It might have offered to pay compensation, but that was not the object of the Swiss Application.[184]

He also dismissed the argument, hinted at in the Senate Debate,[185] which he described as being of "some dialectical complexion" that by performing the automatic function of registering the State's determination, the Court is, in law, exercising its function under Article 36(6):

> It is impossible for the Court to attach importance to the argument that as governments are free to accept or not to accept the obligations of the Optional Clause ... they are free to do so subject to reservations of their unlimited free choice. A person or a State may be free to join an association or accede to a treaty. This does not mean that they are entitled to join or accede on their own terms in disregard of the rules of the association or the provisions of the treaty.[186]

With regard to the "good faith" argument, he felt that the "greatest caution must guide the Court" in attributing bad faith, unreasonableness or an abuse of right to a sovereign State.[187]

Judge Klaestad's Dissenting Opinion involves a direct dialogue with Judges Spender and Lauterpacht. Noting that a finding that the U.S. Declaration was invalid would place the United States in the same legal situation as States which have not accepted the compulsory jurisdiction of the Court, he asked:

> Would such a consequence be in conformity with the true intention of the competent authorities of the United States?[188]

183. Id. at 97.
184. Ibid.
185. See supra note 76 and accompanying text.
186. Supra note 151 at 105.
187. Id. at 111.
188. Id. at 77.

Looking at the Debate in the Senate, he felt that they did not appear to afford sufficient grounds for such a supposition.[189] And we can see that this is true when we note that Senator Morse, along with most of the other Senators, did not regard the Amendment as crippling the declaration.[190]

In Judge Klaestad's view the United States truly intended to issue a "real and effective Declaration" albeit with far reaching exceptions.[191] He favoured severing the offending words from the Declaration[192] although it is not entirely clear whether he wanted to sever the entire reservation or just the self-judging words. He felt that the Court should first have dealt with the question of jurisdiction in Objection 4(a) before it considered the question of Admissibility in the Third Objection.[193] That Objection should have been joined to the merits.[194]

Judge Armand-Ugon also felt that the Third Preliminary Objection should have been joined to the merits.[195] With regard to the United States Declaration, he saw it as being composed of two parts, acceptance of the Court's jurisdiction and reservations to that acceptance. They were not indivisible.[196]

Because reservations cannot limit the Court's power to decide on its own competence, no reservation may be made to Article 36(6). Consequently the Reservation should be regarded "*comme non-écrit et inoperante*".[197]

Aerial incident of 27 July 1955

This case involved an El Al Israel airliner which was blown over Bulgarian territory as a result of inclement weather. It was fired upon by Bulgarian fighter aircraft with the result that all of the passengers, including six United States nationals, were killed and their property on board the aircraft was destroyed.[198]

189. Ibid.
190. See supra note 65 and accompanying text. The one clear dissenter from this position was Senator Pepper, see supra note 81 and accompanying text.
191. Supra note 151 at 77.
192. Id. at 78.
193. Id. at 78-79.
194. Id. at 81.
195. Id. at 90.
196. Id. at 91.
197. Id. at 93.
198. [1959] ICJ Pleadings, pp. 169-170.

On October 28, 1957, the United States filed an Application with the International Court of Justice demanding monetary reparation and such other relief as the Court might deem fit and proper.[199] The jurisdictional basis of the U.S. Application was Bulgaria's Declaration of July 29, 1921, accepting the compulsory jurisdiction of the Permanent Court of International Justice.

Bulgaria invoked the Connally Amendment on the basis of reciprocity. It claimed that the defence of its territory, the security of its airspace over the Southwestern frontier region and the disposition of its anti-aircraft defences were all within its domestic jurisdiction.[200]

The United States Application alleged that the dispute involved, among other questions of international law, "the scope and obligations relating to the overflight of international civil aircraft", the duties of Government and military defence authorities in whose territory the intrusion was alleged to have taken place and the use of force against passengers of intruding aircraft; together with issues of fact which, if resolved in favour of the United States Government would prove to be breaches of international obligations by the Bulgarian Government and if breaches of international law were found to have occurred, it would also have involved a question of the nature and extent of the reparations due to the United States.[201]

In his written observations on the Connally Amendment, Mr. Eric H. Hager, the U.S. Agent, argued:

> Bulgaria cannot determine that the United States claim based on the incident of 1955 is essentially within Bulgaria's domestic jurisdiction, since any such determination would fly in the face of actuality and would ignore the international character accorded the claim by the parties in their previous negotiations. United States reservation (b) does not permit the United States or any other State to make an arbitrary determination in bad faith.[202]

Further on, he said:

199. Id. at p. 167.
200. Id. at pp. 271ff.
201. Id. at pp. 22ff. See Article 36(2) (a)-(d).
202. Id. at p. 308.

The United States does not consider that reservation (b) authorises or empowers this Government or any other Government, to make an arbitrary determination that a particular matter is domestic when it is evidently one of international concern and has been so treated by the parties.[203]

As an example he pointed to U.S. conduct in *Interhandel* in invoking the Connally Amendment only in respect of some issues while leaving the domestic nature of other matters to the Court to decide.[204]

The United States argument at that stage seemed to adopt Judge Read's position in the *Norwegian Loans Case*[205] that the Connally Amendment was neither automatic, nor peremptory, nor completely self-judging but rather that if left to the Court a residuum of decision-making power.[206]

But apparently U.S. authorities thought better of this argument. In a letter of May 13, 1960, the United States abandoned it "on the basis of further study and consideration of the history and background of reservation (b)". It then went on to reiterate the position taken by Becker in arguing the *Interhandel Case.*[207] The case was removed from the Calendar of the Court on May 30, 1960.[208] This was the first and only time that an applicant Government accepted a respondent's preliminary objection as justified.[209]

By this act of withdrawal, the United States appears to have precluded itself from ever challenging the reasonableness of an interpretation that a particular matter was essentially within the domestic jurisdiction of the declarant.[210]

Reasonableness and good faith

The jurisprudence surrounding self-judging reservations seems to involve two conflicting approaches to their interpretation. One

203. Id. at p. 323.
204. Ibid.
205. See supra note 140 and accompanying text.
206. Gross, "Bulgaria Invokes the Connally Amendment", 56 AJIL 357, 368 (1962).
207. See supra note 165 and accompanying text.
208. [1960] ICJ 146.
209. Rosenne, *"La Cour International de Justice 1960"*, 65 *Revue Gen. de Droit International Public* 1, 3 (1961).
210. Schlesinger, supra note 113 at 696.

158

approach takes the self-judging reservation at its word and holds that it cannot be interpreted so as to leave the Court with any residuum of decision-making power although this view leads to polar opposite conclusions. One conclusion, expressed by U.S. Agent Loftus Becker in argument in the *Interhandel Case,*[211] views the reservation as a valid one which automatically excludes the jurisdiction of the Court once a determination of domestic jurisdiction has been made. The opposite conclusion is drawn by Judges Lauterpacht and Spender is that such reservations are fundamentally inconsistent with Article 36(6) and therefore they invalidate a declaration of acceptance containing them.

A third variant of this approach, suggested by Judges Armand-Ugon and Klaestad, among others, involves severing either the self-judging words from the reservation or severing the self-judging reservation from the entire declaration. This view also assumes that such a reservation is invalid because it leaves the Court no power to decide and therefore conflicts with Article 36(6).

The alternative approach, suggested by Judge Read is that any understanding or determination of domestic jurisdiction must be reasonable and that the Court can decide whether it is reasonable. On this view, such a reservation leaves a residuum of decision-making authority to the Court. Thus, it is not inconsistent with Article 36(6).

Of the four views just canvassed, Judge Lauterpacht's position is the most intransigent and the Court will be very unwilling to accept it.[212] But that ought not to prevent us from examining it as a proposition of law.

There is fairly impressive authority on either side of the question. The view that the Court has the power to decide if the determination of domestic jurisdiction is reasonable was supported by Professors Bourquin[213] and Guggenheim[214] in arguments be-

211. See supra note 165 and accompanying text. The U.S. is unlikely to have succeeded in any event. In *Israel v. Bulgaria* [1959] ICJ 127, the ICJ held that, because Bulgaria was not an original Member of the United Nations, Article 36(5) did not operate to transfer its Declaration of July 29, 1921, to the ICJ.
212. Guggenheim, *"Der sogenannte automatische Vorbehalt der inneren Angelegenheiten gegenüber der Anerkennung der obligatorischen Gerichtsbarkeit des Internationalen Gerichtshofes in Internationalen Gerichtspraxis"*, in Zemanek, K. (ed), *Völkerrecht und rechtliches Weltbild (Festschrift für Alfred Verdross, 1960)*, p. 131.
213. Supra note 126 and accompanying text.
214. Supra note 166 and accompanying text.

fore the Court. In an editorial in the *American Journal of International Law* in 1946, shortly after promulgation of the Connally Amendment, Pittman B. Potter expressed the view that there was no ground for fear that the reservation would be used to nullify the acceptance of compulsory jurisdiction completely. He pointed out that it would be the Executive who acted under the reservation and professed to see that as some assurance that it would be applied with prudence and responsibility. But beyond that, he felt that the reservation envisaged a fundamental principle of international law which 'no brave — or are they timorous? — words can overthrow". That principle was that no State can entirely decide for itself what matters are left to its domestic jurisdiction, "either practically or in legal principle".[215] Lawrence Preuss made similar comments.[216]

On the other hand, during a discussion at the *Institute de droit international*, in 1950, a number of eminent authorities expressed the view that States had a right to make such a reservation and that this view is not open to challenge.[217]

Professor Charles De Visscher in discussing the *Interhandel Case* studied the debates in the United States Senate and concluded that the question of conformity with Article 36(6) was clearly in the minds of the Senators. Therefore, because the Court's jurisdiction is based on the consent of the respondent State, the Court cannot ignore such a clear expression of intent. Its function is therefore limited to recording the determination and giving it its full effect. There was no question that the Court could assume for itself the power to decide whether the U.S. determination accords with reason and good faith. To so interpret the reservation would give the Court precisely what the U.S. intended to exclude from it.[218]

Among U.S. writers, Quincy Wright and Oliver Lissitzyn, took the position that the United States' obligations under the Connally Amendment were moral rather than legal obligations.[219]

215. 40 AJIL 792 (1946).
216. 40 AJIL 720, 726 (1946).
217. (1950-I) 43 *Annuaire de l'institut de droit international* 25, 27 and 29.
218. (1959) 63 *Révue général de droit international public* 413, 418-419.
219. Lissitzyn, O., *The International Court of Justice* (1951), p. 65; Wright, Q. "The International Court of Justice and the Interpretation of Multilateral Treaties", 41 AJIL 445, 452 (1947).

160

In the United Kingdom, Sir Humphrey Waldock, later to be a Judge on the International Court of Justice, supported the view that the Connally Reservation rendered the U.S. Declaration invalid.[220] He felt that there was abundant evidence that the United States intended its reservation to give it a complete right to insist upon its own determination of matters essentially within domestic jurisdiction.[221]

Those who essentially favour severance include Herbert W. Briggs[222] and Leo Gross. Briggs' approach seems more like one of ignoring a self-judging reservation rather than severing it. Discussing the Connally Amendment, he feels that the Court can take jurisdiction of a matter which the United States has determined to be within its domestic jurisdiction. The Court can base its jurisdiction on "the United States Declaration and the *Nottebohm* rule that a unilateral attempt to withdraw jurisdiction in a case already pending before the Court cannot deprive the Court of jurisdiction already established".[223]

There is a distinction however. In *Nottebohm* there was a declaration in force at the time the application was filed. It was a valid declaration which did not purport to exclude the jurisdiction of the Court. It expired subsequently. In the *Interhandel* and *Norwegian Loans* cases, the validity and status of the declarations were in doubt at the time of filing. So we cannot say that the jurisdiction was established at the moment of filing.

Gross notes that the ICJ Statute is an integral part of the United Nations Charter and Article 103 of the Charter provides that the Charter shall prevail in the event of a conflict between obligations under the Charter and under any other international agreement. Therefore Article 36(6) is "hierarchically superior to the will of the parties".[224]

Those who argue that the U.S. Reservation cannot be interpreted so as to give the Court any power of review base their arguments on one or more of the following grounds.[225]

220. Waldock, "The Plea of Domestic Jurisdiction Before International Legal Tribunals" (1954) 31 BYIL 96, 133.
221. "Decline of the Optional Clause" (1955-56) 32 BYIL 244, 272 note 3.
222. "Reservations to the Compulsory Jurisdiction of the International Court of Justice" (1958) 93 *Recueil des Cours* 229, 362-363.
223. Id. at 363.
224. Supra note 206 at 380-381.
225. For a summary of these arguments see Shihata, *The Power of the International Court to Determine its Own Jurisdiction* (1965), p. 291.

1. United States intent is clear and the Court cannot arrogate competence to itself.[226] But the Court is very clearly given competence by Article 36(6) of the Statute. The question is whether the United States has successfully taken it away by arrogating competence to *itself*. This argument is basically circular. Reduced to its constituent propositions, it reads something like this:

a. The reservation deprives the Court of the power to determine its own jurisdiction.

b. Therefore it is inconsistent with Article 36(6).

c. We must reject any interpretation which renders it consistent with Article 36(6) because the reservation deprives the Court of the power to determine its own jurisdiction.

As to United States intent, what emerges from the legislative history is that the Senators were not very clear on the reservation's effects. Even the opponents of the Connally Amendment, such as Senator Morse, denied that the Amendment would have the effect of crippling the obligation. Only Senator Pepper hinted that the declaration might be invalid.[227]

The Senators seemed to feel that the good faith of the United States in exercising its power of determination would vitiate any inconsistency with the Statute. Thus, Senator Connally was able to say on the one hand that:

> ... when it comes to submitting a question to the International Court, if we [the United States] say that it is a domestic question, the International Court cannot take jurisdiction of it.[228]

And on the other hand:

> I do not believe that the United States would adopt a subterfuge, a pretext or a pretence in order to block the judgment of the Court on any such grounds.[229]

Judge Read is probably correct in his assertion that an interpretation which rendered the declaration invalid would do more

---

226. Lauterpacht, supra note 100 at 101-102.
227. Supra note 81 and accompanying text.
228. 92 Cong. Rec. at p. 10695.
229. Id. at p. 10833.

162

violence to U.S. intentions than a holding that left some decision-making power in the hands of the Court. The same remarks can be made about an interpretation involving severance.

The United States would ultimately be free to withdraw its declaration if the Court held that it had a residuum of decision-making power and the U.S. disapproved of that decision. Parenthetically, the present author's hunch is that it would not. What is more likely is that the attitude of the U.S. Government and of many U.S. Senators would be one of relief at a solution which removed a persistent problem without the U.S. Senate having to do anything about it.

2. The second argument, somewhat akin to the first, is the suggestion of Sir Percy Spender that any interpretation which left it to the Court to decide whether the determination was made in good faith would amount to amending the U.S. Reservation so as to add the proviso "provided it is so determined by the United States in good faith".[230]

But good faith is a general principle of law recognised by civilised nations.[231] In the *Nuclear Test Cases* [*Second Phase*], the Court said:

> One of the basic principles governing the creation and performance of legal obligations, whatever their source, is the principle of good faith.[232]

Article 31, paragraph 1 of the Vienna Convention on the Law of Treaties[233] says:

> A treaty shall be interpreted in *good faith* in accordance with the ordinary meaning to be given to the terms of a treaty in their context and in the light of its object and purpose [emphasis added].

So we are justified in regarding good faith as an implied term or

---

230. See supra note 179 and accompanying text.
231. See Cheng, *General Principles of Law as Applied by International Courts and Tribunals* (1953), Part II, pp. 105-160.
232. Supra note 30 at 473.
233. See Waldock, "Decline of the Optional Clause" (1955-56) 32 BYIL 244, 351-352.

condition in most international obligations, at least where it is not expressly excluded.[234]

This brings us to the third argument.

3. It would be odious and difficult for the Court to be placed in the position of having to accuse a sovereign State of unreasonableness, bad faith or abuse of right.

The odiousness or difficulty of the exercise ought not to prevent the Court from doing it. If we accept that good faith is a general principle of law, then it would seem that the Court is bound to apply it under Article 38 (1)(c) of the Statute. In doing so, it can be as diplomatic and circumspect as it wishes. To ignore the principle, however, would be to rely on a *jus strictum* interpretation of international obligations which is wholly unwarranted. Application of the Article 31 of the Vienna Convention on the Law of Treaties, quoted above, must necessarily place the Court in a position where it will have to say, in some future case, that an interpretation advanced by a State does not comport with the principle of good faith. The Permanent Court of International Justice has in fact held the behaviour of a State to be contrary to the principle of good faith and thus unlawful.[235]

There are two very good arguments for an interpretation of a Connally type declaration which would recognise a residuum of decision-making power in the Court. One is Judge Read's point that a contrary interpretation would lead to an absurd and unreasonable result.[236]

The second argument stems from Leo Gross' point that the declaration must be consistent with the United Nations Charter. If it is not, then the Charter must prevail. But that is a necessary conclusion only if the two are inconsistent.[237]

In the *Right of Passage Case*, the Court said:

> It is a rule of interpretation that a text emanating from a
> Government must, in principle, be interpreted as producing

---

234. For a possible example of an express exclusion of good faith as an implied term in an obligation see *Rights of Minorities in Upper Silesia (Minority Schools) Case* [1928] PCIJ, Ser. A, No. 15, p. 4.

235. *Free Zones Case* [1932] PCIJ, Ser. A/B, No. 46, p. 96 at p. 167; *Oscar Chinn Case* [1934] PCIJ, Ser. A/B, No. 63, p. 65 at p. 86. On the place of "abuse of right" in international law, see Iluyomade, "The Scope and Content of a Complaint of Abuse of Right in International Law," 16 Harv. ILJ 47 (1975).

236. See supra notes 141-142 and accompanying text.

237. See supra note 224 and accompanying text.

164

and as intended to produce effects in accordance with existing law and not a violation of it.[238]

So the U.S. and other, similar reservations should be read as consistent with Article 36(6) if at all possible.

Those, like Judge Lauterpacht, who would void the entire declaration and those who would give it peremptory effect are alike in their willingness to place on it an interpretation which would both lead to an absurd result, as Judge Read has suggested, and also result in its being read in a manner which is inconsistent with the Charter.

"Essentially"

Judge Lauterpacht felt that a reservation of matters essentially within domestic jurisdiction of a State as understood by that State is so wide as to cover practically all disputes in which it may become involved.

> ... practically every matter can be plausibly, though not necessarily accurately, described as a matter essentially within the domestic jurisdiction... .[239]

If that is so, then no State can ever be seen to be acting unreasonably or in bad faith when making such a determination. But Lauterpacht's object was not to indicate what were matters of domestic jurisdiction but the fact that States might plausibly make that claim in order to invoke a self-judging reservation. His real view was that very little remained which, from the standpoint of international law was "essentially" a matter of domestic jurisdiction.[240]

Granted that States can find domestic elements in almost every dispute. But the issue in any given dispute is whether a State's characterization of the matter as domestic is plausible. The key question is, what is meant by the word "essentially"?

238. [1957] ICJ 125, 142. See also Vienna Convention on the Law of Treaties, Art. 31(3)(c).
239. Supra note 100 at 52.
240. Fitzmaurice, "Hersch Lauterpacht – The Scholar as Judge, Part I," (1961) 37 BYIL 1, 28-29.

As we have seen,[241] the words "essentially within the domestic jurisdiction" in the Connally Amendment was drawn from Article 2(7) of the United Nations Charter. The initial reservation introduced by Senator Morse used the word "exclusively" which was more in line with the League of Nations Covenant. But, as Sir Humphrey Waldock has pointed out, it seems rather difficult to see what advantage this formula provides over the formula used in the Covenant.[242]

At the San Francisco Conference, one U.S. delegate said that the word "essentially" meant "the essence, the heart of the matter".[243] This seems to imply that if the "essence" of the matter is domestic, then the dispute is domestic. If, on the other hand, the "essence" of the matter is international, then the dispute is international. In determining what the essence of the dispute is, it seems necessary to determine what law is necessary to resolve it. If it must be resolved by the application of rules of international law, then it is essentially international. If it is to be resolved by the application of municipal law then it is essentially within the domestic jurisdiction. The only problem arises when the question is a mixed one of international and municipal law. But such a question must inevitably involve the extent to which rules of municipal law fulfill international obligations. So, here too, we may say that the question is "essentially" international.

In the *Interpretation of Peace Treaties Case* [*First Phase*], the International Court of Justice declined to treat the word "essentially" as different from the word "solely" when the matter involved the interpretation of a treaty. It rejected a plea of domestic jurisdiction as ill-founded where the matter at issue involved a treaty obligation.[244] It should be noted that the treaty in question involved the protection of the human rights of the citizens of Bulgaria, Hungary and Romania. The way in which a State treats its own citizens is generally a question of municipal jurisdiction. But when a State undertakes by treaty with others States to treat its citizens in a certain way, then the interpretation of that treaty is "essentially" a matter of international law. Other matters of concern to the U.S. Senate such as immigration and tariffs are also

241. Supra note 41 and accompanying text.
242. Supra note 220 at 129.
243. 6 UNCIO, p. 45.
244. [1950] ICJ 65; 70-71.

generally domestic. The U.S. is not obliged to enter into a treaty on these matters. But if it does, then the interpretation and application of such a treaty would be essentially international.[245]

It may well be that the standard non-self judging domestic jurisdiction reservation is completely unnecessary. If a case does not involve questions which fall within paragraph 2(a)-(d) of Article 36 relating to international law, then a State accepting the compulsory jurisdiction of the Court under Article 36(2) has not agreed to submit that particular dispute.[246] Thus Article 36(2) itself prevents the Court from deciding "domestic" cases. Likewise sub-paragraphs (b)-(d) all relate specifically to international law and international obligations.[247] In the *Case of Polish Nationals in Danzig*, the Permanent Court of International Justice held that it was improper for the League of Nations to consider whether municipal law was being properly applied since no violation of international law was involved.[248]

Furthermore, Article 38(1) of the Statute makes it clear that the Court's function is to "decide in accordance with international law such disputes as are submitted to it". It may not decide disputes to which international law is irrelevant. International law, by definition, governs the rights and duties involved in the relationships between and among States.[249]

In the *Anglo-Iranian Oil Co. Case*, the International Court of Justice held that it had no jurisdiction because the matters were essentially domestic.[250] The *Tunis and Morocco Nationality Decree Case* involved certain decrees conferring French nationality and liability for military service upon persons who were born in Morocco and Tunis to a parent who was born in one of those territories. The British Government protested the application of those Decrees to British Nationals. It referred the matter to the Council of the League of Nations. France invoked Article 15(8) of

245. See Article 2, paragraph 1(a) of the Vienna Convention on the Law of Treaties: "treaty" means an international agreement concluded between States in written form and governed by international law.

246. Hudson, *The Permanent Court of International Justice, 1920-1942* (1943), pp. 190, 471.

247. Friedman, *The Changing Structure of International Law* (1964), pp. 141-143; Bleicher, "ICJ Jurisdiction: Some New Considerations and a Proposed American Declaration", 6 Col. J. Trans'l L. 61, 66 (1967).

248. [1932] PCIJ Ser. A/B, No. 44, p. 4 at p. 25.

249. Bleicher, supra note 247 at 78. See debate in the U.S. Senate supra note 51 and accompanying text.

250. [1952] ICJ 92.

the Covenant. The Council asked the Permanent Court of International Justice for an Advisory Opinion on whether the dispute was, by international law, solely within the domestic jurisdiction.[251]

The Court said that, to make a dispute international, it is not enough that the matter may affect the interest of more than one State. It must be a matter which is in principle regulated by international law:

> The question of whether a certain matter is or is not solely within the jurisdiction of a State is an essentially relative question, it depends upon the development of international relations. Thus, in the present state of international law, questions of nationality are, in the opinion of the Court, in principle within this reserved domain.[252]

This is of particular interest to us when we recall that the prospect of the International Court of Justice interfering in questions of nationality was one of the motivating fears behind the Connally Amendment but then the Court said:

> ... It may well happen that, in a matter which, like that of nationality, is not in principle regulated by international law, the right of a State to use its discretion is nevertheless restricted by obligations which it may have undertaken towards other States. In such a case, jurisdiction which, in principle, belongs solely to a State, is limited by rules of international law. Article 15, paragraph 8, then ceases to apply... .[253]

The Court then examined the issues and found that they related to the continued validity of British treaties with Tunis and Morocco and the extent of Britain's rights under those treaties particularly under a most − favoured − nation clause and also the question of whether Britain had recognised France's right to legislate in those territories in respect of nationality.[254] It concluded that each of

---

251. [1923] PCIJ, Ser. B, No. 4, p. 7 at pp. 7-10.
252. Id. at p. 24.
253. Ibid.
254. Id. at pp. 27-31.

those issues could only be solved by recourse to international law.[255]

This would seem to be the basic meaning of the word "essentially" and it would seem to be fairly readily ascertainable in most cases. If a dispute involving two or more States is one that involves a treaty or requires the application of principles of international law for its solution, then it would be unreasonable for a State to assert that the matter is essentially a domestic one. If it does not, then the Court will not take jurisdiction.

The proper effect of the explicitly self-judging reservation, if it is to be read both consistently with Article 36(6) and in a way which gives at least partial effect to the intent of the declarant State, is that it shifts the burden of proof as to the reserve domain. Once the declarant State has made its determination, that determination prevails unless the respondent State demonstrates that it is a dispute which can be resolved only through the application of principles of international law.[256]

SELF-JUDGING CONDUCT

The purpose of the foregoing extended discussion is to show that explicitly self-judging reservations were initially intended as an alternative to defiance of judgments which certain United States Senators feared that the Court might render on the question of jurisdiction, judgments which were highly unlikely in view of Articles 36(2) and 38.

The Senators wanted to have their cake and eat it as well. They wanted credit for adhering to the compulsory jurisdiction of the Court. But, at the same time, they wanted a legally justifiable excuse for refusing to appear when the United States Government felt that the matter was an invasion of the reserved domain. What they wanted was non-appearance without default.[257] They pro-

255. Id. at 32.
256. *Case Concerning Certain German Interests in Polish Upper Silesia* [1926] PCIJ, Ser. A, No. 7, p. 4 at p. 30; but see the opinion of Judge Lauterpacht in the *Interhandel Case*, supra note 150 at 112 where he said that he found it "judicially repugnant" to acquiesce in the suggestion that the Court must be guided by a presumption in favour of the determination made by the Government responsible for the automatic reservation.
257. Other examples are, the Portuguese Reservation in its Declaration of December 19, 1955 reserving the right to exclude "any given category or categories of disputes" at

duced an instrument which has inspired volumes of debate and considerable confusion. But the one thing that is clear is that the objectives of the Connally Amendment are mutually exclusive.

If the reservation invalidates the United States declaration, then the United States has not accepted the compulsory jurisdiction of the Court. That is certainly a justifiable ground for non-appearance.[258] But it is not what the United States Senate intended.

If, on the other hand, the reservation or the self-judging words are severable from the declaration, then the United States will not have the justification for refusal to appear which it seeks. The same is true if, as in the present author's view, the Court is left with the power to decide whether the determination is reasonable or made in good faith.

But the United States declaration is a written document the legal effect of which is subject to interpretation. And it is possible to interpret it consistently with Article 36(6) of the Court's Statute. It may be an attempt to autointerpret the jurisdiction of the Court in a way which is inconsistent with Article 36(6). But it is by no means clear that it is a successful one.

When a State refuses to appear, claiming that the Court is without jurisdiction, we again have a case of self-judgment. But here we have a different situation. There is no written document to interpret. There are no words that the Court can look at to determine whether a residuum of decision-making power is left to it.

What is involved here is the *conduct* of the State which is ignoring the Court's process. This conduct may be described as self-judging conduct. It purports to deprive the Court unilaterally of the power to determine whether it has jurisdiction.

In this situation, it would seem that Judge Lauterpacht's reason-

---

any time during the validity of the Declaration. See *Case Concerning Right of Passage Over Indian Territory [Preliminary Objections]* [1957] ICJ 125, 131. The Indian Declaration of August 1, 1956 was terminable upon notice. See [1955-56] ICJYB, p. 186. The 1980-81 edition of the ICJ Yearbook shows that Australia, Barbados, Canada, The Gambia, India, Israel, Malawi, Malta, Mauritius, Pakistan, The Philippines, Somalia, Sudan, Swaziland and the U.K. had reservations terminable upon notice at that time. Panama, Nigeria, Colombia, The Dominican Republic, Egypt, Haiti, Honduras, Uganda, Hungary, Liechtenstein, and Nicaragua had reservations which either said nothing about duration or provided for an indefinite period. Botswana, El Salvador, Kenya, Portugal and Togo reserved the power to amend their declarations at any time.

258. Briggs cites a number of instances in which States have terminated acceptance of compulsory jurisdiction in order to avoid the jurisdiction of the Court in pending disputes, supra note 222 at 275.

ing is inescapable. There is nothing equivocal in self-judging conduct. The conduct would seem to constitute a *de facto* renunciation of compulsory jurisdiction. We might say that France's formal renunciation after the *Nuclear Test Cases* merely ratified the existing position. In the *Fisheries Jurisdiction Cases*, the *Aegean Sea Case*, the *Hostages Case*, and the *Nuclear Test Cases* (insofar as the General Act was raised), the claims for jurisdiction were grounded in "treaties and conventions in force" and/or "special agreements". These cases involved attempts to unilaterally abrogate Article 36(6) of the Statute as it relates to Article 36(1) and to Article 94 of the United Nations Charter.

It would seem that, where a State, which has filed a declaration under Article 36(2), refuses to appear on the ground that the Court has no jurisdiction, the Court would be justified in concluding that it has not really accepted the compulsory jurisdiction of the Court and in holding the declaration to be a nullity. In this situation, Eisemann's reasoning[259] is probably correct. The declaration can only be considered a nullity if the respondent State continues to refuse to appear once the Court has held that it possesses jurisdiction. If a State were subsequently to decide to renew its declaration, we might assume that it would then be willing to comply with the Statute, with whatever judgment the Court has given and with Article 94 of the United Nations Charter.

Likewise, where a State refuses to come to Court under a treaty or convention in force, then, should that State ever seek to invoke the treaty as an applicant, the Court could probably hold, at the request of the respondent, that its past non-appearance has barred it from invoking the treaty in that way.[260] Such a ruling could be made subject to an undertaking by the defaulting State to cure the effects of its default and to comply with Article 36 of the Statute in the future.

---

259. See Ch. 3, supra notes 54-56 and accompanying text.
260. See Vienna Convention on The Law of Treaties, Art. 60.

CHAPTER 6

CONCLUSION – THE WILLINGSNESS OF STATES
TO SUBMIT TO JURISDICTION

The International Court of Justice has no power to compel attendance or to punish States for non-attendance. Thus the chief penalties suffered by the non-appearing party involve procedural disadvantages. Discussion in the preceeding Chapters casts light on some of these. The following rights are forfeited:

1. The right to appoint a judge *ad hoc*;[1]
2. The right to submit a detailed memorial, although apparently there is no limit to the length or detail of postal or telegraphic submissions which a State may submit to the Court;[2]
3. The right to participate fully in both the oral and written proceedings relating to jurisdiction;[3]
4. The right to rebut the applicant's case on the merits with full written and oral submissions;[4]
5. The right to raise affirmative defences;[5]
6. The possibility that non-appearing conduct will result in a State's acceptance of compulsory jurisdiction being regarded as having no legal effect.[6]

Although it does not emerge from the foregoing Chapters, the suggestion has been made that the appearing respondent in interim protection cases might be able to prevail upon the Court to require

---

1. See supra Ch. 3 note 34 and accompanying text.
2. See supra Ch. 3 notes 40-46 and accompanying text.
3. See supra Ch. 3 notes 53 & 54 and accompanying text.
4. See supra Ch. 3 notes 53 & 54 and accompanying text.
5. See supra Ch. 3 notes 64-72 and accompanying text.
6. See supra Ch. 5 notes 258-260 and accompanying text.

172

the applicant to provide some sort of bond or security as compensation for any detriment which the respondent might suffer by complying with such an order should the Court later find either that it has no jurisdiction or that the respondent should prevail on the merits.[7] Article 75, paragraph 2 of the Rules of Court provides that the Court may indicate provisional measures that ought to be taken or complied with by the requesting party. This does not specifically empower the Court to order security. But it would seem to indicate that the Court has the power to do so.

But we may assume that governments are well aware of the procedural rights and protections which they forfeit by failing to appear. The decision to appear or not to appear is a tactical one in which a government undoubtedly wieghs a number of considerations including *inter alia*; the possibility that appearance will contribute to a judgment in its favour, the odium which it may incur by refusal to appear, the advisability of maintaining that a particular dispute is not suitable for adjudication and the possibility that participation in the suit will weaken its case for refusing to comply with a judgment once given.

Similarly, the decision as to whether to accept the compulsory jurisdiction of the Court and the way in which to qualify that acceptance is a tactical decision.

So the problems for those who are interested in advancing the cause of international adjudication are whether and how it can be made more attractive to States.

PROCEDURAL REFORM

Efforts in this area have combined pleas and exhortations with proposals for reform of procedure opening new modes of access to the Court and with proposals for structural change to "depoliticise" recourse to the Court.

---

7. Mendelson, "Interim Measures of Protection in Cases of Contested Jurisdiction" (1972-73) 46 BYIL 259, 312. Developed by Elkind, *Interim Protection: A Functional Approach* (1981), pp. 238-241.

Pleas and exhortations

In 1959, the *Institut de Droit International* passed a resolution aimed at encouraging States to make more use of the compulsory jurisdiction of the Court.

The resolution said that the *Institut* was convinced that submission to law through recourse to international courts and tribunals was an essential complement to the renunciation of the use of force in international relations. It considered that a more general acceptance of compulsory jurisdiction would be an important contribution to respect for law and noted with concern that the development of such jurisdiction lagged behind the need for a satisfactory administration of international justice. It considered that Article 36(2) of the Statute should remain as a means for securing a more general acceptance of the compulsory jurisdiction of the Court and resolved that recourse to the International Court of Justice or to some other court or arbitral tribunal constitutes a normal method of settlement of the legal disputes. Consequently, it urged that recourse to such a court or tribunal could never be regarded as an unfriendly act towards a respondent State.

It also urged that acceptance of the compulsory jurisdiction of the International Court of Justice should be effective and not illusory. Acceptance should be in precise terms and should allow the Court to settle any disputes concerning its own jurisdiction in accordance with the Statute. It specifically urged States to withdraw any self-judging reservations they might have made having regard to the judgments and opinions in the *Norwegian Loans* and *Interhandel* cases and the risk that other States might invoke such reservations against them.

The resolution also maintained the desirability of inserting clauses in general conventions conferring compulsory jurisdiction on the Court under Article 36(1). It also suggested that it was desirable to link the compulsory jurisdiction of the Court (as far as the Statute allows) or of some other tribunal to financial agreements concerning economic development schemes whether concluded between States or between States and international organisations or international public corporations.[8]

---

8. (1959-II) 48 *Annuaire de L'Institut de Droit International*, 381 [hereinafter *Annuaire*]. Reproduced 54 AJIL 136 (1960); Jenks, *The Prospects of International Adjudication* (1964), pp. 113-116. See also Jessup, "International Litigation as a Friendly Act", 60 Colum.L.R. 24 (1960).

But representatives of States in the political arena are less willing to recommend or advocate recourse to the Court or to compulsory jurisdiction. In 1966 the United Nations Special Committee on Friendly Relations discussed the reluctance of States to accept compulsory jurisdiction.[9] A number of representatives stressed the advantages of judicial settlement. The debate focused on whether specific mention should be made of the role of the International Court of Justice and whether it was advisable to recommend that States accept the compulsory jurisdiction of the Court in accordance with Article 36(2) of the Statute.[10] It was argued that, since the Court was the principal judicial organ of the United Nations and that since each Member was *ipso facto* a party to the Statute of the Court, no formulation of the principle of peaceful settlement of disputes would be complete without reference to the Court. The proposal submitted by Dahomey, Italy, Japan, Madagascar and The Netherlands was the strongest proposal in that respect:

> (a) Legal disputes should as a general rule be referred by the parties to the International Court of Justice, and in particular States should endeavour to accept the jurisdiction of the International Court of Justice pursuant to Article 36, paragraph 2, of the Statute of the Court.
> (b) General multilateral agreements concluded under the auspices of the United Nations, should provide that disputes relating to the interpretation or application of the agreement, and which the parties have not been able to settle by negotiation, or any other peaceful means, may be referred on the application of any party to the International Court of Justice or to an arbitral tribunal, the members of which are appointed by the parties, or, failing such appointment, by an appropriate organ of the United Nations.[11]

The sponsors explained that they were not trying impose any par-

---

9. *Report of the Special Committee on Friendly Relations*, U.N. Doc. A/6230, pp. 56-57, paras. 215-220 (1966).
10. Id. at p. 56, para. 211.
11. Id. at p. 48, para. 159.

ticular line of conduct on States but only to make the principle of the peaceful settlement of disputes more effective.[12]

In opposition to this proposal, some representatives argued that, if States rarely had recourse to the International Court of Justice and preferred other means of settlement, they did so because they had strong reasons.[13] They stressed that recent international practice did not justify attempts to extend the compulsory jurisdiction of the Court. They also pointed to the need to take into account the freedom of parties to a dispute to settle it by the means which they considered most appropriate.[14] Compulsory jurisdiction had been rejected at the San Francisco Conference and at subsequent international conferences.[15] One representative urged a revision of the Court's Statute so as to eliminate those factors which reduced the efficiency of the Court as a means of settling international disputes.[16]

The text which emerged from the Committee was incorporated into the Declaration on Principles of International Law concerning Friendly Relations and Cooperation with Respect to the Settlement of Disputes of October 24, 1970.[17]

Paragraph 5 provided:

> International disputes shall be settled on the basis of sovereign equality of States and in accordance with the principle of free choice of means. Recourse to, or acceptance of, a settlement procedure freely agreed to by States with regard to existing or future disputes to which they are parties shall not be regarded as incompatible with sovereign equality.

Leo Gross, clearly disappointed at this result, called it "a paean to the liberty of States in which Vattel would have rejoiced".[18] He proposed that an appeal by the General Assembly, addressed to all States along the lines of the resolution of the *Institut* would be "the logical first step in order to get the Court off dead centre".[19]

12. Id. at p. 56, para. 214.
13. Id. at p. 57, para. 215.
14. Ibid., para. 217.
15. Ibid., para. 218.
16. Ibid., para. 216.
17. U.N. Doc. A/Res/2625 (XXV) reprinted 65 AJIL 243 (1971).
18. Gross, "The International Court of Justice: Consideration of Requirements for Enhancing Its Role in the International Legal Order", 65 AJIL 253, 265 (1971).
19. Id. at 274.

Such an appeal should simply point out that the Court is open to all States and that recourse to international adjudication is never an unfriendly act.

Such an appeal would only be a first step. On the other hand, as the debate of the Special Committee demonstrates, mustering a majority in the General Assembly for such a proposal would be no easy matter. If it were achieved, proponents of international adjudication could take some comfort from the fact that a majority of States in the General Assembly were committed, at least in principle, to that position. But that is precisely the problem. Most States are not committed to that position even in principle.

Recommendations for procedural reform

One proposal emerging from this work is the suggestion advanced by Judge Jessup of a "special appearance" procedure whereby a respondent can challenge the jurisdiction of the Court with confidence that this challenge will not be taken to confer jurisdiction by means of *forum prorogatum*.[20] He also feels that the Court should refuse to consider communications from non-appearing parties.[21]

In the 1950s, the *Institut de Droit International* considered proposals for revision of the Statute of the International Court of Justice in some detail, particularly with a view to improving the disposition of States to accept the compulsory jurisdiction of the Court.

Other proposals were made by C.W. Jenks who devoted considerable space to the problem in his book *The Prospects of International Adjudication*.[22] Leo Gross, in his article, "The International Court of Justice: Consideration of Requirements for Enhancing Its Role in The International Legal Order",[23] discussed these proposals and added a number of proposals of his own.

It is not proposed to recapitulate here all of the many reforms suggested. But generally they can be said to fall into two classes, those involving mere modification of procedure and those which

20. See supra Ch. 3, notes 47-48 and accompanying text.
21. See supra Ch. 3, note 40 and accompanying text.
22. Jenks, *The Prospects of International Adjudication* (1964).
23. Supra note 18.

would involve a change in the Statute of the Court, possibly even a structural change in the nature of the Court[24] although Gross cautioned that changes to the Court's Statute are, under Article 69 of the Statute, equivalent to amendments to the United Nations Charter requiring, under Article 108, "a vote of two thirds of the members of the General Assembly and ratification by two thirds of the Members, including all the permanent members of the Security Council".[25] And, as Jenks put it, "How far new developments in the contentious procedure of the Court are possible within the present framework of the Statute depends in part on how liberally the Statute is interpreted by the Court in the light of developing needs".[26]

Many of the proposals suggested by Jenks were aimed at de-politicising reference of disputes to the Court. One of these was the citation of nominal respondents in cases relating to the construction of treaties. A provision in a treaty might provide that any State wanting to refer a question relating to its interpretation would automatically name all other parties to the treaty as respondents. Any case stemming from such a provision would, in substance, be an *ex parte* application.[27] Other variants of this are the recognition of *ex parte* applications *per se* or *ex parte* applications in which the Court determines who the other necessary parties should be.[28]

Leo Gross has made an even more far reaching proposal. He suggests the possibility of making the Court an organ to ensure "the authoritative and uniform interpretation of conventions in the domestic forum. It should be given a power similar to that of the Court of Justice of the European Communities of making preliminary decisions regarding questions of interpretation of treaties and even questions involving customary international law involved in disputes before domestic tribunals.[29] One of the chief virtues which he sees in this proposal is its "prophylactic effect". No State needs to appear before the Court as either applicant or respondent. A State need not even appear in the procedure at all unless it desires to submit written comment.[30] It combines desir-

24. Id. at 269, 275.
25. Id. at 275.
26. Supra note 22 at p. 152.
27. Id. at pp. 155-156. See supra note 18 at 280.
28. Id. at p. 157.
29. Supra note 18 at pp. 308-313.
30. Id. at 311.

able features of advisory and contentious procedures. At the same time, the Court would render binding decisions on the proper interpretation of treaties.

He also suggested the possibility of giving advisory opinions to parties to a dispute.[31]

Jenks[32] also proposed an Amendment to Article 34 of the Statute to allow public international organisations access as parties to contentious disputes before the Court. In this he was following a suggestion by the *Institut*, which, in 1954, adopted a resolution declaring that it was a matter of urgency to widen the terms of Article 34 of the Statute so as to grant access to the Court to international organisations of States.[33] It is not at all clear, however, whether the prospect of being sued by an international organisation would encourage a State to submit to the jurisdiction of the Court or increase its determination not to do so.

IMPARTIALITY

Impartiality and procedure

It would seem axiomatic that if States are going to submit their disputes to international adjudication they must have confidence in the impartiality of the justice meted out by the tribunal.

There are three separate facets to the question of impartiality; impartiality of procedure, impartiality of judges and impartiality of the law itself. In a recent book, V.S. Mani examined the procedural aspects of international adjudication.[34] In order to be considered impartial, a tribunal's rules of procedure must be seen to be upholding two fundamental procedural rights "*audi alteram partem*" (the right of the parties to be heard) and "equality of the parties". These two procedural norms are really two sides of the same coin. They both ensure that neither party is given a procedural advantage over the other and they both "instill confi-

---

31. Id. at p. 171. See in this regard the *North Sea Continental Shelf Case* 1969] ICJ 3. In that case, the Court was not called upon to delimit the continental shelf between the parties (at 46) but rather to decide "what principles of international law are applicable to the delimination as between the Parties of the area of the continental shelf in the North Sea which appertains to each of them... ." (at 6).
32. Supra note 22 at pp. 208-221.
33. (1954-II) 45 *Annuaire* 298. See also supra note 18 at 302.
34. Mani, *International Adjudication: Procedural Aspects* (1980).

dence in the minds of the litigant States in the efficiency and impartiality of the tribunal's mechanism". These two procedural norms serve other important functions as well. They "tend to serve the sovereign sensibilities of States". They facilitate the effective conduct of adjudication, enabling the tribunal to gather adequate material information concerning the dispute and [to] adjudicate the controverted claims". Finally, "they ensure effective participation by the disputant parties in the communicative process".[35]

But Mani was not proposing reform. His approach was to examine a variety of topics such as initiation of proceedings, written proceedings, oral arguments, presentation of evidence and interim protection in terms of the fundamental procedural norms which he had identified.

Impartiality of judges

Most of the proposals for reform, particularly those canvassed by the *Institut*, relate to procedures for the selection of judges. It should be noted initially that there are provisions in the Statute designed to safeguard the independence of the judges.

Article 18 declares that:

> No member of the Court can be dismissed unless, in the unanimous opinion of the other members, he has ceased to fulfill the required conditions.

Article 19 gives diplomatic privileges and immunities to judges who are engaged in the business of the Court. Article 32 provides that their salaries may not be decreased during their tenure in office. Article 16 provides that no member of the Court may exercise any political or administrative function. Article 17, paragraph 1 says that no member of the Court may act as agent, counsel or advocate in any case and paragraph (2) prevents judges from participating in cases in which they have previously taken part as counsel, agent or advocate or even as a member of some other

35. Id. at p. 15.

international tribunal or of a municipal court. Article 24 allows a Judge to recuse himself for "special reasons".

But there is still a general feeling that the questions of qualifications of the judges tend to be submerged in a quest for representation of "voting blocs made up of regional and/or social, economic and political 'affinity' groups".[36] In response to this feeling, the *Institut* proposed, in 1954, that judges of the Court should be elected on the basis of their personal qualifications in accordance with Article 2 of the Statute, although it did caution that this resolution was without prejudice to the necessity of maintaining a certain geographical balance on the Court as provided in Article 9.[37]

One thing which may affect the independence of judges is their eligibility for re-election. The current term is 9 years after which a judge is eligible for re-election. If a judge feels that his voting recod is likely to be taken into consideration when he stands for re-election, this may affect his independence. Thus, the *Institut* proposed in 1954, that judges should be elected for one term of 15 years with no eligibility for re-election.[38]

One particularly intriguing proposal, related specifically to acceptance of compulsory jurisdiction, was not considered by the *Institut* but rather in the Sixth Committee deliberations on the principles of friendly settlement discussed above.[39] The representative of Japan, Mr. Hattori, proposed that acceptance of the Court's compulsory jurisdiction should be a factor in deciding its composition.[40]

Lauterpacht has isolated two separate issues concerning the impartiality of judges or international arbiters. One is the question of their personal integrity. He noted that this question was given prominence in the second half of the nineteenth century, when arbitration first became the subject of scientific legal discussion. He dismissed it by suggesting that the lack of reality which characterised international arbitration in that period was responsible for the detailed treatment of a subject "whose gravity and practical application has proved to be altogether imaginary". Today we

---

36. Supra note 18 at 282.
37. (1954-II) 45 *Annuaire* 296; 49 AJIL 14 (1955); Gross, id. at 282-283.
38. (1954-II) 45 *Annuaire* 421-422; Gross, id. at 291.
39. See supra notes 9-16 and accompanying text.
40. GAOR, 18th Sess., Sixth Committee, 821st Mtg. (Nov. 27, 1963), p. 226. Discussed supra note 18 at 283-284.

hardly ever see that problem discussed.[41] In the words of one commentator:

> ... the personal integrity of the judges may be taken for granted. In fact in the history of permanent courts, no judge has ever been accused of being swayed by consideration of personal gain, nor, it may be asserted, has any doubt been cast on the independence of the Court as a whole.[42]

The far more serious problem, which has exercised scholars and laymen alike, has been the question of the political impartiality of the judges on the International Court of Justice. Historically, a "deep-rooted distrust and scepticism about the impartiality of 'alien' judges"[43] has affected the policy of many States. It has never been cited specifically as a reason for any State's refusal to appear before the Court. But it did play a considerable part in the United States' national debate over the Connally Amendment. If we recall our discussion of the Connally Amendment in Chapter 5, we noted that a considerable suspicion was manifested by the Senators that the Court might assume jurisdiction over a matter which was essentially within the domestic jurisdiction of the United States if the U.S. did not protect itself with that Amendment.

Debate over the retention of the Connally Amendment in 1960 revealed an even deeper suspicion on the part of most of the witnesses who appeared before the Senator Foreign Relations Committee. The Texas Bar Association, for instance passed a resolution which it submitted to the Committee stating that the World Court was:

> ... essentially foreign, not necessarily competent, probably political rather than judicial in its attitudes and decisions, possibly dominated by our enemies and therefore likely dis-

41. One general discussion of the problem is found in Wetter, *The International Arbitral Process: Public and Private* (1979) Vol. III, pp. 408-444. See also Ch. VIII, Vol. III at pp. 3-355 which deals with "the *Venezuela-Guyana Boundary Dispute*: An In Depth Study of Nullity of An Arbitral Award".

42. Anand, "The International Court of Justice and Impartiality Between Nations" (1963) 12 Ind.Y.B.Intn'l Affairs 12, 37.

43. Id. at 13.

posed to be hostile to the major interests of the United States.[44]

Some witnesses were upset that there were "Communist" Judges on the Court[45] and some even imagined that the Court was packed with Communists.[46]

It is very difficult to resist the inference that nationality exerts a powerful influence on a judge. In fact a committee of the Permanent Court of International Justice consisting of Judges Loder, Moore and Anzilotti, lent credence to this notion:

> Of all influences to which men are subject, none is more powerful, more persuasive, or more subtle, than the tie of allegiance that binds them to the land of their homes and kindred and to the great sources of the honours and preferments for which they are so ready to spend their fortunes and risk their lives.[47]

Sir Hersch Lauterpacht strongly resisted this view. He felt that conscious bias in favour of a judge's own State is both a dereliction of duty and an abuse of the powers of his office. A judge's nationality may influence him subconsciously.[48] However, the Statute of the International Court of Justice (and the Permanent Court of International Justice before it) specifies that one qualification of the judge is that he should be of the "highest moral character". This standard, he felt, is aimed at combatting, not so much personal corruption, but judicial bias stemming from national sympathies.[49] He also felt that the occasons on which judges conspicuously fail to overcome political bias or prejudice is in the nature of an exception.[50]

He concluded that:

44. *Compulsory Jurisdiction: International Court of Justice*, Hearings before the Committee on Foreign Relations, U.S. Senate, 86th Congress, Second session on S. Res. 94 (January 27 and February 17, 1960), p. 70. Cited id. at 18.
45. See Schweppe, "The Connally Amendment Should not be Withdrawn", 46 ABAJ 732, 732-3 (1960).
46. Supra note 42 at 18.
47. PCIJ, Ser. E, No. 4, p. 75. See also Hudson, *The Permanent Court of International Court of Justice* (1943), p. 355; Rosenne, *The International Court of Justice* (1957), p. 152; Anand, supra note 42 at 39.
48. Lauterpacht, *The Function of Law in the International Community* (1933), p. 215.
49. Id. at pp. 215-216.
50. Id. at pp. 216-217.

To deny the very possibility of international judges being impartial is to exhibit a shallow scepticism which ignores both human nature and ... historical experience.[51]

However, when he surveyed the judgments given by the Permanent Court of International Justice, he found that in sixteen cases in which "the parties have availed themselves of the right to appoint a national judge", the national judges voted with the majority in favour of their States' positions. In one case, the record did not disclose the names of all the dissenting judges. In the remaining 12 cases the national judges dissented in favour of their own losing Governments.[52] But it appears that he was talking about judges *ad hoc* rather than all national judges.

In 1969, Il Ro Suh conducted a study of the voting behaviour of national judges on the Permanent Court of International Justice and the International Court of Justice. He considered a total of two hundred and three votes in fifty-four contentious cases and eight advisory opinions. He found that only four judges dissented from a majority opinion favouring their Governments, none of them were judges *ad hoc*. Thirty-two votes, including eleven by judges *ad hoc* were cast with the majority against their Governments, ninety-seven votes including 56 votes by judges *ad hoc* were cast with the majority in favour of their Governments and seventy votes, of which eighteen were by judges *ad hoc* were cast in dissent in favour of their Governments.[53]

What the study shows is that national judges, even judges *ad hoc* have not always supported their own Governments' positions although they did so in a substantial (but not overwhelming) majority of situations (about 82.3%).

He did feel that the seventy minority votes cast in favour of their own Governments by national judges did tend to suggest rather strongly that those judges were influenced by national

51. Id. at p. 218.
52. Id. at p. 230.
53. Il Ro Suh, "Voting Behaviour of National Judges in International Courts", 63 AJIL 222, 227-228 (1969). Similar studies were done by Liacouras, *The International Court of Justice* (1962) Vol. II, p. 527b; Larsen, "The Facts, the Law and the Connally Amendment", (1961) Duke L.J. 110; Samore, "National Origins v. Impartial Decisions: A Study of World Court Holdings", 34 Chicago-Kent L.R. 201 (1956). The latest study done on the question of judicial impartiality was devoted exclusively to judges *ad hoc*, Nsereko, "The International Court, Impartiality and Judges Ad Hoc" (1973) 13 Indian J.I.L. 207.

184

interests particularly since in eleven cases, national judges were the only dissenters in an otherwise unanimous Court.[54]

It would take another similar study to determine whether, in 1984, 15 years after Il Ro Suh's study, the situation has remained static, or there has been a swing against, or in favour of judicial support for the home State. None the less, it must be regarded as defamatory of the judicial independence of the judges to regard them as representatives of their home States (although the institution of judges *ad hoc* lends credence to this notion).

What we may say, however, is that the judges are people who have risen to positions of prominence in their home States. Such people are unlikely to be rebels either politically or by temperament.

Lauterpacht admits that, even in States which have judiciaries possessed of the highest degree of integrity, "birth, training and community of sentiment or interest to one section of the population may pose a problem in matters involving economic policy and in disputes involving the opposing interests either of capital and labour, or generally of the wealthy and the poor".[55]

That judges do bring value judgments to their interpretation of the law was recognised and, in fact, welcomed by European and American jurists in the late nineteenth century.[56]

It was the view of these jurists that policy choices inevitably play a role in judicial decision making.[57] The law cannot "be worked out like mathematics from some general axiom of conduct".[58] But, if the law is to remain impartial, policy must stem, not from the political bias of the judge, but from enquiry into the interests which society[59] or, more accurately, the law[60] wishes to protect. It is concerned with social and economic facts from which a judge can determine the most just solution in any given situa-

54. Id. at 229.
55. Supra note 48 at p. 217.
56. See Pound, "The Scope and Purpose of Sociological Jurisprudence", 25 Harv. L.R. 140, 143 (1911).
57. Holmes, "The Path of the Law", 10 Harv. L.R. 457, 466 (1897).
58. Id. at 467.
59. Gény, *Method d'Interpretation et Sources en Droit Privé Positif* (1899) § 11, *The Modern Legal Philosophy Series* (Transl. Husik 1913), Vol. 9 at pp. 35-39.
60. Gmelin in *The Modern Legal Philosophy Series*, ed. at pp. 85-145 (Translated by Bruncken from a collection of essays published under the title *Quosque* in 1910).

tion.[61] Roscoe Pound called this form of jurisprudence "Sociological Jurisprudence".[62]

In our day, the Sociological School of Harold Lasswell and Myres McDougal seeks to extend these insights about value judgment and the law to the study of international law.[63]

Bringing value judgments to their decisions may indeed have been what judges were doing all along.[64] But a jurisprudence which recognises that value judgments play a role in judicial decisions strikes at the heart of the notion of judicial impartiality.

Impartiality of the law

This type of jurisprudence can work in a municipal society which is, at least notionally, a community of shared values. But it inevitably raises serious questions of confidence for those who do not share the values of the judges.

Western democratic nations tend to pride themselves on the fact that their legal systems operate under the "rule of law" a principle which aims at ensuring impartiality of technique. But, in a modern pluralistic nation-state, a value oriented approach works best if the different segments of society see the law as protecting competing interests with some impartiality. In short, the most important interest which the law must protect is the interest of diversity. The law must not be seen as an instrument of coercion in the hands of one particular dominant race or class.

In International society, the common denominator of ethics and values is even wider. Thus, if States of widely different ideological and cultural backgrounds are going to be induced to submit to a process of adjudication according to the law, the law must be impartial, not merely as a matter of technique but in its substantive rules as well. Otherwise, the notion that the judge must apply values based on the interests that the law protects can easily be taken to confirm the Soviet view of international law, based on

61. Supra note 59.
62. Pound, "Mechanical Jurisprudence", 8 Col. L.R. 605, 609 (1908).
63. See *inter alia* McDougal, Lasswell and Reisman, "Theories About International Law: Prologue to a Configurative Jurisprudence", 8 Va.J.I.L. 188 (1968).
64. Lawson, *A Common Lawyer Looks at the Civil Law* (1969), pp. 82-83.

the Marxist theory, that law is the instrument of the ruling class.[65] According to the Soviet view, as long as "Socialist" judges are in the minority on the International Court of Justice, it is a tool of Anglo-American imperialism and cannot be expected to render impartial justice.[66]

It may be difficult, if not impossible, to overcome an ideological commitment to a view of the Court as biased. But progress may be possible with those non-aligned, Third World States whose views are not set in ideological concrete. The views of many of them are comparable to that of "Socialist" States but for different reasons.[67] They observe that international law has historically developed amongst Western European Nations and is consequently a reflection of European values.[68]

The decision of the International Court of Justice which did more than anything else to reinforce this view was its 1966 decision in the Second Phase of the *South West Africa Case*[69] dismissing, as inadmissible, the applications of Ethiopia and Liberia against South Africa concerning its administration of the territory in question under a League of Nations Mandate. This decision was widely seen as upholding Western values at the expense of the values and interests of the Third World:

> Not only were the new states disappointed with the result of the South West Africa Case, they found so very little force of conviction in the majority justification of that decision that they were unwilling to accept the Court's work in other areas.[70]

If the Court is to interpret the law in the light of the values pro-

65. Lissitzyn, *International Law in a Divided World* (1963), pp. 14-18; Hazard, "Renewed Emphasis Upon a Socialist International Law", 65 AJIL 142, 143 (1971); Anand, supra note 42 at 19; Merrills, "The Justiciability of International Disputes" (1969) 47 Can. Bar R. 241, 256-258.

66. As to the record of "Socialist" judges see Grzybowski, "Socialist Judges in the International Court of Justice" (1964) Duke Law Journal 536. But see Franck, *The Structure of Impartiality* (1968), p. 34. "In appraising Russian attitudes towards the third-party decision making system it behooves us to mix our heady brew of *J'accuse* with a dash of sobering *mea culpa*".

67. Stone, *International Court and World Crisis* (1962), p. 36.

68. Anand, supra note 42 at 20; Merrills, supra note 65 at 256; Nsereko, supra note 53 at 217.

69. [1966] ICJ 6.

70. Prott, "The Style of Judgment in the International Court of Justice" (1970-73) 5 Aus. YBIL 75, 81. See also Gross, supra note 18 at 267.

tected by the law, and States are to gain confidence in the impartiality of the Court and the judges, then they cannot proceed on the basis of seat-of-the-pants hunches about what the values are. The values need to be worked out systematically and with the participation of all States. To a certain extent, this is being done by the United Nations pursuant to its Article 13 duty to encourage the progressive development and codification of international law as manifested in such codification conferences as the Third United Nations Conference on the Law of the Sea and in the work of the International Law Commission.[71] More work needs to be done, particularly in the area of "general principles of law recognised by civilised nations".[72]

JUSTICIABILITY

States which lack confidence in the impartiality of the Court are unlikely, as a rule, to accept compulsory jurisdiction whereas, the problem of non-appearance usually involves States which have accepted the compulsory jurisdiction and have then refused to appear as respondents in specific actions. Failure to appear and failure to accept the compulsory jurisdiction of the Court are both aspects of the same problem, a refusal to accept the principle of third-party settlement of disputes. Thus the two issues share many of the same conceptual problems. But there are differences.

States which have accepted compulsory jurisdiction and subsequently refused to participate in a case, do not usually base their refusal on claims about the lack of impartiality of the Court. They are more likely to argue that the dispute is non-justiciable.

Justiciability has been defined as the "fitness of a dispute for settlement on the basis of legal principles".[73] A distinction must be made between legal and political non-justiciability. There are matters which, according to the rules of international law are not suitable for adjudication. These rules relate to the admissibility of

71. On the recent work of The International Law Commission see El Baradei, Franck & Trachtenberg, *The International Law Commission: The Need For a New Direction* (UNITAR 1981). This work is discussed by Franck and El Baradei at 76 AJIL 630 (1982).

72. See supra note 7, Ch. 1 at pp. 3-22.

73. De Visscher, *Theory and Reality in Public International Law* (Transl. Corbett 1959), p. 331.

the application. They include such rules as the exhaustion of local remedies rule applied in the *Interhandel Case*[74] and the nationality of claims rule applied in the *Nottebohm Case.*[75]

In the *Nuclear Test Cases*, the Court dismissed the New Zealand and Australian applications on the ground that, since the objectives of the applicants had been achieved, there was no longer a justiciable claim before it.[76]

In the *Northern Cameroons Case*, the Republic of Cameroon attempted to challenge a plebiscite held by the United Kingdom under the terms of a United Nations Trusteeship Agreement concerning the territory in question. The people of the Northern Cameroons had opted to join Nigeria instead of Cameroon.[77] The Agreement had terminated and was no longer in force. But the applicant sought a declaratory judgment that the United Kingdom had breached the terms of the agreement relating to the plebiscite.[78]

The Court refused to agree that the judicial protection which the applicant claimed under the Agreement survived after the agreement had terminated and the Trust had come to an end.[79] The Court said:

> ... it is not the function of the Court merely to provide a basis for political action if no question of legal rights is involved.[80]
>
> ... the Court must discharge the duty to which it has already called attention — the duty to safeguard the judicial function. Whether or not at the moment the application was filed there was jurisdiction in the Court to adjudicate the dispute submitted to it, circumstances that have since arisen render any adjudication devoid of purpose. Under these conditions, for the Court to proceed further in the case would not, in its opinion, be a proper discharge of its duties.[81]

74. See supra Ch. 5, note 178 and accompanying text.
75. See supra Ch. 2, note 113 and accompanying text.
76. See supra Ch. 2, notes 158-165 and accompanying text.
77. [1963] ICJ 15, 23.
78. Id. at 36.
79. Ibid.
80. Id. at 37.
81. Id. at 38.

In the *Asylum Case*,[82] the Court held that Colombia had no right to grant asylum in its embassy to the Peruvian political fugitive, Haya de la Torre under the 1929 Havana Convention on Asylum.

Subsequently, a dispute arose over how to give effect to the Court's Judgment. The Colombian Government filed a new application in which it asked the Court to state in what manner the judgment was to be carried out and to declare that Colombia was not bound to surrender Haya de la Torre to Peruvian authorities.[83]

The Court found that it was being asked to make a choice amongst the various courses by which the asylum could be terminated. These courses were, however, conditioned by facts and possibilities which the Parties alone were in a position to appreciate. The choice amongst them could not be based on legal conditions but rather on conditions of practicability and political expediency. It was not part of the Court's judicial function to make such a choice.[84]

Other questions of non-justiciability involve the reserved domain which has been considered in Chapter 5. Only in very unusual circumstances, involving a clear international undertaking, would the International Court of Justice dictate to a State who its Head of State should be or the manner and method of choosing its Government or whether it should pursue a socialist or a free-market economic policy. These would be regarded as internal matters. But, in addition, the Court would not normally dictate to a State how it should vote in the United Nations or what Governments or States it should recognise or what other States it should ally itself with in a political crisis. These are generally regarded as matters of policy. Thus, the reserved domain includes not only matters exclusively or essentially within the domestic jurisdiction of States, but also matters which international law recognises to be matters of State policy.

But, as with matters of domestic jurisdiction, a State may enter into certain undertakings with other States in respect of such matters or its discretion may be circumscribed by rules of customary international law. In such a case, a dispute involving such treaties or rules of customary international law becomes justiciable and there is no legal reason for the Court to refuse to resolve such matters.

82. [1950] ICJ, 266.
83. *Haya de la Torre Case* [1951] ICJ 71, 75.
84. Id. at 79.

In the Advisory Opinion on the *Legal Consequences for States of the Continued Presence of South Africa in Namibia (South West Africa) Notwithstanding Security Council 276 (1970)*, the Court said that Members of the United Nations are under a duty to refrain from entering into treaty relations with South Africa in all cases where the Government of South Africa purports to act in relation to Namibia. Member States are under a duty to refrain from sending diplomatic or special missions to South Africa which include Namibia in their jurisdiction, to refrain from sending consular agents to Namibia, to refrain from entering into economic or other relationships re Namibia and to refrain from recognising certain of South Africa's administrative acts in Namibia.[85]

The usual reason given for not participating in a case already submitted to the Court is that the dispute is of a political nature and not a proper one for judicial settlement.[86] Thus, in the *Fisheries Jurisdiction Cases*, the Icelandic Government argued that this was a matter involving "the vital interests of the people of Iceland".[87] In the *Nuclear Test Cases*, the French Government protested that the matter was too closely connected with the national security and defence of France and in the *Hostages Case*, the Iranian Government complained that the hostage problem was only a part of a larger problem inherent in the relationship between the United States and Iran of over twenty years duration.[88]

The non-responding respondents argued that the Court did not possess jurisdiction with varying degrees of authority and conviction. In the *Anglo-Iranian Oil Case*, and in the *Aegean Sea Case*, the Court ultimately held that it did not have jurisdiction. In the *Nuclear Test Cases*, France's claim that the Court had no jurisdiction was supported in part by an actual reservation of matters connected with the national defence. But there were other jurisdictional issues in those cases which were not as clearcut and it is doubtful that France would have participated in the Case if the Court had found that it had jurisdiction.

In the *Hostages Case*, the Court did not even deem it necessary to waste time with a jurisdictional phase. Iran might ultimately have got around to denouncing the treaties on which jurisdiction

85. [1971] ICJ 16, 55-56.
86. See generally supra Ch. 2.
87. Correspondence from the Minister for Foreign Affairs of Iceland to the Registrar [1975] ICJ Pleadings.
88. [1979] ICJ 7, 10-11.

was based. But during the early stages of a revolution it is rare to sit down to review treaty commitments. Revolutionary ferment does not usually permit such detached reflection.

In all of the above cases, it would seem that, while lack of jurisdiction was one professed motive for abstention from the judicial process, the primary motive was the claim in each case that the action was non-justiciable.

Any discussion of non-justiciability inevitably involves a dialogue with Sir Hersch Lauterpacht, the most articulate critic of the doctrine of non-justiciability. In his book *The Function of Law in the International Community*, written before he received his knighthood and well before his elevation to the bench of the International Court of Justice, he identified "four clear — although not mutually exclusive — conceptions of legal or justiciable disputes". These are:

(a) Legal disputes are such differences between States as are capable of judicial settlement by the application of existing and ascertainable rules of international law.

(b) Legal disputes are those in which the subject-matter of the claim relates to questions of minor and secondary importance not affecting the vital interests of States, or their external independence, or internal sovereignty, or territorial integrity, or honour, or any of the other important interests usually referred to in the so-called "restrictive clauses" in arbitration conventions.

(c) Legal disputes are those in regard to which the application of existing rules of international law is sufficient to ensure a result which is not incompatible with the demands of justice between States and with a progressive development of international relations.

(d) Legal disputes are those in which the controversy concerns existing legal rights as distinguished from claims aiming at a change of existing law.[89]

Of these, the second conception is the oldest and probably more accurately reflects the thinking of Government leaders than the others.

89. Supra note 48 at pp. 19-20.

Traditionally, treaties involving international arbitration exempted disputes which might affect the vital interests, independence and international honour of the contracting parties. Later treaties limited the obligation to arbitrate "legal disputes" or disputes "with regard to which the parties are in conflict as to their respective rights". Such clauses were inserted into declarations of acceptance of the compulsory jurisdiction of the Permanent Court of International Justice as a means of excluding "political" disputes or disputes related to interests and not to rights.[90] In his book, *Theory and Reality in Public International Law*, De Visscher expresses the view that, when a State takes a political position, it is expressing the priority that its government assigns to the interests involved:

> The specifically political quality is to be seen in the particularly close relation that rulers assert from time to time between the State and certain goods or values that they hold indispensible to its security or greatness.[91]

Iceland, for example, regarded the conservation of its fisheries resources as non-justiciable because, as a nation dependent upon its fisheries, it regarded the matter as vital.

De Visscher also pointed out that the political nature of a dispute was not constant. A dispute may be political one day and non-political the next.[92] A relatively unimportant question may suddenly flare into a political question of the first magnitude.

Whether something is a political question also depends on whom the State is dealing with. An act by a State which is considered unfriendly is likely to be "Taken as an attack upon the State's honour" whereas the same act by a friend may be considered negligible.[93]

Thomas Franck points out that *"since the importance of a dispute is a subjective reaction to an event and not an inherent quality of the event itself*, the test is nearly useless from the point of view of good order" [Franck's emphasis].[94]

90. Ibid.
91. Supra note 73 at p. 73.
92. Ibid.
93. Id. at p. 285.
94. *The Structure of Impartiality* (1968), p. 178.

Hence:

> ... the only useful guide from the legal point of view, is the external behaviour of interested States.[95]

This underlines the difficulty of developing legal norms which can be applied by a Court to determine what is a legal dispute and what is a political one. Political questions, according to De Visscher, are the expression of "vital and moving forces". They are subject to constant change. Thus they cannot be locked up in a definition.[96] He did, however, acknowledge that certain matters generally have a political character while others are political only on exceptional occasions.[97] But his book demonstrates throughout, the operation of political factors in all areas of international law and the fact that there is no clear demarcation between political and other disputes. With regard to domestic matters he notes that there is hardly any matter which "looked at from a certain angle or a certain level of generalisation or specialisation, may not raise now a question within the exclusive jurisdiction, now one subject to international regulation".[98]

There are many rules of international law which are designed to contain the exercise of internal powers within certain limits. De Visscher gives, as an example, the delimitation by each State of its territorial sea, a vital question in the *Fisheries Jurisdiction Cases*.

This is in fact precisely the kind of rule which has been at issue in most cases of non-appearance. In the *Sino-Belgian* dispute, it was the treatment of foreign nationals within the territory of the Republic of China. The *Anglo-Iranian Oil Case* involved the nationalisation of the property of aliens in Iran. The *Nottebohm Case* involved the right of a State to determine who its nationals were, a matter clearly within the reserved domain, and the right of a State to protect the interests of those nationals before an international tribunal, a matter which was not. The *Nuclear Test Cases* involved the right of a State to use its own territory in a way which might result in nuclear pollution of the territory of other States. The *Aegean Sea Case* involved the right of a State to delimit its continental shelf.

95. Supra note 73 at p. 73.
96. Supra note 73 at p. 73.
97. Ibid.
98. Id. at p. 222.

194

Finally, the *Hostages Case* dealt with some of the most hallowed rules of international law, those concerning what a State may do with foreign diplomats in its own territory whom it suspects of committing espionage or other criminal acts.

> All that can be said about the content of the reserved domain is that the problem of its demarcation arises most often in connection with matters which, owing to their projection into the international sphere or their repercussions there, are most likely to bring into play the interests of more than one State.[99]

Other writers are of the opinion that the distinction between legal and political disputes has no real validity.

Lauterpacht argued that all disputes which can be resolved by the application of legal rules are legal whether or not they affect the vital interests of States.[100] Thus, all conflicts in the sphere of international politics can be reduced to conflicts of a legal nature.[101]

One writer points out that there have been quite a few situations in which cases involving political tension have been brought before the Court.[102] He cites as examples the *Anglo-Iranian Oil Case*, the *Corfu Channel Case*, the *Cases of Treatment in Hungary of Aircraft of the United States of America,*[103] the *Asylum Case,*[104] the *Aerial Incident Cases,*[105] and the *Antarctic Territory Cases.*[106]

Lauterpacht points to the historical paradox that many disputes of political importance were settled by the judicial process while many other disputes which were "obviously" capable of decision

99. Ibid.
100. Lauterpacht, supra note 48 at p. 139. See also Doecker, "International Politics and The International Court of Justice", 35 Tulane L.R. 767, 770 (1961); Brown "Reserved International Rights", 38 AJIL 281 (1944); Schwarzenberger, *Power Politics* (2d Rev.ed. 1951), p. 450, although Schwarzenberger argues that "an organised society based upon a community spirit and founded upon the rule of law seems to be an illusion."
101. Lauterpacht, id. at p. 164.
102. Doecker, supra note 100 at 782.
103. [1954] ICJ 99, 103.
104. Supra note 82.
105. *Aerial Incident of October 7, 1952* [1956] ICJ 9; *Aerial Incident of March 10, 1953* [1956] ICJ 6.
106. [1956] ICJ 12, 15.

along strictly legal lines were withheld from adjudication or arbitration on the ground that they were essentially political.[107]

In fact, all international disputes including legal controversies are political in character because the State is a political institution and all questions which affect it, particularly those which deal with its relationship with other States are political.[108]

Arthur Larsen, the Director of the World Peace Through Law Centre demonstrated this point. In a paper which he gave to the American Society of International Law[109] in 1960, he examined some of the most vital political problems of the day such as Berlin, Suez, the Sino-Indian Border, refugee problems and the Gulf of Aquaba and showed, in each case, how they involved legal issues although he cautioned that he did so with no illusions as to whether the Parties to those disputes could realistically be expected to adjudicate them.[110]

With respect to the Berlin problem, he identified the legal issues as:

(1) The extent, if any, of the obligation of the U.S.S.R. to permit German personnel and goods traffic between West Germany and West Berlin under the Jessup-Malik agreement of 1949;

(2) The extent, if any, of the obligations of the Soviet Union to permit allied military (a) rail, (b) motor vehicle or (c) air communication between West Germany and West Berlin under:

(i)   an alleged agreement by Presidential correspondence, acceptance by non-reply or action or estoppel in 1945,

(ii)   an alleged agreement by practice,

(iii) an alleged agreement by incorporation into techncial day-to-day agreements in Kommandatura committees especially the Committee on Air Travel;

(3) The extent, if any, of the obligation of the Soviet Union to permit the Western Allies to communicate between West Germany and West Berlin under an alleged rule of customary international law such as easement by necessity...;

107. Supra note 48 at p. 163.
108. Id. at p. 153. See also supra note 10 at p. 172.
109. Larsen, "Peace Through Law: The Role and Limits of Adjudication – Some Contemporary Problems", 54 Proc. ASIL 8 (1960).
110. Id. at 9.

(4) The right, if any, of the U.S.S.R. to transfer the execution of its obligations, if any, under the above headings to the German Democratic Republic without divesting itself of its own liabilities to the Western Allies;

(5) The right, if any, of the U.S.S.R. to divest itself of these alleged obligations completely by according to the German Democratic Republic "full sovereignty".... .

(6) The obligations, if any, of the German Democratic Republic under (4) and (5) above;....[111]

The nature of the judicial task is isolation of the legal problems from the political situation and solution of the legal problems on the basis of objective rules of international law to the exclusion of political, moral and other extra-legal considerations.[112]

In the words of Judge Hardy C. Dillard:

Just as men are neither a pack of wolves nor a choir of angels and marriages are sometimes happy and sometimes sad, so with disputes. Most of them, as we all know, have both a political and a legal component. And surely, the legal component can usually be syphoned off for analysis.[113]

Such matters as the sovereignty and independence of States are fundamental legal principles. The rules of international law stem from concern on the part of States to protect those interests. Therefore, as Lauterpacht has pointed out, they "are safe under international judicial settlement, because nothing − except force − can alienate them".[114]

Commenting on this, Jenks said:

The logic of this position is unanswerable, but a quarter of a century has elapsed and it still appears to fail to carry any conviction to men of affairs.[115]

In an attempt to determine why this is so, some writers have

111. Id. at 9-10. Contra Stone, supra note 67 at p. 7. His arguments will be discussed infra notes 160-162 and accompanying text.
112. Rosenne, *The International Court of Justice* (1957), p. 66.
113. Address to the American Society of International Law, "The World Court − An Inside View", 67 Proc. ASIL 296, 299 (1972-73).
114. Supra note 48 at p. 173.
115. Jenks, "Hersch Lauterpacht: Scholar As Prophet" (1960) 36 BYIL 1, 15.

pointed out that recourse to judicial settlement is, in itself, a political step.[116] Also, a judicial decision to the effect that the law is on one State's side is a powerful political argument.[117] By the same token, a State which has argued and lost its case in the International Court has visibly had its legal arguments defeated and its political position weakened.[118]

As De Visscher points out, lawyers and politicians look at these matters through different lenses. A lawyer is likely to ask whether there are rules of international law which can be brought to bear on the issue. To a politician, the question is the extent to which State interests, or even Government policy (which is often identified with State interests) are affected by the dispute. A Government may refuse to submit a dispute to judicial settlement without disputing the existence of legal rules which can be applied by a judge or arbitrator.[119] Thus, the attempt to measure the justiciability of disputes in terms of their political importance is illusory.

Other attempts to define "political questions" relate to the existence of ascertainable rules of law. In the *Nuclear Test Cases*, Judge Petrén argued that the admissibility of the application depended on the existence of an applicable rule of customary international law.[120] Because he was unable to discern the existence of such a rule, he thought that the claim should have been inadmissible. In short, he would have declared a *non liquet*.

The view that there are gaps in the rules of international law which make certain disputes incapable of legal settlement was strongly contested by Lauterpacht who argued that a judicial decision is a choice between interests which are worthy of legal protection and that such a choice was always both possible and necessary.[121] He strongly believed in the principle of completeness of the legal order.[122]

Other writers have supported the notion of completeness of the legal order on the ground that, where there are no principles of

116. Jenks, supra note 22 at p. 124; Doecker, supra note 100 at 784; see also Merrills, supra note 65 at pp. 241-242.
117. Grzyboski, supra note 66 at 547.
118. Merrills, supra note 65 at 251.
119. Supra note 73 at p. 331.
120. [1974] ICJ 253, 305.
121. "'Non Liquet' and the Completeness of Law" (1958) *Symbolae Verjil* 196.
122. Lauterpacht, *Development of International Law by the International Court* (1958), pp. 4-5.

international law, a Court is bound to dismiss the applicant's case[123] (whatever is not prohibited is permitted).[124] To a certain extent, the Permanent Court of Justice supported this view in the *Lotus Case*.[125] However Lauterpacht felt that the approach was dangerous in that a rigid application of such a test would reduce the activity of a judge to a merely automatic function.[126] He criticised the *Lotus Case* as a "misguided insistence upon the explicitness of rules of international law".[127] He felt that, if it was false to assume that there were gaps in the law, it was equally false to assume that the "consequence of a presumed silence of the law is a rigidly negative attitude toward interests claiming legal protection".[128] The necessary aim of any legal system is not only formal completeness, but material completeness in which the judge must consider not only the letter of the law, but also its spirit and purpose.

In answer to this, De Visscher argued that international law is not a hierarchic order which embraces all of the interests or values of States.[129] He assailed "doctrinal complacency on the subject of what is called the plenitude of the legal order".[130]

But, the drafters did not intended to allow the International Court of Justice to declare *non liquet*. What is now Article 38(1) (c) was inserted in the Statute precisely to prevent that.[131] As far as the *Nuclear Test Cases* are concerned, one author has demonstrated the existence of "general principles of law" applicable to the question of whether one State may use its territory so as to interfere with other States' peaceful enjoyment of their territory.[132]

Allied to the suggestion that there are gaps in international law which render some disputes unsuitable for judicial settlement is

123. See Fitzmaurice, "Hersch Lauterpacht – The Scholar as Judge Part I" (1961) 37 BYIL 1, 15.
124. Supra note 48 at p. 85.
125. [1927] PCIJ, Ser. A, No. 10, p. 4 at p. 18.
126. Supra note 48 at p. 85.
127. Id. at p. 94.
128. Id. at p. 86.
129. Supra note 73 at p. 328.
130. Id. at p. 352.
131. See Cheng, *General Principals of Law as Applied by International Courts and Tribunals* (1953), pp. 7-21. See League of Nations, *Procès Verbaux of the Committee of Jurists to Draft a Statute for a Permanent Court of International Justice* (1920), 14th Mtg., at pp. 307, 322-324.
132. Elkind, "Footnote to the Nuclear Test Cases: Abuse of Right – A Blind Alley for Environmentalists", 9 Vand.J. Transn'l L. 57 (1976).

the idea that a legal dispute involves a conflict of interests whereas a political dispute involves a conflict of rights. This notion arises from a perception that international law is not adequate to deal with certain problems.

In municipal societies, change in the law is usually effected by a legislature and is the result of a political decision. In international law there is no legislature capable of modifying or supplementing existing law.[133] Since international law is deficient in this respect, conflicts, which in municipal law are usually resolved by the legislature assume, in international society, the form of conflicts of interest.[134]

According to De Visscher, wars arising from disputes as to rights have been rare. In most cases, wars spring from conflicts of interest. Even where legal reasons were given for recourse to arms, the motives for doing so were political.[135]

Talking further about conflicts of interests, he cites the *Asylum Case* as an example of a case in which the problem was stated too narrowly. The nub of the problem was the surrender of a political prisoner to territorial authorities. The Havana Convention was the only law on the problem. But, as the Court recognised, there were many extra-legal problems involved in the dispute. Thus by putting the problem "on the narrow plane of the Havana Convention the parties put themselves into a position from which the Court could not extricate them".[136] An agreement by the Parties to submit the dispute to a settlement *ex aequo et bono* would have been more successful in depoliticising the dispute.

Many of our cases of non-appearance can be analysed in this way. In the *Sino-Belgian Treaty Case*, the Government of China was seeking a revision of its legal relationship with Belgium. It refused to go to Court unless Belgium agreed to allow the dispute to be settled *ex aequo et bono*.[137] The Treaty which it was seeking to overturn gave Belgium extraterritorial rights in Chinese territory. The Chinese position was not unlike that of present day Third World States and "Socialist" States which would regard such a treaty as an "unequal treaty" contravening *jus cogens* norms of

133. Supra note 48 at p. 245.
134. Id. at p. 352.
135. Supra note 73 at p. 327.
136. Id. at pp. 334-335.
137. Supra note 48 at pp. 199-200. See also, supra Ch. 2, note 2 and accompanying text.

customary international law.[138] Similarly, in the *Anglo-Iranian Oil Co. Case*, Iran was trying to extricate itself from an unequal position and gain sovereignty over its natural resources.

In the *Fisheries Jurisdiction Cases*, the law was truly in a state of flux. In his letter to the Court of January 11, 1974, the Icelandic Minister of Foreign Affairs noted that the Third United Nations Conference on the Law of the Sea had been convened and that:

> It is now a fact that the concept of an exclusive economic zone... of up to 200 miles in extent enjoys very wide support. This finds expression in a number of legislative enactments, conclusions of international meetings of the Sea-bed Committee as well as in the General Assembly of the United Nations.[139]

Unfortunately, this bare statement was the only argument that there was on the point. It was open to Iceland to appear and argue that there was a developing rule of customary international law permitting it to undertake management of its fisheries resources within the disputed zone. Had it done so, it is quite possible that the argument would have received more serious attention.

It may be that Judge Petrén was voicing a similar view in the *Nuclear Test Cases*. The New Zealand Application had noted "a growing juridical perception of the nature and quality of [nuclear testing] and a rapid development of law concerning it".[140] Petrén undoubtedly felt that this law had not yet emerged.

Iran's letter in the *Hostages Case*[141] suggests that Iran was seeking no less than a radical restructuring of its entire legal relationship with the United States.[142]

These cases illustrate that, since the mechanisms for changing

---

138. Brownlie, *Principles of Public International Law* (1966), pp. 495-496; Falk, "New States and the International Legal Order" (1966) 118 *Recueil des Courts* 7, 15-17.
139. [1975] ICJ Pleadings Vol. II at pp. 462-463.
140. [1974] ICJ Pleadings Vol. II at p. 8.
141. See supra Ch. 2, note 227 and accompanying text.
142. See Falk, "The Iran Hostage Crisis: Easy Answers and Hard Questions", 74 AJIL 411 (1980). On the other hand the Islamic Republic of Iran may recognise no law but the Law of God as revealed in the Koran. Arnold & Guillaume, *The Legacy of Islam* (1931), p. 288. But see Bassiouni, "Protection of Diplmats Under Islamic Law", 74 AJIL 609 (1980) which suggests that holding diplomatic hostages contravenes Islamic law as well as international law.

the law are decentralised, when the law on a particular topic is in the process of change, States may be reluctant to submit to judicial settlement for fear that a judicial decision might result in a premature crystallisation of the dispute.[143]

In international law, law violation may sometimes have a law-creating function. Where a rule of customary international law is violated and, rather than challenging the violation effectively, the preponderance of nations decides to follow suit, a new, permissive rule emerges by which the formerly prohibited conduct becomes lawful. This can be illustrated by the new rules relating to Exclusive Economic Zones. The initial impetus for this development was provided by a small number of "unlawful" attempts, such as Iceland's Declaration of July 15, 1971,[144] to appropriate an area of sea exceeding the 12-mile limit of the territorial sea which was the maximum permitted under the Geneva Convention on the Territorial Sea and Contiguous Zones 1958.

Where the parties do want to settle a dispute involving a conflict of interest, they have the option of submitting to settlement *ex aequo et bono* thus allowing the judge scope for judicial legislation although De Visscher suggests that this is more properly the function of an arbiter whose powers are fixed in a *compromis*, who is chosen by the parties and who therefore commands their confidence.[145]

Lauterpacht denied that the distinction between conflicts of rights and conflicts of interests was relevant to the problem of the scope of the judicial function in international law although he found no objection to it as a matter of political theory. It merely "states a fact in the domain of international politics". In so far as as the distinction is used to secure a machinery for binding settlement of conflicts of interests, it is impracticable. In so far as it is used to differentiate between disputes appropriate for binding judicial settlement and disputes which have to be dealt with by purely persuasive methods, it is unnecessary and perhaps even mischievous. It is unnecessary because a judicial agency cannot, by the very nature of its function, decide disputes which are not concerned with existing legal rights.[146]

143. Doecker, supra note 100 at 790.
144. See supra Ch. 2, note 116 and accompanying text.
145. Supra note 73 at p. 338.
146. Supra note 48 at pp. 369-370.

There is one more type of problem which has been labelled unsuitable for judicial settlement. In a paper given to the American Society of International Law, Professor Lon Fuller referred to "polycentric" problems which he defined as problems in which there can be no single solution or issue toward which a party can direct proofs and arguments.[147] He gave as examples: setting prices and wages within a managed economy; redrawing of boundaries of electoral districts to make them conform to shifts in population; assigning players on a football team to their respective positions; designing a system of throughways into a metropolitan area; allocating scarce funds for projects of scientific research; allocating air routes among various cities; drawing an international boundary across terrain that is complicated in terms of geography, natural resources and ethnology, etc.[148] The *Haya de la Torre Case* may have involved such a polycentric decision although the Judgment is by no means clear on that point.

Polycentric decisions are usually made by a commission which does not perform a legal function but an administrative one. But it is worth noting that when such a commission is accused of acting *ultra vires*, or failing to conform to its terms of reference, or using inappropriate standards, that is a legal matter, and courts will adjudicate on the question.[149]

In Lauterpacht's view, it is not the nature of a dispute which makes it unfit for judicial settlement, but the unwillingness of a State to have it settled by the application of law.[150] Speaking from the same platform as Fuller, Arthur Larsen made the same point:

> ... the real obstacle to adjudication is not inherent in the nature of things, but it is largely a matter of deliberate choice. As of today nations stay away from the Court not because of polycentricity, political nature or insufficient

147. Fuller, "Adjudication and the Rule of Law", 54 Proc. ASIL 1, 4 (1960).
148. Id. at 3-4.
149. See e.g., *Baker v. Carr*, 396 U.S. 186 (1962) decided after Fuller's paper was given. The U.S. Supreme Court decided that legislative districts must be of roughly equal proportion if they were to comply with the 14th Amendment guarantee of "equal protection" for the voters.
150. Supra note 48 at p. 369. But see Rosenne, "Sir Hersch Lauterpacht's Concept of the Task of an International Judge", 55 AJIL 825, 832, note 34 (1961). Rosenne believes that there are other extra-judicial factors which may establish the non-justiciability of a particular dispute.

shared content of principles, but simply because they prefer to retain their unilateral freedom of action, and in many cases because they apparently prefer to live with continuing controversy than take a chance on an unfavourable decision. In short, the problem isn't "can't" — its "won't".[151]

So we are left with the fundamental problem of the reluctance of States to submit their disputes to third-party settlement.

THIRD PARTY SETTLEMENT

It may be that a dispute is susceptible to settlement by the application of legal norms but that other modes of settlement are preferable. A negotiated settlement, for instance, may be more likely to result in a compromise from which each party can derive some satisfaction. This is not open to a court applying the law.[152] Thus a negotiated settlement may be preferable to the risk of an unfavourable judgment.[153] Nonetheless, most applications to the International Court of Justice detail the unsuccessful attempts which have been made to negotiate a solution and such attempts are widely regarded as a precondition to judicial settlement.

It has also been suggested that the uncertainty and unpredictability of international law are important factors in deterring States from submitting their disputes to the Court.[154] Since there are no international legislators as such, judges are not supposed to declare *non liquet* but to find applicable rules by recourse to "general principles of law".

Because it is not always easy to predict the outcome of a case which may affect matters of vital interest, States are reluctant to submit such disputes to adjudication.[155] If the judge is too bold, he will be accused of lack of predictability. If he is too cautious, the Tribunal "may fall into disuse and sterility".[156]

Of course, as Judge Dillard points out, municipal law is often possessed of this same uncertainty.[157]

151. Supra note 109 at p. 15.
152. Supra note 65 at 241-242.
153. Id. at 246-247.
154. Supra note 115 at 26.
155. Nsereko, supra note 53 at 218.
156. Supra note 18 at 254.
157. Supra note 113 at 298.

204

Thomas Franck goes even further when he says:

> ... third party law, unlike other order-creating systems, can
> only be understood as a process — and a fallible, existential
> human process at that — rather than a compendium of rules
> that are certain and immutable. Principles, concepts, evi-
> dence, there are; but certainty is impossible, even if it were
> desirable, and immutability is undesirable, even if it were
> possible.[158]

But Lauterpacht points out that there are a number of factors
which aggravate the problem in the domain of international law:

> They are the scarcity and indefiniteness of substantive rules
> of international law as a result of the comparative immaturity
> of the system, of the scarcity of precedent, both judicial and
> in the practice of States, and of the imperfections of the law-
> creating and the law-amending processes; the difficulties in
> the ascertainment of the existing law and the consequent
> uncertainty as to the exact legal position in many of its
> branches; the revealed lack of agreement between States on
> a number of subjects; the emphasis laid on the principle of
> independence and presumptive freedom of action with the
> resulting check upon a creative interpretation of existing
> law; ... .[159]

There seems to be a general assumption that greater certainty and
predictability in the law is likely to induce States to come to the
Court. But judicial settlement may actually be promoted by the
existence of uncertainty. Certainty in the law may, in fact, be a
powerful incentive to one party to go to court, the one that is
assured of success by clear and ascertainable legal rules. But what
of its adversary? It would seem to be assured of failure by the
same clear and ascertainable legal rules. It is likely to declare
defensively that the dispute is non-justiciable.

It has also been suggested that adjudication may produce
answers "rather distinct from the realities of the dispute as seen

158. Franck, *The Structure of Impartiality* (1968), pp. 60-61.
159. Supra note 48 at p. 70.

by the States in conflict".[160] Looking at the Berlin crisis,[161] Julius Stone answered Larsen by pointing out that the real concern of the disputants involved *realpolitik*. Berlin was a show-window of the West and the Western powers were interested in keeping it that way. The interest of the Soviet Union was to gain Western recognition of the German Democratic Republic.[162] These reasons and not the legal issues were the reason why the dispute threatened the peace. In fact, the Court might have made matters a good deal worse by answering the wrong question.

Franck believes, however, that this is simply another way of restating the "important matter" theory of non-justiciability.[163] Whether a dispute should end up in Court or not, he argues, should not depend on a facile shibboleth, such as the "political disputes" doctrine. What is wanted is rather a reasoned examination of the dispute and of the various alternative techniques of dispute settlement and Kelsen argues that the legal or political character of a dispute refers to the nature of the norms to be applied to the dispute.[164]

If a State files an application with the International Court of Justice, then we may assume that that State feels that the dispute concerns a conflict of legal rights which ought to be settled by the application of legal norms as opposed to political norms. In the *Hostages Case*, the United States was initially concerned to demonstrate to the world that it had taken every step to settle the dispute peacefully. That it later attempted to rescue the hostages by force seems to indicate that it ultimately lost patience with those efforts and the suggestion has been made that the rescue attempt evinced disrespect for the juridical process.[165]

If the dispute is truly non-justiciable according to the rules of international law, then the Court will declare the application inadmissible. If not, it will then decide whether it has jurisdiction.

---

160. Stone, supra note 67 at p. 8.
161. See supra notes 109-111 and accompanying text.
162. Supra note 67 at p. 8.
163. Supra note 94 at p. 178.
164. Kelsen, *Principles of International Law* (1952), pp. 381-382.
165. *Hostages Case* [1980] ICJ 3, 43-44. Even stronger condemnation of the rescue mission came from Judge Morozov (at 52) and Judge Tarazi who also criticized other extra-judicial actions by the United States aimed at securing release of the hostages (63-64). See Stein, "Contempt, Crisis, and the Court: The World Court and the Hostage Rescue Attempt", 76 AJIL 499 (1982).

206

If it does, it will then decide upon the merits of the dispute. So, we are back to our original question. Why does its opponent refuse to appear?

States like to present themselves, especially to their own subjects or citizens, as guardians of the rule of law. The two primary sanctions for violation of international law are force and the risk of being seen to behave in a lawless manner (international responsibility). Force, or rather, aggressive force is a violation of the United Nations Charter. But in matters which States regard as affecting vital interests, they prefer to sacrifice troops in a war or to incur the risk being labelled lawless, to sacrificing policy objectives.

Usually, they can minimise the damage of these two sanctions if they can interpret their legal obligations for themselves (auto-interpret).[166] Even war can be handled in this way if a Government can characterise its acts as a response to aggression without fear of authoritative contradition. Thus, with a few notable exceptions,[167] States do not readily submit to tribunals which can authoritatively interpret their legal obligations if they regard compliance with an adverse verdict as undesirable.

A State which would be a judge in its own cause is not a judge but an advocate. But an advocate pleading before what bar? The bar of public opinion?

Internal public opinion is too unreliable and too easily manipulated by the propaganda organs of the State.[168] Adverse international public opinion can often serve to unify a population behind its leaders.

No, it is not public opinion. A State which would be a judge in its own cause is an advocate pleading into a void from which no clear answer is returned. It will retain its freedom of action unless and until other forces are brought to bear upon it.

If, at the end of the exercise we face nuclear confrontation, if lesser battlefields are strewn with dead and mangled bodies, cities are devastated and the living weep, starve and suffer, so be it — as long as the States involved have not been labelled lawless by an authoritative law-determining agency.

166. Cheng, "Epilogue: On the Nature and Source of International Law" in Cheng (ed.), *International Law Teaching and Practice* (182), pp. 211-212.
167. Such as the European Convention on Human Rights with its provision for individual petition to the European Commission on Human Rights, Art. 25.
168. Supra note 73 at pp. 55-56.

BIBLIOGRAPHY

American Law Institute, Restatement (second) of conflict of laws (1971).

Amos, S., History of the civil law of Rome (1883).

Annual practice, The (Whitebook of U.K. civil procedure) (1920).

Arnold, Sir I. and Guillaume, A., The legacy of Islam (1980).

Ashraf, M., Interim relief in civil suits (1973).

Berger, A., Encyclopaedic dictionary of Roman law (1953).

Bigelow, M.M., History of procedure in England (1880).

Brownlie, I., Principles of public international law (1960).

Bruncken, E. (transl.), Science of legal method-selected essays, Modern legal philosophy series, vol. 9 (1917).

Brunner, H., *Deutsche Rechtsgeschichte* (1892).

Buckland, W.W., A textbook on Roman law (2d ed. 1932).

Campbell, J., A compendium of Roman law (2d ed. 1982).

Carbonnier, J., *Droit civile* (5th ed. 1954).

Cheng, B., General principles of law as applied by international courts and tribunals (1953).

–, (ed.), International law: Teaching and practice (1982).

Cohen, E.J., Manual of German law (1971).

Constantopolous, D.S., et al. (ed.), *Grundprobleme des Internationalen Rechts, Festschrift für Jean Spiropolous* (1957).

Cuche, P. et Vincent, J., *Précis de procédure civile et commerciale* (12th ed. 1960).

Deutsch, K. and Hoffman, S., Relevance in international law: Essays in honour of Leo Gross (1968).

Dumbauld, E., Interim measures of protection in international controversies (1932).

El Baradei, M., Franck, I. and Trachtenberg, R., The international law commission: The need for a new direction (UNTTAR 1981).

Elkind, J.B., The impact of American law on English and commonwealth law: A book of Essays (1978).

–, Interim protection: A functional approach (1981).

Engelmann, A., A history of continental civil procedure (1928).

Fachiri, A.P., The Permanent Court of International Justice (2d ed. 1932).

Franck, T., The structure of impartiality (1968).

Friedman, W., The changing structure of international law (1964).

Guggenheim, P., *Les mesures provisoires de procédure international et leur influence sur le développement du droit des gens* (1931).

Guyomar, G., *Commentaire du réglement de la Cour Internationale de Justice* (1973).

–, *Le défaut des parties a un différend devant les juridictions internationales* (1960).

Herzog, P.E., Civil procedure in France (1967).

Holdsworth, Sir W.S., A history of English law (3d ed. 1944).

Hübner, R., History of Germanic private law (transl. Philbrick) (reprinted 1968).

Hudson, M.O., International tribunals past and future (1944).

–, A treatise on the Permanent Court of International Justice (1933).

–, A treatise on the Permanent Court of International Justice, 1920-1942 (1943).

Huigman, R., Steiner, E., Piccard, R. and Thilo, E., *Dictionaire juridique français-allemand* (1939).

Jenks, C.W., The common law of mankind (1958).

–, The prospects of international adjudication (1964).

Jessup, P.C., The price of international justice (1971).

Jowitt, Earl W.A.J.I, Dictionary of English law (1977).

Karlowa, O., *Der Römische Civilprozess zur Zeit der Legisactionen* (1872).

Keith, K.J., The extent of the advisory jurisdiction of the International Court of Justice (1971).

Kelsen, H., Principles of international law (1952).

Kerr, W.W., A treatise on the law and practice of injunctions (1878).

Lapradelle, A. de, *Maîtres et doctrines du droit des gens* (2d ed. 1950).

Lauterpacht, Sir H., The development of international law by the International Court (1968).

–, The function of law in the international community (1933).

–, Private law sources and analogies of international law (1927, reprinted 1970).

Lawson, F.H., A common lawyer looks at the civil law (1969).

League of Nations, Documents concerning the action taken by the Council of the League of Nations under article 14 of the covenant and adoption of the statute of the Permanent Court of International Justice (1921).

–, *Procès verbaux* of the Committee of Jurists to draft the statute for a Permanent Court of International Justice (1920).

Liacouras, P.J., The International Court of Justice (1962).

Lipsky, G.A. (ed.), Law and politics in the world community (1953).

Lissitzyn, O., International law in a divided world (1963).

–, The International Court of Justice (1951).

Livy (Titus Livius), *Ab urbe condito*, The history of Rome, vol. 4 (transl. M'devitt, W.A. 1915).

Maitland, F., Equity (2nd ed. reprinted 1944).

Mani, V.S., International Adjudication: Procedural Aspects (1980).

Mommsen, T. and Kreuger, P., *Corpus iuris civilis* (1889).

Niemeyer, H.G., *Einstweilige Verfügungen des Weltgerichtshofes: Ihr Wesen und ihre Grenzen* (1932).

Oellers-Frahm, K., *Die einstweilige Anordnung in der internationalen Gerichtsbarkeit* (1975).

Oppenheim, L.L., International law (Lauterpacht ed., 8th ed. 1955).

Parry, C., The sources and evidence of international law (1965).

PCIJ, Acts and documents concerning the organization of the court (2d ed. 1947).

Planck, J.J.W. von, *Das Deutsche Gerichtsverfahren im Mittelalter nach dem Sachsenspiegel und dem verwandten Rechtsqueblem* (1874).

Plucknett, T.F.T., A concise history of English law (5th ed. 1956).

Politis, N., *La Justicio International* (1924).

Puchta, G.F., *Geschichte des Römischen Civilprozess* (10th ed. 1893).

Report on the project concerning the establishment of the proposed International Court of Arbitral Justice, *IIe Conférence Internationale de paix*, 1 *Actes et documents* (1907).

Rosenne, S., The International Court of Justice (1957).

–, The law and practice of the International Court of Justice (1965).
Sandars, T.C., The institutes of Justinian (1918).
Schatzel, W. and Schlochaur, H.J., *Rechtsfragen international ein Organization Festschrift für Hans Wehberg* (1956).
Schwarzenberger, G., Power politics (2d rev. ed. 1951).
Scott, J.B., The project of a Permanent Court of International Justice and Resolutions of the Advisory Committee of Jurists (1920).
Scott, S.P., *Corpus juris civilis* (English translation 1973).
Shihata, I.F., The power of the International Court to determine its own jurisdiction (1965).
Sohm, R., The institutes: A textbook of the history and system of Roman private law (Transl. Ledlie 3d ed. 1907).
Spiropoulos, J., *Théorie générale du droit international* (1930).
Spry, I.C.F., Equitable remedies (1971).
Stone, J., International Court and world crisis (1962).
–, Legal control of international conflicts (1958).
Supreme court practice (U.K. Whitebook 1982).
Sztucki, J., Interim measures and The Hague Court (1983).
United Nations, Report of the special committee on friendly relations, U.N. Doc. A/6230 (1966).
Visscher, C. De, Theory and reality in public international law (transl. Corbett 1959).
Wetter, J.G., The international arbitral process: public and private (1979).
Zemanek, K. (ed.), *Völkerrecht und rechtliches Weltbild (Festschrift für Alfred Verdross)* (1960).

ARTICLES, ESSAYS AND LECTURES

Adede, A.O., *The rule on interlocutory injunctions under domestic law and the interim measures of protection under international law: Some critical differences*, 4 Syr. J.Int'l L. and Comm. 277 (1977).
Anand, R.P., *The International Court of Justice and impartiality between nations*, (1963) 12 Ind.Y.B.Int'l Affairs 12.
Arbour, J.M., *Quelques réflexions sur les mesures conservatoires indiquées par la Cour Internationale de Justice* (1975) 16 *Cahiers de Droit* 532.
Bassiouni, M.C., *Protection of diplomats under Islamic law*, 74 AJIL 609 (1980).
Bastid, Suzanne, *La jurisprudence de la Cour Internationale de Justice* (1951) 78 *Receuil des Cours* 579.
Bernhardt, J.P.A., *The provisional measures procedure of the International Court of Justice through U.S. staff in Tehran: Fiat Iustitia, Pereat Curia?*, 20 Va. J.Int'l L. (1986).
Bleicher, S.A., *ICJ jurisdiction: Some new considerations and a proposed American declaration*, 6 Col. J. Trans'l L. 61 (1967).
Borel, E. and Politis, N., *L'extension de l'arbitrage obligatoire et la compétence de la Cour Permanente de Justice Internationale* (1927-II) *Annuaire de l'institut de droit international* 675.
Briggs, H.W., *Interhandel: The Court's judgment of March 21, 1959, on the preliminary objections of the United States*, 53 AJIL 547 (1959).
–, *Reservations to the compulsory jurisdiction of the International Court of Justice* (1958) 93 *Receuil des Cours* 229.
–, *The United States and the International Court of Justice*, 55 AJIL 301 (1959).
Brown, P.M., *Reserved international rights*, 38 AJIL 281 (1945).
Cavaglieri, A., *Règles générales du droit de la paix* (1929) 26 *Receuil des Cours* 311.

210

Cheng, B., *Comparative law and the practice of courts*, in Report on the Conference on Law and Science (David Davies Memorial Institute of International Studies 1958).

–, *Epilogue: On the nature and sources of international law* in Cheng (ed.), International law teaching and practice (1982).

Collier, C.S., *Judicial world supremacy and the Connally reservation*, 47 ABAJ 68 (1961).

Crockett, C.H., *The effects of interim measures of protection in the International Court of Justice*, 7 Calif. W.I.L.J. 348 (1977).

Dillard, H.C., *The World Court – an inside view*, 67 Proc. ASIL 296 (1972-73).

Doecker, G., *International politics and the International Court of Justice*, 35 Tulane L.R. 767 (1961).

Dumbauld, E., *Relief pendente lite in the International Court of Justice*, 33 Pennsyl. Bar Assn. Q. 265 (1962).

–, *Relief pendente lite in the Permanent Court of International Justice*, 39 AJIL 391 (1945).

Editorial, *International Court of Justice: Optional clause: Withdrawal of automatic reservation by France* (1959) 8 ICLQ 735.

Eisemann, P.M., *Les effets de la non comparution devant la Cour Internationale de Justice* (1973) 19 *Annuaire français de droit international* 351.

Elias, T.O., *The International Court of Justice and the indication of provisional measures of protection* (Gilbert D'Amado Memorial Lecture 1978).

Elkind, J.B., *Footnote to the nuclear test cases: Abuse of right – A blind alley for environmentalists*, 9 Vand. J. Trans'l L. 57 (1956).

–, *French nuclear testing and Article 41 – another blow to the authority of the Court?*, 8 Vand. J. Transn'l L. 39 (1974).

–, *The Aegean Sea Case and Article 41 of the Statute of the International Court of Justice* (1979) 32 *Révue Hellenique de droit international* 285.

Falk, R., *New states and the international legal order* (1966) 118 *Recueil des Cours* 7.

–, *The Iran Hostage Crisis: Easy answers and hard questions*, 74 AJIL 411 (1980).

Finch, E.H., *United States policy regarding compulsory arbitration*, 46 ABAJ 852 (1960).

Fitzmaurice, Sir Gerald, *Hersch Lauterpacht – the scholar as judge, Part I* (1961) 37 BYIL 1.

–, *Hersch Lauterpacht – the scholar as judge, Part II* (1962) 38 BYIL 1.

–, *The problem of the 'Non-appearing' defendant government* (1980) 51 BYIL 89.

Franck, T. and El Baradei, M., *The codification and progressive development of international law: A UNITAR study of the role and use of the International Law Commission*, 76 AJIL 630 (1972).

Fuller, Lon, *Adjudication and the rule of law*, 54 Proc. ASIL 1 (1960).

Gény, F., *Méthod d'interpretation et sources en droit privé positif* (1899) in The Modern Legal Philosophy Series, Vol. 9 (transl. Husik 1913).

Giverdon, C., *La réform par la procedure par défaut* (1959) *Recueil Dalloz section chronique* 201.

Essays, The Modern Legal Philosophy Series, Vol. 9 (transl. Bruncken 1913).

Goldsworthy, P.J., *Interim measures of protection in the International Court of Justice*, 68 AJIL 258 (1974).

Gross, L., *Bulgaria invokes the Connally Amendment*, 56 AJIL 357 (1962).

–, *The case concerning United States diplomatic and consular staff in Tehran: Phase of provisional measures*, 74 AJIL 395 (1980).

–, *The dispute between Greece and Turkey concerning the continental shelf in the Aegean*, 71 AJIL 31 (1977).

–, *The International Court of Justice: Consideration of requirements for enhancing its role in the international legal order*, 65 AJIL 253 (1971).

–, *States as organs of international law and the problems of autointerpretation*, in Lipsky, (ed.) Law and politics in the world community (1953).

Grzybowski, K., *Socialist judges in the International Court of Justice* (1964) Duke L.J. 536.

Guerrero, J.G., *La qualification unilatérale de la compétence nationale*, in Constantopolous et al. (ed.), *Grundprobleme des internationalen Rechts, Festschrift für Jean Spiropoulos* (1957).

Guggenheim, P., *Der sogenannte automatische Vorbehalt der inneren Angelegenheiten gegenüber der Anerkennung der obligatorischen Gerichtsbarkeit des internationalen Gerichtshofes in internationalen Gerichtspraxis* in Zemanek, K. (ed.), *Völkerrecht und rechtliches Weltbild (Festschrift für Alfred Verdross*, 1960).

–, *Les mesures conservatoires dans la procédure arbitrale et judiciaire*, (1932) 40 Receuil des Cours 649.

Hambro, E., *The binding character of provisional measures of protection indicated by the International Court of Justice* in Schatzel, W. and Schlochaur, H.J., *Rechtsfragen international ein Organization, Festschrift für Hans Wehberg* (1956).

Hammarskjöld, Å., *Quelques aspects de la question des mesures conservatoires en droit international positif* in *Zeitschrift für ausländisches öffentliches Recht und Völkerrecht* (1935).

–, *Sidelights on the Permanent Court of International Justice*, 28 Mich. L. Rev. 327 (1927).

Haver, P., *The status of interim measures of the International Court of Justice after the Iranian Hostage Crisis*, 1 Calif. W. Int. L.J. 512 (1981).

Hazard, John, *Renewed emphasis upon a socialist international law*, 65 AJIL 142 (1971).

Holmes, O.W. Jr., *The path of the law*, 10 Harv. L.R. 457 (1879).

Hudson, M.O., *The new arbitration treaty with France*, 22 AJIL 371 (1938).

–, *The United States Senate and the World Court*, 29 AJIL 301 (1935).

–, *The World Court: America's declaration accepting jurisdiction*, 32 ABAJ 832 (1946).

Il Ro Shu, *Voting behavior of national judges in international courts*, 63 AJIL 222 (1969).

Iluyomade, B.O., *The scope and content of a complaint of abuse of right in international law*, 16 Harv. I.L.J. (1975).

Jenks, C.W., *Hersch Lauterpacht: Scholar as prophet* (1960) 36 BYIL 1.

Jessup, P.C., *International litigation as a friendly act*, 60 Colum. L.R. 24 (1960).

Jiménez de Aréchaga, E., *The amendments to the rules of procedure of the International Court of Justice*, 67 AJIL 1 (1973).

–, *International law in the past third of a century*, 159 Recueil des Cours 1 (1978).

Lalonde, P.V., *The death of the Eastern Carelia Doctrine: Has compulsory jurisdiction arrived in the World Court?* (1979) U.Tor.Fac.L. Rev. 80.

Larsen, A., *Peace through law: the role and limits of adjudication - some contemporary problems*, 54 Proc. ASIL 8 (1960).

–, *The facts, the law and the Connally Amendment* (1961) Duke L.J. 110.

–, *The self-judging clause and self interest*, 46 ABAJ 729 (1960).

Lauterpacht, Sir Hersch, *Non-liquet and the completeness of law* (1958) Symbolae Verjil 196.

–, *The British reservations to the optional clause* (1930) 10 Economica 137.

Lellouche, P., *The nuclear test cases: Judicial silence v. atomic blasts*, 16 Harv. J.I.L. 614 (1975).

Mc Dougal, M., Lasswell, H. and Reiseman, W.M., *Theories about international law: Prologue to a configurative jurisprudence*, 8 Va. J.I.L. 188 (1968).

Mani, V.S., *Interim measures of protection: Article 41 of the I.C.J. Statute and Article 94 of the U.N. Charter*, (1968) 10 Indian J.I.L. 359.

–, *On imterim measures of protection: I.C.J. practice* (1973) 13 Indian J.I.L. 262.

212

Mendelson, M.H., *Interim measures of protection in cases of contested jurisdiction* (1972-73) 46 BYIL 259.

Merrills, J., *Interim measures of protection and the substantive jurisdiction of the International Court* (1977) 36 CLJ 86.

–, *The justiciability of international disputes* (1969) 47 Can. Bar R. 241.

Nsereko, D.D., *The International Court, impartiality and judges ad hoc* (1973) 13 Ind. J.I.L. 207.

Ober, F.B., *The Connally Reservation and national security*, 47 ABAJ (1961).

Padelford, N.J., *The composition of the International Court of Justice: Background and practice* in Deutsch, K. and Hoffman, S. (eds), Relevance in international law: Essays in honor of Leo Gross (1968).

Potter, P.B., *Editorial* 40 AJIL 792 (1946).

Pound, Roscoe, *Mechanical jurisprudence*, 8 Col. L.R. 605 (1908).

–, *The scope and purpose of sociological jurisprudence*, 25 Harv. L.R. 140 (1911).

Preuss, L., *Editorial*, 40 AJIL 720 (1946).

–, *The International Court, the senate and matters of domestic jurisdiction*, 40 AJIL 720 (1946).

Prott, L.V., *The style of judgment in the International Court of Justice (1970-73)* 5 Aus. YBIL 75.

Rague, M.A., *The reservation power and the Connally Amendment* 11 NYUJIL & Pol. 323 (1978).

Rhyne, C.S., *An effective world court is essential*, 46 ABAJ 749 (1960).

Rogers, William P., *United States 'automatic' reservation to the optional clause jurisdiction of the ICJ* (1958) 7 ICLQ 758.

Rosenne, S., *La Cour Internationale de Justice en 1960* (1960) 65 Révue generale de droit international public 1.

–, *Sir Hersch Lauterpacht's concept of the task of an international judge*, 55 AJIL 825 (1961).

Samore, W., *National origins v. impartial decisions: A study of world court holdings*, 34 Chicago-Kent L.R. 201 (1956).

Schachter, O., *The enforcement of international judicial and arbitral decisions*, 54 AJIL 1 (1960).

Schlesinger, R.B., *The Connally Amendment – amelioration by interpretation*, 48 Va.L. Rev. 685 (1962).

Schweppe, A.J., *The Connally Amendment should not be withdrawn*, 46 ABAJ 732 (1960).

Sohn, L.B., *The exclusion of political disputes from judicial settlement*, 38 AJIL 694 (1944).

Stein, T., *Contempt, crisis and the court: The world court and the hostage rescue attempt*, 76 AJIL 499 (1982).

Tiewul, S.A., *International law and nuclear test explosions on the high seas*, 8 Cornell ILJ 45 (1975).

Visscher, Charles De, *Editorial* (1959) 63 Révue generale de droit international public 413.

Waldock, Sir H., *The decline of the optional clause* (1955-56) 32 BYIL 244.

–, *The plea of domestic jurisdiction before international legal tribunals* (1954) 31 BYIL 96.

Watson, J.S., *Autointerpretation, competence and the continuing validity of Article 2(7) of the U.N. Charter*, 71 AJIL 60 (1977).

–, *Legal theory, efficacy and validity in the development of human rights norms in international law* (1969) U.Ill Law Forum 609.

Wright, Q., *The International Court of Justice and the interpretation of multilateral treaties*, 41 AJIL 445 (1947).

Wortley, B.E., *Interim reflections on procedures for interim measures of protection in the International Court of Justice*, in Milano, Università, Instituto di Diritto Internationale e Straniero Communicatione e Studi Vol. 14, Festschrift – Il processo internazionale studi in onore di Geatano Morelli, p. 1009 (1975).

TABLE OF CASES

NAME INDEX

220

SUBJECT INDEX

224

Martinus Nijhoff Publishers BV

Kluwer academic publishers group
Spuiboulevard 50
P.O. Box 989 / 3300 AZ Dordrecht
The Netherlands
Telephone: 078-334887 / Telex: 29245

To the Book Review Editor of:

We are pleased to send you a review copy of our new publication:

Title:	NON-APPEARANCE BEFORE THE INTERNATION COURT OF JUSTICE
	Functional & Comparative Analysis
Series:	Legal Aspects of International Organization
Author:	J.B. Elkind
Editor:	
Price:	Dfl. 110.00/US$ 42.00/£27.95
ISBN:	90-247-2921-1
Bibl. data:	224 pp., cloth
Publication date:	1984

We would appreciate receiving two clippings of your review in due course.

Sincerely yours,
Promotion Department